Birnbaum's

WITHOUT KIDS

by Pamela S. Weiers

Jill Safro
EDITOR

Suzy Goytizolo
SENIOR EDITOR

Keith Groshans
ASSOCIATE ART DIRECTOR

Andrea Rotondo Hospidor
PROJECT EDITOR

THE OFFICIAL GUIDE

Linda Calderon
EDITORIAL ASSISTANT

Alice Garrard
CONTRIBUTING EDITOR

Alexandra Mayes Birnbaum
CONSULTING EDITOR

DISNEY EDITIONS AND HEARST BUSINESS PUBLISHING, INC.

Table of Contents

8 PLANNING AHEAD

First things first: Lay the groundwork for an unforgettable vacation by timing your Walt Disney World visit to take advantage of the best weather, crowd patterns, and special goings-on. We set forth information about package and ticket options, offer time- and money-saving strategies, and present the keys to the World's extensive transportation system. Our custom-designed sample schedules will help you plan your days and nights. And a round of specialized advice offers the promise of no regrets.

36 CHECKING IN

Whether it's elegant, rustic, whimsical, or romantic digs you're seeking, you'll find them among Walt Disney World's 21 resorts and two Bahamas-bound cruise ships, themed as only Disney knows how. Choose from hotels whose architecture and ambience evoke such locales as Africa, New Orleans, Martha's Vineyard, Polynesia, or an early 1900s mountain lodge. Within our listing we explain the advantages of staying on-property and the big draws of each resort. You'll also find recommendations for lodging outside the World.

78 THEME PARKS: THE BIG FOUR

Enchanting, engaging, entertaining . . . overwhelming. The Magic Kingdom, Epcot, Disney-MGM Studios, and Disney's Animal Kingdom can rekindle even the most sluggish sense of wonder. But where to begin? Right here: We've devised strategies to help you make the most of each day. We've also provided an orientation to each park; detailed walking tours that highlight the most alluring stops for adults; a primer on Fastpass, Disney's new time-saving service; and lists of touring priorities that rank every attraction. From "Don't Miss" to "Don't Knock Yourself Out," we've scoped out the grown-up fun quotient.

144 DIVERSIONS: SPORTS, SHOPPING & OTHER PURSUITS

Because the World's attractions extend way beyond the theme parks, so does our guidance. Here, discover the options, including five first-rate 18-hole golf courses, tennis, boating, fishing, and biking. Shoppers will have a field day checking out our favorite shopping spots. For those who prefer soaking and sliding, we dive into all three water parks. Our in-depth report on romantic (and private) sunset and fireworks cruises reveals the creative essence of this adult-minded retreat. We also visit the natural realms of Fort Wilderness, and indulge in the sinful splendor of Walt Disney World's three spas.

184 DINING & ENTERTAINMENT

Here's your insider's guide to adult best bets for full-service restaurants and casual eating spots in the theme parks, resorts, and elsewhere in Walt Disney World. We've found dining rooms with prime views, cheap eats, sweet treats, afternoon tea, wines by the glass, and hearty microbrews. After dark, you'll know where to go to watch the big game, hear cool jazz, join in a rollicking sing-along, and dance the night away (disco, country, or hip-hop), as well as how to navigate the newest Downtown Disney hot spots, find a dinner show or a comedy club, or catch a theme park spectacular.

ISBN: 0-7868-5316-6

Printed in the United States of America

A truckload of gratitude to my fabulous supporting cast of family and
friends (especially Michael, Mum & Dad, and Marianne) for their patience,
understanding, and tireless support. Ears all around! —Pam

Other 2001 Birnbaum's Official Disney Guides

Disneyland
Walt Disney World
Walt Disney World For Kids, By Kids

A Word from the Editors

When you stop to think about it, a Walt Disney World guide for adults makes a lot of sense. Look at it this way: How many kids do you know who have been there alone? As it happens, Disney has been catering to grown-up sensibilities for a long time; the most obvious example is one entire theme park, namely Epcot.

The Birnbaum editorial team: Andrea Rotondo Hospidor (left), Jill Safro, Suzy Goytizolo, Keith Groshans, and Linda Calderon (seated)

For true movie buffs, the Disney-MGM Studios is close to heaven. The Magic Kingdom sprinkles guests with pixie dust and transports them to the giddy, fantasy-filled days of their youth. And Disney's Animal Kingdom, a lush celebration of all creatures great and small, is sure to lure the nature lover out of even the most civilized, buttoned-down sophisticate. Add to the above a hopping nightlife district and an all-out sports complex, and you have proof positive that the World is expanding in precisely our direction. Chic resort hotels and restaurants, world-class golf courses, and sensuous spa treatments only add to the allure.

But there's also another, more subtle level on which Walt Disney World has always appealed to grown-ups. We're referring to the little jokes, both visual and verbal, that keep popping up where you least expect them. More than ever before, Disney's creative efforts are crossing over to the grown-up side of the street. Lots of adults, both younger ones ("pre-kid") and older people whose children have flown the coop ("post-kid"), are descending on the parks with needs and notions that are vastly different from those of the parental persuasion.

It is with great pride that we present the sixth edition of our guide for adults, and we like to think we've come a long way since the original version. Letters from grateful readers have affirmed our instincts and inspired us to pursue our cause with even greater purpose. Clearly, an adult-oriented book is a perfect complement to our ongoing series of Birnbaum Guides to Walt Disney World and Disneyland. We already publish what we immodestly believe is the definitive annual guide to Walt Disney World. Anyone who wants the complete word on everything there is to see and do there is well advised to accept no substitutes.

The book you hold in your hands is special in several important respects. First, as you may have already noticed from the title page, it is written by one very talented person, Pamela S. Weiers, aided and abetted by the rest of the

We Couldn't Have Done It Without...

Acela Baldwin

Keith Card

Christian Compagnuolo

Danielle Courtenay

Craig Dezern

Walt Disney

Gene Duncan

Dave Fisher

Clark Galbreath

Sandy Hawkins

Karen Haynes

Terry Hayt

Janice Hilliard

Chris Howd

Tim Lewis

Rob Machado

Sanjay Patel

Eric Skubish

Rick Sylvain

Bob Weiers

Birnbaum staff. Pam's distinctive voice, equal parts authority, experience, and humor, makes her the perfect person to lead a tour of this vast enterprise. Second, this book is by no means comprehensive. Rather, it skips the kid stuff and delivers the goods on adult amusements in Walt Disney World.

Put another way, this guide is selective in the very best sense. We have spent the past year debating which of the attractions, hotels, and restaurants—both new and old—continue to merit special attention by adults. Final decisions were reached after making countless trips to Orlando and putting everything to the test.

For the most part, these visits are not the sort we would recommend for the casual traveler. Consider the time Pam made a sweep through 15(!) hotels in one day, looking for the best adult nooks and crannies. The mere memory of it still sends chills up her spine, as does the recollection of a plunge into River Country's unheated (read: almost numbing) swimming cove one cool January afternoon.

The result is that anything that doesn't live up to expectations is bumped from our "standout" list to the "good bets" rankings or banished entirely. Attractions that are awash in a sea of kids are simply given short (or at least shorter) shrift. And when we find something that just tickles us with pleasure, we aren't subtle about mentioning it.

Even with research aplenty, we have to fess up to the fact that this book would never have seen print were it not for the dedication and talent of many, many other people. To begin, we owe enormous thanks to the people who manage and run Walt Disney World. It is their willingness to open their files and explain operations to us in the most accurate way possible (not to mention letting us—and only us—publish pictures of their treasured characters) that makes this the Official Guide, even though it is, in fact, written by non-Disney employees.

In the listing above we've tried to acknowledge Disney staffers, both in the parks and behind the scenes, who contributed their time, knowledge, and experience to this edition. In addition, we want to extend a deep bow to Linda Warren, Ken Potrock, Darlene Papalini, Laura Simpson, Kevin Banks, and Darren Chiappetta for the care and effort they've put into this project. We would also like to thank our favorite off-site Disney expert, Wendy Lefkon,

PHOTO BY TODD SEBASTIAN WILLIAMS

Author Pamela S. Weiers

who edited our guides for many years and is still instrumental in their publication as executive editor at Disney Editions.

For their key roles behind the scenes, we salute editorial director Tom Passavant, press presider Shari Hartford, and copy editor Robert Rohr. Of course, no list of acknowledgments would be complete without our founding editor, Steve Birnbaum, who was surely smiling on this project, as well as Alexandra Mayes Birnbaum, who continues to be a guiding light—to say nothing of a careful reader of every word.

Finally, it is important to remember that Walt Disney World is constantly changing and growing, and with each annual revision we meticulously refine and expand our material to serve your needs even better. For the present edition, though, this is the final word.

HAVE A GREAT VISIT!
THE EDITORS

Don't Forget to Write

No contribution is of greater value to us in preparing the next edition of this book than your comments on what we've written and on your own experiences and discoveries at Walt Disney World. Please share your insights with us by writing to:

The Editors, Official Disney Guides
Birnbaum's Walt Disney World Without Kids 2001
1790 Broadway, Sixth Floor
New York, NY 10019

Anyone can have a magical time at Walt Disney World with advance planning.

Planning Ahead

There are plenty of hotels, restaurants, and theme park attractions for everyone at Walt Disney World. So why sit down with a book to plan ahead? Because a little attention to detail beforehand—we like to think of it as shopping for fun insurance—pays big dividends once you arrive in the Orlando area. Just ask the couple who had the foresight to book a table at the ultradeluxe Victoria & Albert's dining room before they left home. Or the friends who arrived with admission passes in hand and thereby avoided the ticket line at the entrance to Epcot. Or the golfers who were able to snag a coveted midmorning tee time on the Osprey Ridge course during their Easter visit. Our point: You can't be assured of the vacation experience you want without knowing which of the gazillion ways to enjoy Walt Disney World most appeal to you, and how to go about making sure these potential highlights don't become missed opportunities.

This first chapter not only provides the framework for a successful visit but also establishes a vital awareness that helps the information in subsequent chapters fall right in line. On the following pages, you'll find insight on when to visit; advice on tickets, packages, reservations, and how to save money; information on how to get around the World; flexible touring schedules; tips for older travelers, couples, singles, and guests with disabilities; and a whole lot more. This chapter is a straightforward planner that you'll return to again and again—no doubt with greater purpose than the first time through, when you're still eager to learn about Walt Disney World's hotels, theme parks, dining, and nightlife. So go ahead and give it a quick skim if this is your first read, but don't forget to come back.

Much tougher than the (rhetorical) question of *if* you want to visit Walt Disney World is the prickly matter of *when*. In addition to your own schedule, there is the weather to consider; you'd also like to avoid the crowds, although you'd love to get a gander at the Christmas parade or that flower festival you read about in the newspaper. You want to experience Walt Disney World at its best. But when?

Weather and crowd patterns are charted in this section, along with other factors, such as extended park hours, so you can see how possible vacation dates stack up. Timing your visit to meet all expectations may be impossible, but our experience does suggest certain optimum times. Mid-January through early February, late April through late May, September through early November, and the week after Thanksgiving through the week before Christmas stand out as particularly good times to find oneself in the World.

Taking things one step further, we like to underline the period from the Sunday *after* Thanksgiving to the week *before* Christmas as the ultimate timing for a WDW visit. This is a chance to savor Walt Disney World during one of its least crowded and most festive times of

WDW WEATHER

	Average High (°F)	Average Low (°F)	Average Rainfall (inches)
January	71	49	2.3
February	73	50	3.0
March	78	55	3.2
April	83	59	1.8
May	88	66	3.6
June	91	72	7.3
July	92	73	7.2
August	92	73	6.8
September	90	72	6.0
October	85	66	2.4
November	79	58	2.3
December	73	51	2.2

year. The place is wrapped in wonderful holiday decorations, and there are scads of special goings-on, from parades to parties.

If your travel dates fall outside the above-mentioned ideal, don't despair. Walt Disney World makes a spectacle of itself year-round. This listing highlights holidays and happenings that—for their fanfare, their crowd-drawing potential, and in some instances, their accompanying package deals—are worth factoring in to your vacation plans.

Note: We've provided 2001 dates when available, but specifics are apt to change. For the most current details about listed events, be sure to call the number provided or 407-WDW-INFO (939-4636) up to three months before your visit. For more information about package offerings, turn to "The Logistics" later in this chapter.

Holidays & Special Events

WALT DISNEY WORLD MARATHON (January 7): Marathoners lace up for a 26.2-mile race through scenic areas of Walt Disney World. Live bands, Disney characters, and hot-air balloons inspire some 15,000 runners to stay the course. For details, call 407-939-7810. Vacation packages are available.

BLACK HERITAGE CELEBRATION (February): This event salutes African Americans who have made notable contributions to the arts, sciences, and entertainment.

MARDI GRAS (February): Crescent City jazz bands, Creole and Cajun food, and street performances bring New Orleans' biggest party to Pleasure Island. Also on tap: a colorful celebration at Walt Disney World's Port Orleans resort.

ATLANTA BRAVES SPRING TRAINING (March): Some of baseball's greatest gather at Disney's ballpark to get a jump on the season ahead. Packages (407-938-7810) and single-game tickets (407-839-3900) are available.

ST. PATRICK'S DAY (March 17): Impromptu shindigs sprout like shamrocks in the more spirited corners of the World, while the United Kingdom in Epcot offers a taste of Emerald Isle traditions.

EASTER (April 15): Main Street becomes a bunny trail with a special parade that makes for a hopping Magic Kingdom. The theme parks have extended hours—and monumental crowds—throughout the Easter season.

All in the Timing

Consider the following WDW trends before settling on vacation dates. For details on park hours and attraction refurbishments, call 407-939-4636.

■ **Shortest Lines, Smallest Crowds:** The second week of January through the first week of February; late April through late May; the week after Labor Day until Thanksgiving; the week after Thanksgiving through the week before Christmas.

■ **Longest Lines, Biggest Crowds:** Presidents' week; the third week of March through the third week of April, especially Easter week; the first week of June through Labor Day, particularly Fourth of July; Christmas through New Year's Day.

■ **Potential Pitfalls:** The water parks and certain WDW attractions sometimes close for renovations (most often during winter months). Spring break (between February and mid-April) lures many students, as do Grad Nites (weekend events in late April and early May).

■ **Extended Hours:** The two weeks surrounding Easter; summer; Thanksgiving week; Christmas through New Year's Day.

What to Pack

- Comfortable shoes
- Sunglasses and sunscreen
- A bathing suit
- Bug repellent
- T-shirts and shorts for day
- Casual separates for evening (jeans are okay)
- Lightweight sweaters or jackets for summer evenings and air-conditioned rooms; warmer clothing is essential for evening (and often daytime) from November through March
- A jacket for men and a dress or comparable outfit for women if plans include dinner at Victoria & Albert's
- Suitable sporting togs and equipment for tennis, golf, fishing, jogging, or gym workouts (racquets, clubs, balls, golf shoes, and poles are available for rent)
- Lightweight rain gear and a folding umbrella

EPCOT INTERNATIONAL FLOWER & GARDEN FESTIVAL (April 20–June 3): This flowery event—a fragrant affair featuring some 30 million blossoms—not only makes a glorious perfumery of Epcot, but also allows gardeners to learn a trick or two from the folks who care for 10,000 rosebushes and then some. In addition to character topiaries and elaborate display gardens, workshops, behind-the-scenes tours, dining, and entertainment events abound.

BLACK MUSIC MONTH (June): Pleasure Island presents live music—from gospel, reggae, and R&B to rap, jazz, and hip-hop.

FOURTH OF JULY CELEBRATION: Double-fisted fireworks at the Magic Kingdom, Epcot, and the Disney-MGM Studios are glorious. But you pay a price: It's the busiest day of the summer.

OFFICIAL DISNEYANA CONVENTION (September): This five-day convention, the be-all and end-all for Disney enthusiasts, is tentatively scheduled to be held at WDW's California counterpart (Disneyland) in 2001. To get the latest breaking news, call 407-827-7600 or go to *www.officialdisneyana.com.*

NATIONAL CAR RENTAL GOLF CLASSIC (October 14–22): In this exciting tournament, now in its 31st year, top PGA Tour players compete alongside amateurs on two classic WDW venues: the Palm and Magnolia courses. The drama builds until the final day, when the Magnolia's fickle 18th hole has been known to twist fates. For more information, see the "Golf" section in the *Diversions* chapter, or call 407-824-2250. Vacation packages are available.

EPCOT INTERNATIONAL FOOD & WINE FESTIVAL (October 21–November 19): The temptation to eat and drink your way around World Showcase is intensified by cooking demonstrations (past years have brought such notable chefs as Julia Child to the table), plus samples of exotic specialty dishes, international wines by the glass, and worldly desserts ($1 to $3 per taste). Special five-course dinners sponsored by various vinters are also a highlight (call 407-WDW-DINE for reservations).

PLEASURE ISLAND JAZZ FEST (November): Jazz greats from various eras bring live music to the fore in this weekend festival.

FESTIVAL OF THE MASTERS (November): One of the South's top-rated art shows, the three-day event at Downtown Disney draws upward of 200 award-winning exhibitors from around the country. It tends to be least crowded on Friday and Sunday mornings during the festival.

ABC SUPER SOAP WEEKEND (November 10–11): Soap fans will think they've died and gone to Port Charles at this Studios event. Meet actors from the ABC daytime dramas *All My Children, General Hospital, One Life to Live*, and *Port Charles*. You may even get a chance to act out scenes with the stars. Question and answer sessions give fans the opportunity to ask their soap favorites about characters and storylines. Call 407-397-6808 for further information.

DISNEY'S MAGICAL HOLIDAYS (December): The whole wide World is positively aglow with holiday spirit, and it doesn't stop at decorations: Nightly tree-lighting ceremonies are held in three parks. The Magic Kingdom celebrates with Mickey's Very Merry Christmas Parade and Mickey's Very Merry Christmas Party, a special-ticket event held on several nights during the first three weeks of December that includes hot chocolate and a dusting of snow over Main Street. Epcot invites guests to enjoy a candlelight procession and a choral celebration of holidays around the world (inquire about dinner and show packages). The Disney-MGM Studios mesmerizes with an enveloping display featuring some five million twinkling lights. Vacation packages are available; for details, call 800-828-0228.

NEW YEAR'S EVE CELEBRATION (December 31): The theme parks are open after midnight, attracting huge throngs and presenting such high-spirited fun as "Auld Lang Syne" à la Space Mountain. Double-size fireworks are launched over the Magic Kingdom, Epcot, and the Disney-MGM Studios. All of the theme parks are still decked out in full Christmas regalia. Many of the resorts have special celebrations. Pleasure Island unleashes the New Year's Eve spectacular it's been rehearsing for the past 364 nights in a special-admission blowout.

Hot Tickets

Given the snooze-and-you-lose nature of getting into some events, you'll want to add a few numbers to your pre-vacation Rolodex.

■ Consider that a recent month brought such acts as The Pretenders and Bo Diddley to House of Blues, and call 407-934-2583 a good month ahead to reserve your seats.

■ To make a sure thing of witnessing Cirque du Soleil at Downtown Disney, call 407-934-7639 for tickets up to six months ahead.

■ Advance planning also pays off when Disney's Wide World of Sports complex hosts, say, the Atlanta Braves. Call 407-363-6600.

Cruise Patrol

For the vacation *and* the vacation after the vacation, consider a Disney Cruise Line land-and-sea package. After a three- or four-day romp in the theme parks, you'll cruise to the Bahamas on a ship fit for Mickey. Staterooms go from basic to luxe, corresponding to accommodations at Disney resorts, and easy transfers are the rule. See *Checking In* for more information.

THE LOGISTICS
Should You Buy a Package?

Travelers who like the idea of paying for their vacation in one lump sum that includes accommodations, transportation, and park admission have a wealth of choices when visiting Walt Disney World.

Vacation plans put forth by Disney tempt with such extras as unlimited golf, spa treatments, meals at WDW restaurants, and admission to WDW's bounty of attractions. Specifics vary, but package offerings range from the economical Resort Magic Plan to the top-of-the-line Grand Plan. Additional packages are built around the needs of golfers or honeymooners, and still others are tied to a season or special event. Featured accommodations include hotels on and off WDW property; some deals incorporate discounted airfare or meal plans. The Disney Cruise Line provides a seamless Walt Disney World-cruise vacation (to learn more, see the left margin and *Checking In*). For details on packages offered by the Walt Disney Travel Company, call 800-828-0228 or go to *www.disneyworld.com*. (Note that you must pay for packages up front. There is a 45 day cancelation policy.)

Other operators with plans featuring WDW and off-property hotels include American Airlines Vacations (800-321-2121), Delta Vacations (800-872-7786), TWA Getaway Vacations (800-438-2929), United Vacations (877-328-6877), American Express Vacation Travel (800-297-6898), and AAA Vacations (inquire at the nearest AAA office).

Because the value of any package depends wholly on your needs, we have provided a checklist to help you quickly narrow the choices. If you think you might be interested in buying a package, call for brochures, then use these guidelines to help determine which plan, if any, suits you.

The right package: (1) saves you money on precisely the type of lodging, transportation, and recreation you want; (2) includes meaningful extras (meals at restaurants of your choice, for example), as opposed to fluff like welcoming cocktails and so-called privileges that are actually services available to all WDW guests; (3) fits like a glove. No matter what the sale price, you wouldn't buy a pair of gloves that were two sizes too big nor should you buy a package that encompasses much more than you can reasonably expect to enjoy.

Money Matters

A few points of interest related to green matter and its plastic counterparts: Traveler's checks, American Express, Visa, MasterCard, Discover Card, Diners Club Card, JCB, and The Disney Credit Card are acceptable for most charges at WDW. While restaurants in the parks accept credit cards, some refreshment stands operate on a cash-only basis. WDW resort guests who leave a credit card imprint upon check-in may use their hotel ID card to charge meals at all restaurants and some food carts, purchases at shops and lounges, and recreational fees. These guests also receive the benefit of Express Check-out—an itemized bill is slipped under their door on the day of departure—a much appreciated perk when that morning rolls around and last-minute to-dos await.

As for banking services, there are a slew of ATMs accessible for a $2 service fee. Locations include Main Street, Frontierland, and Tomorrowland in the Magic Kingdom; the entrances to Epcot, the Disney-MGM Studios, and Animal Kingdom; Germany and the walkway between Future World and World Showcase in Epcot; the Toy Story Pizza Planet Arcade in the Studios; the Transportation and Ticket Center; Pleasure Island; Downtown Disney Marketplace; Downtown Disney West Side; and the lobby of all WDW resorts. For full-service banking, there is a SunTrust branch opposite the Downtown Disney Marketplace, at 1675 Buena Vista Drive (407-828-6106 or 800-786-8787); hours are 9 A.M. to 4 P.M. weekdays (until 6 P.M. Thursdays), with drive-in teller service from 8 A.M. to 6 P.M.

Cost-Cutting Tips

■ Consider accommodations with kitchen facilities to save on food costs. Or rent a refrigerator (available at WDW resorts for a $10.60 nightly fee).

■ Compare lunch and dinner menus. The same dishes are often available for less at midday. And ask about early-bird dinner specials.

■ Buy a WDW resort mug good for unlimited refills (of soft drinks, coffee, tea, and hot chocolate) at the hotel's food court, snack shop, and pool bar during your stay.

■ When choosing a place to stay, don't break the budget for a resort packed with amenities you won't have time to enjoy. Also realize that often the only difference between the least and most expensive rooms in a hotel is the view, and consider how often you'll be looking out that window.

■ Join The Disney Connection Club (formerly the Magic Kingdom Club) to net discounts on park tickets, vacation packages (including the Disney Cruise Line), and merchandise. Members have access to a private website and a monthly newsletter which reports the latest special offers; call 800-893-4763.

■ Use an American Express card to charge at least two nights at most WDW resorts and receive discounts on merchandise, meals, and more.

Keep in Mind

■ All admission passes are non-transferable.

■ When we say that any unused days on a pass may be used on a future visit, we mean that these days don't expire until you do.

■ Passes bought before Animal Kingdom's debut can be used in that park at no additional cost.

■ As long as you have at least one day remaining on your multi-day pass (except the Ultimate Park Hopper Pass), you can upgrade to the next level within 7 days of first use by paying the difference.

■ If you want to do things like spend the day in the Magic Kingdom and then head to Epcot for dinner, you need a Park Hopper Pass, a Park Hopper Plus Pass, or an Ultimate Park Hopper Pass.

Admission Options

The first thing visitors need to understand is the name game: Disney defines a ticket as admission good for one day only; multi-day admission media are called passes. Once you know this, you're ready to consider your options. **Note:** For the purposes of this section the term *parks* is understood to mean the Magic Kingdom, Epcot, the Disney-MGM Studios, and Animal Kingdom. Adult admission prices quoted include sales tax and are subject to change. Call 407-WDW-INFO (407-939-4636), or visit *www.disneyworld.com* to confirm current prices.

ONE-DAY TICKET ($48.76): Good for one-day admission to one park only.

FOUR- AND FIVE-DAY PARK HOPPER PASSES ($186.56 and $218.36, respectively): Valid in all four theme parks (Magic Kingdom, Epcot, Disney-MGM Studios, and Animal Kingdom) for four or five (not necessarily consecutive) days; include unlimited use of WDW transportation. Any unused days may be used on a future visit.

FIVE-, SIX-, AND SEVEN-DAY PARK HOPPER PLUS PASSES ($250.18, $281.99, and $313.79, respectively): Valid in all four theme parks for five, six, or seven (not necessarily consecutive) days; includes two, three, or four "plus" options, which may be used for admission to Typhoon Lagoon, Blizzard Beach, River Country, Disney's Wide World of Sports, or Pleasure Island; allows unlimited use of WDW transportation. Unused days or "plus" options may be used on a future visit.

ULTIMATE PARK HOPPER PASSES: Available to Walt Disney World resort guests only. Valid for the duration of a guest's stay for admission to the four theme parks, as well as the water parks, Disney's Wide World of Sports complex, DisneyQuest, and Pleasure Island; includes unlimited use of WDW transportation. Prices are $115.55 for two days, $157.96 for three days, $210.95 for four days, $253.36 for five days, $285.16 for six days, and $316.97 for seven days.

THEME PARK ANNUAL PASSES ($343.44; $309.52 for renewal): Valid for unlimited admission to all four theme parks for one year; includes unlimited use of WDW transportation and free parking.

PREMIUM ANNUAL PASS ($460.07; $414.48 for renewal): Valid for unlimited admission to the four theme parks, the water parks, Disney's Wide World of Sports complex, and Pleasure Island for one year; includes unlimited use of Walt Disney World transportation and free parking.

Note: Both annual passes provide savings on theme park admission; they also offer substantial discounts on resort rooms, dinner shows, and more.

Medical Matters

Although medical care is readily available at WDW, travelers with chronic health problems are advised to carry copies of prescriptions and ask their physicians to provide names of local doctors. Diabetics should note that Walt Disney World resorts will provide refrigeration for insulin. More generally:

■ Report emergencies to 911 operators or to Sandlake Hospital (407-351-8550).

■ Each of the theme parks has a First Aid Center staffed by a registered nurse. In the Magic Kingdom, the center is next to Crystal Palace; at Epcot, it's in the Odyssey Center; at the Disney-MGM Studios, it's next to Guest Relations; and in Animal Kingdom, it's near the Creature Comforts shop, in Safari Village.

■ For non-emergency medical care, Doctors On Call Service (407-399-3627) and CentraCare (800-238-2000) offer 24-hour-a-day house-calls. A doctor will be dispatched to your location anytime, day or night.

■ Another option for non-emergency medical care is Centra Care Walk-In Medical Care (407-934-2273), located at 12500 South Apopka-Vineland Road, open 8 A.M. to midnight weekdays and 8 A.M. to 8 P.M. weekends.

■ For referral to a pharmacy or to find out how to have medication delivered, call Centra Care (407-934-2273 or 407-239-7777).

The Pass Word

Admission passes may be purchased at Orlando International Airport, theme park entrances, Guest Services at Downtown Disney, any WDW resort, any hotel on Hotel Plaza Boulevard, and the Transportation and Ticket Center (offerings vary at each location). WDW resort guests may charge passes to their rooms. Cash, traveler's checks, personal checks (with presentation of driver's license and major credit card), Visa, Master-Card, American Express, Discover Card, Diners Club Card, JCB, and The Disney Credit Card are also accepted.

Select multi-day passes can be bought in advance at The Disney Store; by phone at 407-WDW-INFO (939-4636); or through WDW's website at *www.disneyworld.com* (allow two to three weeks for processing); or via mail order (allow three to four weeks). To receive passes by mail, send a check or money order (including $3 for handling) payable to the Walt Disney World Company to: Walt Disney World; Box 10140; Lake Buena Vista, FL 32830-0030; Attention: Ticket Mail Order.

Tips for Drivers

■ Florida state law requires use of headlights in the rain or fog and at dusk.

■ Gas stations opposite Pleasure Island and near BoardWalk are open 24 hours; another, in the Magic Kingdom Auto Plaza, closes two hours after the park does.

■ Be alert to slippery roads when it rains, as a fine layer of oil accumulates between drizzles.

■ It's legal to turn right at a red light anywhere in Florida, unless a sign is posted.

■ Call 407-824-4777 for free AAA towing at WDW. The Auto Plaza's AAA Car Care Center provides service (407-824-0976). Off-property, call Riker's Wrecker Service for 24-hour towing (407-855-7776) and repairs (407-238-9800), or call AAA if you're a member.

■ For traffic reports and news, tune to 90.7 FM (National Public Radio), 580 AM, or 740 AM.

■ Keep coins handy for tolls on roads to and from the airport.

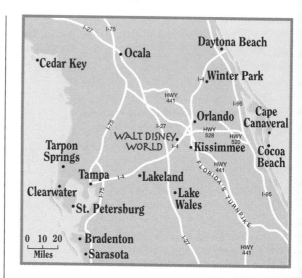

GETTING AROUND

Before you can find your way around Walt Disney World, you must first have a firm sense of where you are (and where you are not). While Walt Disney World is closely associated with the city of Orlando, it is actually located about 22 miles southwest of Orlando proper in a much smaller community called Lake Buena Vista.

The most important highway in the Orlando area is unquestionably I-4, which runs southwest to northeast, cutting through the southern half of Walt Disney World before bisecting Orlando and winding up just shy of Daytona Beach at I-95 (a major coastal artery). All the area's other major highways intersect I-4. Among the more frequently traveled is Route 435 (or Kirkman Road), a north-south route that links I-4 to the major hotel-and-business thoroughfare called International Drive, known locally as I-Drive.

Will you need a car during your stay? Only if you plan to spend time touring and exploring outside the World. Most area hotels offer buses to and from Walt Disney World. And Disney's own resorts and parks are serviced by a legion of buses, monorail trains, and boats, which provide efficient means of getting from point to point within WDW borders. This transportation is available to visitors staying at WDW resorts and to those with a multi-day park pass. If you think reliance on mass transit will cramp your style, by all means rent a car. Disney's transportation is convenient (departing from most areas every 15 to 20 minutes, a bit less frequently during the off-season), but it can accommodate only limited spontaneity and, if the route isn't direct, can take up a bit of time. If you decide to get around by car, note that parking at any of the theme parks costs $6 per day (it's free for WDW resort guests). Also, note that it's easiest to rent a car from one of the companies at the airport (Avis, Budget, Dollar, and National).

The following listing—a compilation of WDW transportation to key destinations—is a quick reference; detailed information is available at WDW resorts. Schedules coordinate with park hours (service begins about one hour prior to park opening, even on special early-entry days, and continues until one hour after closing), so there's little chance of being stranded. Call 407-939-4636 to confirm available routes. We have not included options for guests at the resorts on Hotel Plaza Boulevard, which have separate bus service; call your hotel for a schedule.

MAGIC KINGDOM: From the Grand Floridian, Contemporary, and Polynesian: monorail (the Contemporary also has a walkway). From Epcot: monorail to the Transportation and Ticket Center (TTC), then transfer to the TTC-Magic Kingdom monorail or ferry. From the Disney-MGM Studios, Animal Kingdom, and Downtown Disney: buses to the TTC, then transfer to ferry or monorail. From Fort Wilderness and the Wilderness Lodge: boats. From all other WDW resorts: buses.

Getting to WDW from Orlando Airport

During rush hour take the airport's South exit, and follow the Central Florida Greeneway (Route 417) to State Road 536, which leads right to WDW; tolls total $2. The distance is about 22 miles. For the shortest route, take the airport's North exit, head west on Route 528 (a.k.a. the Beeline Expressway) to I-4 west, and turn off at the appropriate WDW exit; tolls are $1.25.

■ **Exit 27:** Resorts on Hotel Plaza Boulevard

■ **Exit 26B:** Epcot, Typhoon Lagoon, Old Key West, Caribbean Beach, Swan, Dolphin, BoardWalk, Yacht and Beach Club, Dixie Landings, Port Orleans, The Villas at the Disney Institute, or Downtown Disney

■ **Exit 25:** Magic Kingdom, Disney-MGM Studios, Animal Kingdom, River Country, Blizzard Beach, Fort Wilderness, Disney's Wide World of Sports complex, Grand Floridian, Contemporary, Polynesian, Wilderness Lodge, All-Star resorts, Coronado Springs, Animal Kingdom Lodge, Palm and Magnolia golf courses, or Celebration

■ **For those without wheels:** Florida Towncars offers a $75 flat rate round-trip for up to five people to most Disney resorts, $85 round-trip to the resorts near the Magic Kingdom. Call 407-277-5466 or 800-525-7246. Mears Motor Shuttle, though time-consuming, is efficient and economical. Operating 24 hours, Mears serves area hotels at $14 one way or $27 round-trip, per person. For info, call 407-423-5566.

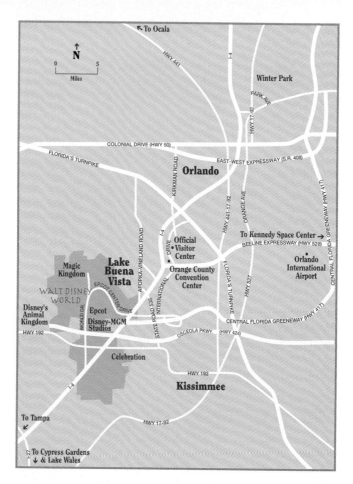

EPCOT: From the Swan, Dolphin, Yacht and Beach Club, and BoardWalk: walkway or boats to the International Gateway entrance, near World Showcase's France pavilion. From the Grand Floridian, Contemporary, and Polynesian: local hotel monorail to the Transportation and Ticket Center, then switch for the TTC-Epcot monorail. From the Magic Kingdom: express monorail to the TTC, then switch for the TTC-Epcot monorail. From Fort Wilderness and Downtown Disney: buses to the TTC, then transfer to the TTC-Epcot monorail. From the Disney-MGM Studios, Animal Kingdom, and other WDW resorts: buses.

DISNEY-MGM STUDIOS: From the Swan, Dolphin, Yacht and Beach Club, and BoardWalk: walkway or water launches. From Fort Wilderness and Downtown Disney: buses to the TTC, then transfer to the Studios bus. From the Magic Kingdom, Epcot, Animal Kingdom, and all other WDW resorts: buses.

ANIMAL KINGDOM: From the Magic Kingdom, Epcot, Disney-MGM Studios, Downtown Disney, and WDW resorts: buses.

DOWNTOWN DISNEY: From The Villas at the Disney Institute: walkway or bus. From Port Orleans, Dixie Landings, and Old Key West: boats or buses. From the Magic Kingdom, Epcot, the Grand Floridian, Contemporary, and Polynesian: monorail to the TTC, then transfer to the Downtown Disney bus (direct buses take guests from these locations after 4 P.M.). From the Disney-MGM Studios, Animal Kingdom, Wilderness Lodge, and Fort Wilderness: buses to the TTC, then switch for the Downtown Disney bus. From all other WDW resorts: buses.

FORT WILDERNESS/RIVER COUNTRY: From the Wilderness Lodge: bus or bike path. From the Magic Kingdom and the Contemporary: boats. From Epcot, the Grand Floridian, Contemporary, and Polynesian: monorail to the TTC, then transfer to the bus to Fort Wilderness. From the Disney-MGM Studios, Animal Kingdom, and Downtown Disney: buses to the TTC, then change for Fort Wilderness bus. For all other WDW resorts: bus to Downtown Disney, switch for bus to the TTC, then take Fort Wilderness bus. **Note:** Visitors who are planning to arrive by car must park in the Fort Wilderness parking lot, then take an internal bus to River Country, Pioneer Hall, and all other Fort Wilderness destinations. Evening transport back to WDW resorts may be direct.

TYPHOON LAGOON: From Fort Wilderness and the Wilderness Lodge: buses to the TTC, then transfer to the Typhoon Lagoon bus. From the Grand Floridian, Contemporary, and Polynesian: monorail to the TTC, then change for the Typhoon Lagoon bus. From the TTC, the theme parks, and all other WDW resorts: buses.

BLIZZARD BEACH: From WDW resorts and theme parks: buses.

BOARDWALK: From Magic Kingdom, Animal Kingdom, Typhoon Lagoon, Blizzard Beach, Coronado Springs, and Downtown Disney: buses. From Epcot and the Disney-MGM Studios: walkway or water launches. From the Swan, Dolphin, Yacht, and Beach Club: walkway. From all other WDW resorts: connecting bus through a theme park, Downtown Disney, or the TTC.

Meet the TTC

Think of the Transportation and Ticket Center (TTC) as the friendly neighborhood hub. Easily the most "connected" place in the World, the TTC is equipped to shuttle guests to most WDW locations. It is most important as a traffic-free link between Epcot and the Magic Kingdom, since WDW's two monorail loops merge here. The TTC also provides connections for day visitors and guests whose resorts do not offer direct transportation to certain parts of the World. Parking here costs $6 per day (free to WDW resort guests). There's an ATM, a kennel, and a picnic area. Park admission passes may be purchased.

DAY-TO-DAY SAMPLE SCHEDULES

The task of deciding how your days at Walt Disney World will be spent only seems daunting. Yes, there is a lot of ground to cover. The Magic Kingdom, Epcot, Disney-MGM Studios, and Animal Kingdom offer so much entertainment, it's easy to feel overwhelmed at the mere thought of choosing which park, let alone which attraction, to see first. In addition to the four major theme parks, there's a splashy trio of water parks, a quintet of fine 18-hole golf courses, an armada of pleasure boats, a nightlife metropolis, and tons of shopping opportunities. It all sounds quite unwieldy, but you'd be surprised how much fits neatly into a week's vacation.

Since the theme parks are the areas most likely to challenge even the obsessively organized traveler, these schedules will simplify days spent in each of the big four. To complement these daytime schedules, we've included evening and rainy-day supplements that offer alternatives such as indoor sporting events, hayrides, dinner shows, movies, and massages. You'll also find helpful hints on arranging golf tee times or tennis lessons. These schedules provide our best guidance and tips for each park; we leave it to you to decide if, when, and how fast. The plans work in tandem with the descriptions provided in the *Theme Parks*, *Diversions*, and *Dining & Entertainment* chapters. Note that we've not included the Fastpass option in our sample schedules. By no means interpret this as an unfavorable review of Disney's new time-saving technology. However, working this service into a daily schedule is an inexact science. That said, we recommend taking advantage of Fastpass at every opportunity. It'll save you time and make you feel like a VIP, to boot. (For more details on Fastpass, turn to page 81.)

Before we set you loose on the schedules, a few touring guidelines are in order. First, we have allotted four self-contained days to the theme parks—including one day each at the Magic Kingdom, Epcot, the Disney-MGM Studios, and Animal Kingdom—because this is the *minimum* amount of time necessary to cover the adult essentials at an unharried pace. As for order, we suggest spending the first day at Animal Kingdom and devoting successive days to touring Epcot, the Disney-MGM Studios, and the Magic Kingdom. These schedules are ideally used at times when extended evening hours are in effect at the parks, but smaller crowds during the off-season can help you cover the same territory. WDW resort guests participating in the early-entry program at the theme parks should take advantage of attractions open during this time and slip into the schedule after the park's official opening.

A Day at Disney's Animal Kingdom

■ Arrive at least a half hour before the park's posted opening time, and prepare to bond with the crowds waiting to enter.

■ Pick up a guidemap, and note the schedules of any performances you may want to see, such as Tarzan Rocks! or Festival of the Lion King. Plan to arrive about 45 minutes before the Lion King show begins, and up to 30 minutes ahead for the Tarzan show.

■ Resist the urge to conduct an informal wildlife census in The Oasis, and walk straight for the bridge to Safari Village (the path on the right offers the most direct route). The animals will be here all day. Minimal lines for your biggest priorities, Dinosaur (the new incarnation of Countdown to Extinction), Kali River Rapids, and Kilimanjaro Safaris, won't.

■ Give The Tree of Life a quick once-over, but don't stop to inspect it now. (We promise to come back later.) Instead, head to the first brachiosaurus skeleton on your right. In DinoLand U.S.A., make the thrilling acquaintance of Dinosaur. The morning jolt should keep you running for the rest of the day. Also, take a peek at The Boneyard playground before it's overrun with little diggers, and swing over to Tarzan Rocks! if the show is starting soon.

■ Next, go to Animal Kingdom's newest land, Asia, and ride the drenching Kali River Rapids. Afterward, take a walk through the Maharajah Jungle Trek and explore the tiny village of Anandapur. While you're in the area, slot in a time to see Flights of Wonder (check your guidemap for the schedule).

■ Beat a path to Africa, making sure to grab a quick bite along the way (we suggest Tusker House, in Harambe). Then make tracks for Kilimanjaro Safaris. Afterward, dally on the Pangani Forest Exploration Trail to watch the gorilla family at play.

■ When afternoon crowds descend, hop on the Wildlife Express to Conservation Station, and get your fill of all the interactive exhibits at journey's end.

■ Make your way to Camp Minnie-Mickey in time for the next Lion King staging.

■ *Now* it's time for It's Tough to be a Bug! in The Tree of Life. Be sure to check out the animal carvings on the tree and around the shops of Safari Village.

■ No fireworks here (imagine the stampede). As an alternative, experience dinner as entertainment at Rainforest Cafe. If you have other dining plans, consider stopping in for an after-dinner Margarilla Spotted Chocolate Monkey.

HOT TIP

Internet users can access *www.disneyworld.com* to receive an interactive preview or update of WDW's offerings. Packed with graphics, the website is everchanging. Among its more valuable features: ticket sales, customized resort recommendations, a reservations desk, maps, details about special events, and park hours during your stay.

Be Prepared*

■ If you want to see a dinner show—particularly the Hoop-Dee-Doo Musical Revue, one of the World's toughest tickets—reserve a table in the same breath that you book your hotel. Reservations are taken up to two years in advance; call WDW-DINE (939-3463).

■ Arrange for priority seating at WDW restaurants (up to four months in advance) by calling WDW-DINE.

■ Plan on attending a Magic Kingdom E-Ride Night. Call up to a month ahead for specific dates. (See page 83 for the E-Ride lowdown.)

■ Call 939-4636 to confirm park hours in effect during your visit, and plan an itinerary using the schedules provided in this chapter.

■ If you're a golfer, reserve tee times as far

•CONTINUED ON NEXT PAGE

A Day at Epcot

■ Guests are often permitted to enter the park a half hour before the scheduled opening time.

■ Once you pass under Spaceship Earth, investigate Innoventions Plaza, but postpone any serious exploration until the less congested hours of the afternoon.

■ Stomach growling? If you haven't had breakfast or need a quick java jolt, slip into Fountain View Espresso and Bakery.

■ If you were unable to secure priority seating arrangements for dinner before arrival, head for Guest Relations or Innoventions Plaza straightaway to book a table at one of the international restaurants of World Showcase. We suggest Les Chefs de France, in the France pavilion.

■ Head to Test Track, followed by Wonders of Life (your priorities: Cranium Command and Body Wars), the Imagination! pavilion (if you miss Honey, I Shrunk the Audience, you'll live to regret it), and, finally, The Land.

■ This should take you up to (at least) 11 A.M., when World Showcase opens. Consider grabbing a bite at The Land's Sunshine Season Food Fair before crossing over into World Showcase.

■ View *O Canada!* at the Canada pavilion. Then wander through the shops, gardens, and pub at the United Kingdom before fully exploring France.

■ Work your way toward The American Adventure to catch the extraordinary show, stopping to take in all the sights along the way.

■ Don't forget about the priority seating dinner arrangements you made earlier in

the day. All this walking has probably jump-started your appetite!

■ After dinner, pop into Mexico and then hightail it back to Future World to visit Spaceship Earth and Innoventions.

■ Keep an eye on the time so you can secure a spot around World Showcase Lagoon to watch the evening's performance of IllumiNations.

A Day at the Disney-MGM Studios

■ Arrive before the posted opening time, as doors often open a half hour early.
■ Pick up a complimentary guidemap; note that many attractions have set show-times, and some don't open until later in the morning. Study the layout of the park—it has been known to confuse even the most skilled of navigators.
■ Haven't had breakfast yet? Consider stopping by the Starring Rolls Bakery for a quick croissant.
■ If you were unable to book a table for dinner before leaving home, just stop at

the kiosk at Hollywood Junction (the corner of Hollywood and Sunset boulevards) and make priority seating arrangements for one of the following: the 50's Prime Time Cafe, Sci-Fi Dine-In Theater, Mama Melrose's, or the Hollywood Brown Derby. Note that this plan assumes a quick lunch taken whenever your personal lunch bell rings (good bets include Sunset Ranch Market and ABC Commissary).
■ If you're up for a couple of early-morning thrills, head directly to Sunset Boulevard for the Rock 'n' Roller Coaster and The Twilight Zone Tower of Terror, but do so *before* you eat. For something much tamer, you might try to get a jump on the notoriously long line at Voyage of The Little Mermaid. (If there is time before the first show, head to the nearby Great Movie Ride or Magic of Disney Animation.)
■ Afterward, head across the park for Sounds Dangerous starring Drew Carey, Disney's Doug Live!, Star Tours, Jim Henson's Muppet*Vision 3-D, and The Hunchback of Notre Dame show.

•CONTINUED FROM PREVIOUS PAGE

in advance as possible—90 days ahead if you've purchased a golf package or if you're staying at either a WDW resort or a resort on Hotel Plaza Boulevard, 30 days ahead if you're not, to secure your preferred time(s) and venue(s). Lessons may be reserved up to 90 days ahead. Call WDW-GOLF (939-4653). See "Sports" in the *Diversions* chapter for more details.

■ Note that tennis lessons and guided fishing trips may be booked up to 90 days in advance. Call WDW-PLAY (939-7529).

■ A few days before you leave home, make a quick round of calls to confirm all arrangements and reservations.

*All area codes are 407. You must dial this area code for all local calls.

In the Evening Hours

Here's more than a week's worth of activities for your consideration. For a complete guide to after-dark amusements, see our "Nightlife Guide" in the *Dining & Entertainment* chapter.

■ Attend a dinner show. All require reservations, and the Hoop-Dee-Doo Musical Revue calls for more forethought than any other.

■ For a cheap thrill (just $6 per person) and an early night, take a hayride at Fort Wilderness.

■ Grab a partner and play the coolest tennis at Walt Disney World. There are a few courts lighted for night play. The courts at Old Key West, Swan, and Dolphin are open 24 hours.

•CONTINUED ON NEXT PAGE

■ Stroll down New York Street. Next, see The Great Movie Ride and The Magic of Disney Animation. Note that the Mulan parade passes through these parts each afternoon (twice during busy seasons).

■ Having now taken care of your highest touring priorities, check your guidemap and slot in times before or after dinner to see the Indiana Jones Epic Stunt Spectacular and the Disney-MGM Studios Backlot Tour.

■ Between attractions, check out the interesting shops on Sunset and Hollywood boulevards. For a relaxing breather, slip into the Tune-In Lounge.

■ Note when the last performance of Beauty and the Beast—Live on Stage takes place, and see it then.

■ Get a spot for Fantasmic! at least 60 minutes before showtime. Filled with dazzling special effects and music, this nighttime spectacle is a nice way to wrap up the day.

A Day at the Magic Kingdom

■ Plan to be in the parking lot at least 45 minutes before the park is scheduled to open, so as to be at the Central Plaza end of Main Street before opening time.

■ If you haven't booked a table in advance, make any desired priority seating arrangements at City Hall. (We recommend Cinderella's Royal Table or Crystal Palace for an early lunch.) Pick up a guidemap here.

■ If you haven't had breakfast, grab a bite at the Main Street Bake Shop.

■ When the park opens, see what you can of the top priorities, moving at your own pace. Begin with Splash Mountain, Big Thunder Mountain Railroad, Pirates of the Caribbean, and anything else you care to see in Adventureland (note that the new Aladdin ride is likely to cause some congestion). Then move on to The Haunted Mansion, followed by a cruise on the Liberty Belle Riverboat.

■ Pausing for lunch when your priority seating time arrives or hunger calls, begin a second sweep of the park, targeting such attractions as the Carousel of Progress, Country Bear Jamboree, and Diamond Horseshoe Saloon Revue. Check out any shops and entertainment en route that catch your eye.

■ About 20 minutes before the afternoon parade (daily at 3 P.M.), either camp out on Main Street or skip the parade and head for Fantasyland to see as many key attractions—Peter Pan's Flight, The Many Adventures of Winnie the Pooh, and It's a Small World—as possible before the crowds swell back to normal.

■ Phobic about long lines? Even when people are swarming about most Magic

Kingdom attractions, The Walt Disney World Railroad, Tomorrowland Transit Authority, The Timekeeper, and The Hall of Presidents all tend to keep wait times to a relative minimum.

■ Breeze through Mickey's Toontown Fair and then head to Tomorrowland to experience two of the Magic Kingdom's biggest thrills—Space Mountain and Alien Encounter—before taking a jaunt through toyland on Buzz Lightyear's Space Ranger Spin.

■ Spend the rest of the day tying up loose ends on your touring checklist and perusing the shops on Main Street.

■ Consider arranging to have dinner at a restaurant accessible via monorail (perhaps California Grill or Cítricos). Return to the park in time to snare a spot on Main Street to watch the evening parade. If there are two runnings of the parade, aim to see the later one, when the crowds are apt to have dwindled and better viewing locations can be had.

•CONTINUED FROM PREVIOUS PAGE

■ For dining as an event, book a table at Victoria & Albert's, Artist Point, California Grill, Cítricos, Yachtsman Steakhouse, or Flying Fish Cafe.

■ If ready-made nightlife appeals, go club-hopping at Pleasure Island—one stop, many different venues (check out the Jazz Company, the Adventurers Club, or 8TRAX), plus a New Year's Eve street party every night. Or swing by Downtown Disney West Side, Pleasure Island's neighbor, to see who's playing at the House of Blues.

■ Take a wine tour. California Grill at Disney's Contemporary resort and Cítricos at the Grand Floridian take crushed grapes seriously and pour wines both by the glass and by the "flight" (two-ounce samples).

■ Prefer the grain to the grape? Beer lovers' hangouts include BoardWalk's working brewpub, Big River Grille & Brewing Works; Crew's Cup lounge at the Yacht Club resort; and The Laughing Kookaburra Good Time Bar at Wyndham Palace Resort and Spa.

■ For a nostalgic evening, stroll the boards at BoardWalk, where everything from saltwater taffy to a dance hall and a sing-along piano bar awaits.

Rainy-Day Inserts

The sun will come out tomorrow (or maybe in a few hours). In the meantime, here are some great ways to pass the time.

■ See a movie with all the comforts in the 24-screen AMC Theatres at Downtown Disney.

■ Sink into a sofa in the lobby of the Grand Floridian and listen to the graceful music. Or curl up by the fireplace at Wilderness Lodge.

■ Pick up a rain poncho (about $5) and head for Epcot, which has more places to escape the rain than any other park.

■ Experience the high-tech interactive games at Downtown Disney's DisneyQuest.

■ Get a massage. Disney spas offer myriad treatments that can be blissful excuses to stay dry.

■ Take afternoon tea at the Grand Floridian's Garden View lounge.

Water Parks

■ Choose from River Country, an old-fashioned swimming hole nestled into a cove of Bay Lake; Typhoon Lagoon, seven times the size of River Country, with one of the world's largest wave pools; and Blizzard Beach, Walt Disney World's newest and biggest water park, themed as a ski resort.

■ Whichever you visit, be at the gate when the park opens, as these places frequently fill up before noon during the warmer months. When the water parks reach a certain capacity, only guests arriving via WDW buses are admitted until crowds subside, usually about 3 P.M. When they hit peak capacity, no one is admitted until the throngs ease up.

■ Blizzard Beach's relative novelty makes it extremely popular with visitors of all ages; guests should expect lots of company and ask an attendant to point out any quiet zones.

■ Note that you may bring a picnic lunch and non-alcoholic beverages into any of the water parks. While fast food is available, it's fun to bring your own.

■ Typhoon Lagoon and Blizzard Beach each feature a lazy waterway that's perfect for a cool respite from the water-slide traffic. Grab one of the inner tubes and settle in.

■ River Country offers a brief but pretty and extremely peaceful nature trail that winds through egret territory on the lake's edge; peer through a trailside telescope for a view across the lake.

CUSTOMIZED TIPS
Guests with Disabilities

Walt Disney World has long earned praise from guests with disabilities because of the attention paid to their special needs. Still, familiarization with the World as it relates to one's personal requirements is essential, and to this end, the comprehensive *Guidebook for Guests with Disabilities* is required reading. The guide is available at all wheelchair rental locations (as well as City Hall in the Magic Kingdom and Guest Relations at Epcot, Disney-MGM Studios, and Animal Kingdom). However, we strongly recommend getting this publication well before you leave home to become familiar with procedures and accessibility. Those interested in guided tours should note: The Society for the Advancement of Travel for the Handicapped (347 Fifth Ave., Suite 610, New York, NY 10016; 212-447-7284) can provide a list of travel agents who are knowledgeable about travel for people with disabilities. To receive the listing, send a check or money order for $5. If you prefer to connect directly with a tour operator, consider Flying Wheels Travel (507-451-5005 or 800-535-6790) or Accessible Journeys (610-521-0339 or 800-846-4537).

While we defer to the *Guidebook for Guests with Disabilities* for its comprehensiveness, the following advice is an indication of WDW facilities and services:

■ Accessible parking is available at the theme parks (inquire at the Auto Plaza upon entering). Valet parking at Downtown Disney (available from 5:30 P.M. to closing) is complimentary for guests with disabilities.

■ All monorail stations are accessible to guests in wheelchairs. WDW buses are frequently, but not always, equipped with wheelchair lifts.

■ Life jackets for guests with disabilities are available at the water parks.

■ Most theme park attractions are accessible to guests who can be lifted to and from their wheelchairs with the assistance of a member of their party, and many can accommodate guests who must remain in their wheelchairs at all times. Consult the *Guidebook for Guests with Disabilities* or a park guidemap, or check in with a host or hostess for additional guidance.

■ Note that all hotels listed in this book's *Checking In* chapter offer rooms specially equipped for guests with disabilities. Walt Disney World resorts are easily explored by wheelchair. While room and bathroom configurations vary among hotels, lending themselves better to guests with certain needs, all resorts offer roll-in showers. For assistance in selecting a Walt Disney World hotel whose public areas and barrier-free rooms best serve your requirements, ask to speak to someone in the Special Requests Department when you call Central Reservations (407-934-7639).

■ WDW resorts provide a limited number of wheelchairs free of charge (with a $250 refundable deposit). Request one when reserving your room. Wheelchairs are available for rent at each of the theme parks, as are Electric Convenience Vehicles (ECVs). At the Magic Kingdom, the rental area is just inside the main entrance on the right; at Epcot, rentals are available inside the entrance plaza on

Don't Forget

the left, at the gift shop to the right of the ticket booths, and at the International Gateway; at the Disney-MGM Studios, rentals are handled at Oscar's Super Service, just inside the gate; at Animal Kingdom, the rental site is Garden Gate Gifts near the entrance. Wheelchair rentals cost $6 per day and require a $1 refundable deposit. Guests planning to visit more than one park on the same day may obtain a replacement at the next park with no additional charge or deposit (save your receipt and return the wheelchair by the end of the day). ECVs can be rented at the parks for $30 (plus a $10 refundable deposit) per park per day. Due to the limited number of ECVs, they usually sell out within the first couple of hours the parks are open.

■ Select spots along most parade routes and at nighttime show areas are marked for guests using wheelchairs. Arrive as early as possible, as these areas are filled on a first-come, first-served basis. See park guidemaps for locations.

■ For guests with visual disabilities, the theme parks offer audio cassettes designed to accentuate enjoyment of each park through detailed description. A $25 refundable deposit is required for use of a tape recorder.

■ Guests who use Text Typewriters (TTYs) may call 407-827-5141 for Walt Disney World Information. Pay phones equipped with TTYs are available throughout the Walt Disney World Resort.

■ Assistive Listening devices, which amplify attraction sound tracks, are available (with a $25 refundable deposit) at City Hall in the Magic Kingdom and at Guest Relations in Epcot, Disney-MGM Studios, and Animal Kingdom. Scripts are also available for guests with hearing disabilities at most attractions. For live performances, guests may request sign language interpretation; to make arrangements, call 407-824-4321 (voice) or 407-827-5141 (TTY) at least two weeks in advance. Also, Reflective Captioning devices that project dialogue onto a panel placed in front of guests are available for use in some theater shows. Check park guidemaps for locations.

Older Travelers

Walt Disney World is a friendly and welcoming place, but its sheer enormity and energy level, and its mere heat, particularly during the summer, have the potential to overwhelm. While knowing what to expect is half the battle, knowing how to plan accordingly is even more important. The keys to an enjoyable, relaxed visit apply to everyone. Our suggestions:

■ Plan your visit for one of the least crowded times of year (see "When to Go" earlier in this chapter). In the parks, eat early or late to avoid mealtime crowds.

■ Florida residents net discounts on selected nonpeak dates. Call 407-939-4636 for details. Also, some off-property hotels offer discounts to AARP members.

■ Take frequent rest stops in the shade (for the best locales in each park, see the "Quiet Nooks" lists in the margins of the *Theme Parks* chapter).

■ Don't underestimate the distances to be covered at Epcot and Animal Kingdom. These parks are huge, and visitors often log a few miles in a full day of touring. Lots of older travelers who enjoy walking around the other parks choose to treat themselves to a wheelchair at these two. Wheelchairs and Electric Convenience Vehicles are easily rented at the park entrances. However you're getting around, take it slowly. Broken into small increments with plenty of air-conditioned and tree-shaded breaks, it's not so tiring. The *FriendShip* launches that cross World Showcase Lagoon in Epcot provide a nice break for weary feet, especially when there are short queues.

■ Not all of Pleasure Island's clubs are inundated with exuberant twenty-somethings. Show off your two-step to live country bands at the Wildhorse Saloon, modeled after the one in Nashville. The polished atmosphere of Stone Crab lounge at Fulton's Crab House is a fine social setting, as well.

■ Don't miss the four-star tribute to Hollywood's heyday that is the Disney-MGM Studios. The Art Deco design, retro restaurants, and Technicolor tributes to Tinseltown make for a day of nostalgic amusement.

Single Travelers

While Walt Disney World may not exactly be the last word for singles, the fact is, singles and independent travelers can have an absolute blast here. Some ideas:

■ Pleasure Island's clubs typically attract lots of locals on weekends. The restaurants and lounges at Downtown Disney West Side, particularly the concert hall at House of Blues, also attract a hip crowd.

■ Teppanyaki Dining Rooms and the Biergarten restaurant at Epcot, where smaller parties are seated together, offer especially social settings.

For Woofers & Meowers

No pets other than service animals are permitted in the parks. Travelers may lodge Fluffy or Fido in one of WDW's five air-conditioned Pet Care Kennels: near the TTC; at the entrances to Epcot, the Disney-MGM Studios, and Animal Kingdom; and at Fort Wilderness. WDW resort guests pay $9 for overnight pet stays, including food; others pay $11. Day rates are $6 and include one feeding. Pets must have proof of vaccinations. Accommodations are available on a first-come, first-served basis. Guests are encouraged to walk their pets at least three times a day, as the animals are not otherwise sprung from their cages. For hours and other information, call 407-824-6568.

Important Numbers

AMC Theatres:
407-298-4488

Behind-the-Scene
Tours: **407-WDW-TOUR
(939-8687)**

Central Reservations:
**407-W-DISNEY
(934-7639)**

Disney's Wide World
of Sports Complex:
407-363-6600

Donald Duck: **Unlisted**

Golf Reservations/
Lessons:
**407-WDW-GOLF
(939-4653)**

Lost and Found:
407-824-4245

Priority Seating:
**407-WDW-DINE
(939-3463)**

Recreation:
**407-WDW-PLAY
(939-7529)**

Sandlake Hospital:
407-351-8550

Walt Disney Travel
Company:
800-828-0228

WDW Information:
**407-WDW-INFO
(939-4636)**

Weather:
407-824-4104

■ At WDW's 18-hole golf courses, company is a given; players are assigned to a foursome when tee times are allotted.

■ Some of the World's more compelling restaurants have an area with counter seating, which helps take the sting out of dining solo. These noteworthy spots include Flying Fish Cafe, Narcoossee's, Cítricos, Fulton's Crab House, and Portobello Yacht Club.

■ The casual atmosphere along the BoardWalk makes it a fun place to people-watch, and the slew of eateries, shops, and clubs provide interesting diversions. The sing-along at Jellyrolls dueling piano bar never fails to entertain. Another favorite, and an especially good destination for sports fans, is ESPN Club. The environment is conducive to frenzied rooting for your home team, as well as calmer discussions about the intricacies of the game with fellow fans.

■ If you're a tennis player sans partner, consider the player matching program at Disney's Racquet Club (407-824-3578).

■ Tour programs are engaging alternatives to exploring Epcot solo (see page 107 for details).

Couples

There is a place for lovebirds at Walt Disney World. Actually, there are many spots in the World perfectly suited to those with romantic intentions. The Magic Kingdom's carousel-and-castle combo invokes enchantment in true fairy-tale tradition. Epcot's World Showcase has the aura of a whirlwind tour (and inspiration for a future trip?), with countries as exotic and far-reaching as Japan and Morocco (and it has even bottled France). The Disney-MGM Studios recaptures an era of starry-eyed elegance. And what could be more titillating than sharing a surprise-filled safari through Africa at Animal Kingdom? By day, there is romance in the theme parks for those already inclined to hold hands; by night, the parks sparkle with an intensity that inspires sudden mushiness in those who never considered themselves the type, and that's *before* the fireworks.

As the themed resorts of Walt Disney World go about transporting guests to various times and places, they make quite a few passes through settings straight out of the vacation fantasy textbook. From the endearing Victorian charms of the Grand Floridian to the exotic island getaway that is the Polynesian, it's safe to say that Disney has romantic notions that go way beyond heart-shaped tubs.

You won't find a more inspiring backdrop than the wondrously rustic Wilderness Lodge, marked by geysers, waterfalls, steamy hot springs, and the grandest stone fireplace you've ever seen. At the nostalgic BoardWalk resort, unique surrey bikes are available for romantic rides (or high speed escapades!) along the waterfront. You can pedal all the way to Epcot's International Gateway.

And there's more. Consider a restaurant that starts with candlelight, then goes a step further by setting the dining room inside a Mayan pyramid fitted out with such decorative flourishes as a moonlit river and a smoking volcano. (See the margin on page 34 and the *Dining & Entertainment* chapter for more of our romantic picks.)

For those too lovestruck to bother with taking pictures themselves, there's the Romance Photographic Session. For $295, a photographer follows you and your sweetheart around the park of your choice, clicking away. For more information, call 407-827-5029.

Couples with bigger things in mind, like tying the knot, might consider "I do"–ing it here. Each year, more than 2,300 couples flock to Walt Disney World to exchange vows. Why this place? For some couples it's a matter of mutual Disney adoration; for others it's a convenient answer to the dilemma posed by the bride being from one area of the country and the groom from quite another (they figure if everybody's going to be traveling for the wedding, they might as well get a vacation out of it). While no one yet has likened Mickey Mouse to Eros, newlyweds have beaten such a path to Mickey's doorstep over the years that Walt Disney World rates as one of the most popular honeymoon destinations in the country.

Even popping the question can become a Zip-A-Dee-Doo-Dah operation. Romantic settings and appearances by the lovestruck duo themselves (Mickey and Minnie, of course) make the most magical place on earth the perfect setting for a couple's special beginning.

ENGAGEMENTS: Looking for the ultimate place to pop the question? Disney makes it easy for any guest to create a magical moment for Princess or Prince Charming. Several romantic packages are available. Imagine being led into the private Rose Garden at the Magic Kingdom to find a floral bouquet, chilled

Keeping the Faith

Among the religious services most convenient for WDW guests are those held at the Polynesian resort (407-824-2000). Every Sunday at the Polynesian's Luau Cove, a Protestant service is offered at 9 A.M. and Catholic masses are held at 8 A.M. and 10:15 A.M.

Jewish visitors may attend Conservative services at Temple Ohalei Rivka, located at 11200 Apopka-Vineland Rd. (407-239-5444). Guests may also attend reform and Shabbat services at the Congregation of Liberal Judaism at 928 Malone Dr. (407-645-0444), near Winter Park. Muslim services are held five times a day at Jama Masijid at 11543 Ruby Lake Rd. Call 407-238-2700.

The Most Romantic Places in the World

sparkling cider, engraved Mickey and Minnie goblets, wedding "ears," and a glass slipper waiting for you. As the man of the hour kneels to make his proposal, the nightly fireworks extravaganza at the Magic Kingdom begins. The couple is then whisked back to their resort via a private limousine. The cost for a basic Rose Garden afternoon package (sans the fireworks and limo) is $295; evening packages with a private viewing of the fireworks start at $450. Other packages set the tone with a yacht cruise around Seven Seas Lagoon and music by a string trio. A photographer is always an option. Packages, complete with appearances by Mickey and Minnie in formal attire, range from $1,295 to $2,995. For information, call 407-824-5130.

WEDDINGS: In these parts, the sky is truly the limit. Intimate weddings for up to eight guests start at about $3,300; for larger affairs, figure $7,500 minimum during the week, $10,000 on Fridays, Saturdays, and Sundays. Coordinators work with couples from three months to a year in advance to create a wedding tailored to their needs—from elegant affairs without a hint of Disneyana to the sort in which the bride arrives in Cinderella's coach and Goofy "crashes" the reception. These wedding gurus can handle any imaginable detail and a litany of unimaginables.

Nuptials in the theme parks (which range from $7,500 in Epcot to $45,000-plus in the Magic Kingdom) take place before and after park closing and allow couples to take their vows in front of Cinderella Castle in the Magic Kingdom or in an English courtyard in Epcot's World Showcase, among other places. For an extra $15,000, a free-spending couple will get a sprinkling of pixie dust and a personal exhibition of Fantasy in the Sky fireworks.

Then there's the Wedding Pavilion, a dainty structure, reminiscent of a Victorian summerhouse, which sits on a lushly landscaped man-made island between the Grand Floridian and Polynesian resorts. Surrounded by roses, palm trees, and beaches, the pavilion seats 250 and offers a prime view of Cinderella Castle, perfectly framed in a window behind the altar. Picture Point—a trellised archway set among the pavilion's gardens, with the castle in the background—is also available for intimate ceremonies. For couples still in the planning stages, the tasteful on-site wedding salon—known as Franck's—is like a three-dimensional bridal magazine.

Ceremony settings are available at many WDW resorts; the garden gazebo at the Yacht Club, Sunset Point at the Polynesian, Sea Breeze Point at the BoardWalk, and Sunrise Terrace at Wilderness Lodge are all popular spots.

Wedding packages vary broadly, depending upon the type of ceremony and reception desired, and can include discounted passes and rates at certain WDW resorts for family and friends attending the wedding. When booking a wedding package, the bride and groom receive a complimentary room for their first night. For information about weddings at Walt Disney World, call 407-828-3400.

HONEYMOONS: Most WDW resorts have designated suites. You needn't buy a honeymoon package to get special treatment; just let the reservations agent know that you're newlyweds. For information on packages, call 800-370-6009.

Disney Wedding Tips

■ Event locations and times can't be booked with Disney until one year before your wedding date. For those with long engagements, use this time to research the choices.

■ For those on a limited budget, select the Deluxe Intimate Wedding package which includes a ceremony followed by a minimum four-night honeymoon (starting at $3,300, based on a woods-view room at the Wilderness Lodge).

■ Reception sites are as individual as each couple. Consider BoardWalk's Atlantic Dance hall for an afternoon celebration or Epcot's American Adventure Rotunda for an elegant evening soiree.

■ Don't let the party end! After the wedding reception, treat your guests to a dessert party and private viewing of Epcot's IllumiNations: Reflections of Earth. (It will set you back about $30 per person.)

At Walt Disney World, there's a hotel to suit every taste, budget, and mood.

Checking In

L ike a photograph whose mood changes depending upon the frame in which it is displayed, a Walt Disney World vacation is colored by the context in which it is experienced. Guests have quite a variety of frames—rather, resorts—from which to choose, and each yields a unique perspective on the World. Some hotels imbue the mousedom with surprising elegance; others render it especially whimsical, homey, or romantic. Looking for grand seaside digs or a home base straight out of New Orleans? They're here. Something Polynesian? No problem. From campsites and economy-priced rooms to villas and suites, there are accommodations in Cinderella's neighborhood to suit most every taste and billfold.

If you're the sort who favors a gilded frame for your vacation, you'll find the chandelier quotient you're seeking—and a rich Victorian aura—at Disney's turreted Grand Floridian Resort and Spa. Here, the WDW experience is defined by private verandas, a whirlpool surrounded by roses, and room service that delivers the likes of chocolate-covered strawberries "dressed" in tuxedos.

If rustic romance is more your style, your ultimate WDW roost is the Wilderness Lodge, which patterns its grandeur after National Park Service lodges of the early 1900s. The resort's soaring totem poles and teepee chandeliers, bubbling hot spring, and roaring water-fall will forever alter your conception of a log cabin.

If you simply must make every dollar count, the All-Star resorts come through with perfectly comfortable accommodations starting at $77 a night. The brightest dwellings you'll ever want to call home, augmented by three-story sports, music, and movie icons, ensure you'll not forget for a moment that you're staying on WDW turf.

Amenities Checklist

While there are significant differences in the amenities offered at Disney's Value and Deluxe properties, certain conveniences are provided at all WDW hotels. Namely: voice mail, TVs with the Disney Channel and ESPN, clock radios, in-room safes, guest laundry facilities, dry-cleaning service, an ATM, and either room service or more limited food delivery options.

If you're not quite sure what you want, that's fine, too. This chapter provides descriptions of every WDW resort, from the overall atmosphere to the rooms, facilities, and amenities. In addition to the basic rate information, you'll find summaries of each hotel's big draws, plus tips that will help you make a choice that's in line with your budget, interests, and touring priorities. We've covered all of the Disney-owned resorts and their favored siblings, the Swan and Dolphin, plus the Disney Cruise Line. Careful readers will easily discern those we recommend most highly for adults (Hint: look for clues in the "Big Draws" category). Be aware, too, that within each entry, the information provided is selective, encompassing details most relevant to the adult visitor. When it comes to the resorts that line Hotel Plaza Boulevard—seven properties that are within Disney's borders but independently managed—we've included our top three choices for adults. Finally, for those willing to give up the convenience of staying on-property, we've also listed some hotels worth considering outside the World's boundaries. So think about what's important to you in a resort and on this trip to Walt Disney World. Then read on for all the information you'll need to choose the perfect frame.

WALT DISNEY WORLD RESORTS

Unless otherwise noted, all phone numbers are in the area code 407.

As an example of the meticulous theming that is a hallmark of the Disney hotels, consider Port Orleans, a moderately priced resort designed to evoke New Orleans' French Quarter. As you check in, you might catch the aroma of fresh beignets wafting over from the resort's food court, decorated as a Mardi Gras warehouse. The lobby has French horns for light fixtures and restrooms with such great jazz coming over the speakers they could almost impose a cover charge.

In addition to compelling theming, Disney's resorts are marked by staffs trained to bend over backward to ensure guests' happiness and well-kept, comfortably furnished accommodations comparable in size to those found outside WDW borders. There are also practical advantages to staying on-property. Chief among these benefits are convenience and easy access to Disney services. Other privileges enjoyed by WDW resort guests include use of WDW transportation; early admission to the Magic Kingdom, Epcot, and Disney-MGM Studios on designated days; discounted golf fees; and the option to reserve tee times on Disney golf courses up to 90 days prior to their check-in date. At all WDW resorts except the Swan and Dolphin, amenities also include free package delivery and the ability to charge meals, merchandise, and recreation fees to one's room.

This resort listing is organized according to price tiers—Deluxe, Moderate, and Value—with the exception of the Home Away from Home category, used to distinguish all-suite and villa-type accommodations. These categories are consistent with Disney's rating system for its resorts (explained on page 41). But consider location as well as price, particularly if you know you'll be spending a lot of time touring a particular theme park. The "Vital Statistics" section of each entry will help you place the resorts on the World map. You'll notice in this listing that certain hotels are earmarked as "sister resorts"; these are adjacent properties that feature complementary designs and shared facilities. With the exception of Port Orleans and Dixie Landings, whose greater separation and distinct identities we feel merit individual attention, sister resorts descriptions are combined.

We've packed in as much detail as possible about the offerings at each resort, but to learn more about restaurants and lounges, see our recommendations in the *Dining & Entertainment* chapter. For further details about WDW transportation, including a description of options at the Transportation and Ticket Center (TTC), consult *Planning Ahead.* For additional information on recreational opportunities available at the resorts, turn to the "Sports" section of the *Diversions* chapter.

The Last Word On...

RESERVATIONS

Rooms at WDW are in high demand, so book at least six months in advance by calling 407-934-7639 or visiting *www.disneyworld.com*. A deposit of one night's lodging is required within 14 days of the time a reservation is made. The deposit will be refunded only if the reservation is canceled at least 5 days before the scheduled arrival.

CHECKING IN

Check-in time is 3 P.M., except at The Villas at the Disney Institute, BoardWalk Villas, All-Star resorts, Old Key West, and The Villas at Wilderness Lodge, where it's 4 P.M., and Fort Wilderness, where it's 1 P.M. Check-out time is 11 A.M.

•CONTINUED ON NEXT PAGE

Deluxe
Animal Kingdom Lodge

The zebras, ostriches, and antelopes out back are no mascots, not exotic props planted for the resort's much-anticipated spring 2001 grand opening. Nor are they escapees from the nearby Animal Kingdom theme park. They and their hoofed and feathered comrades—about 200 animals, in all, mostly African expats—live on the resort's carefully plotted pasturelands, giving round-the-clock credence to its claims as Florida's only African wildlife reserve lodge. Of course, this ambitious theme is not carried entirely by the storks and giraffes whose habitat comes within 30 feet of guests' domain. Hardly. The lodge's hut foyer opens to an immense thatched-ceiling lobby with the tantalizing depth of a lion's yawn. Here, pupils swell as the eyes dart from the rope bridge to the huge mud fireplace, from the gushing approximation of Victoria Falls to the blur of African masks and artifacts and the chandeliers made of Zulu shields. Oh, yes, and the four-story welcome-to-the-savanna window, which is sure to make momentary bumper cars of slack-jawed new arrivals. Romance and adventure cling to every richly appointed inch of the semicircular lodge, which serves as a five-story animal-observation platform from its viewing parlors to its vibrant restaurants and its expansive swimming pool. Although with 1,293 rooms, the resort is bigger than its African counterparts, it hides the fact well: Built into the landscape, its front drive leads to the third-floor lobby. Traditionally, such semicircular buildings protect against predators; here, it merely creates 180 degrees of ogling. Nine out of 10 guestroom balconies overlook the savanna.

BIG DRAWS: Luxury laced with an undeniable spirit of adventure and romance. Private balconies that double as box seats for viewing animals on the savanna.

WORTH NOTING: Accommodations at this resort are comparable to those at most deluxe hotels in the World; both the deluxe rooms and the smaller standard guestrooms typically include two queen-size beds. Deluxe rooms also include a child's daybed. Ask and you may receive a king-size bed or the polar opposite: bunk beds. Within each room's sandy-colored walls is a unique amalgam of African art pieces, traditionally patterned textiles, and dark-wood furniture handcrafted in Zimbabwe and South Africa. All rooms have private balconies;

(Continued on page 42)

Mickey Rates the Resorts

Disney's ranking system for its resorts provides a convenient framework for considering WDW lodging options. Categories reflect not only price, but the style of the accommodation and the level of service. The hotels fall into Deluxe, Moderate, and Value classifications. Home Away from Home encompasses villa-type lodgings (and the Wilderness Cabins at Fort Wilderness), while Disney's Campground category is occupied solely by the Fort Wilderness campground.

For the sake of clarity and comparison, we have used these same categories in this chapter, with a few exceptions for Fort Wilderness and other properties with two types of accommodations. In general, here's what to expect in our categories:

■ Deluxe properties (rates for double rooms range from about $189 to $565 per night) are defined by large, graciously appointed rooms, several restaurants, and such amenities as 24-hour room service.

■ Home Away from Home (rates from about $34 to $540) applies to villas, vacation homes, all-suite hotels, wilderness cabins, and campsites.

■ Moderate properties (rates from about $129 to $209) feature comfortably sized rooms, full-service restaurants as well as food courts, and bellman luggage service.

■ Value properties (rates from about $77 to $109) offer fewer frills and smaller, yet adequate, quarters. Meals are provided at food courts. Recreation options at these resorts are usually limited.

•CONTINUED FROM PREVIOUS PAGE

SEASONAL RATES

Rates quoted in resort entries are subject to change.

■ **Value** rates apply January 1 to February 14, August 26 to September 26, and November 4 to December 20 for all Value and Moderate resorts, Wilderness Lodge and Villas, Animal Kingdom Lodge, and the Fort Wilderness Cabins; January 1 to February 14 and August 5 to December 20 for the Fort Wilderness Campground; January 1–15 and May 1–December 22 for the Swan and Dolphin; and January 1 to February 14, July 4 to September 26, and November 4 to December 20 for all other WDW properties.

■ **Regular** rates apply April 29 to August 25 and September 27 to November 3 for all Value and Moderate resorts, Wilderness Lodge and Villas, Animal Kingdom Lodge, and Fort Wilderness Cabins; April 29 to August 4 for Fort Wilderness Campground; and April 29 to July 3 and September 27 to November 3 for all other WDW properties (except the Swan and Dolphin).

■ **Peak** rates apply February 15 through April 28 for all WDW properties except the Swan and Dolphin; and January 16–April 30 and December 23–31 for the Swan and Dolphin.

■ **Holiday** higher-than-peak rates apply December 21–31 for all WDW resorts except the Swan and Dolphin.

Animal Kingdom Lodge Tips

■ Although you can view animals from many vantage points, it is not possible to touch or feed them without participating in a special program. Visit Guest Services for more information.

■ Recreational activities are limited due to the presence of animals. For example, no bike rentals are available and there is no jogging path. Guests may indulge in these pursuits at neighboring Disney resorts.

■ Willing to forego wildlife-watching from your balcony? Rooms sans animal views are significantly cheaper.

■ This 33-acre tropical savanna is inhabited by 100 grazing animals and 130 birds—the safari begins as soon as you enter the five-story resort.

(Continued from page 40)

animals and their habitats are visible from 90 percent of the rooms. Lest guests lose their sense of place while reading in bed or brushing their teeth, there are (purely decorative) mosquito nets in every room and some rooms even have a map of Africa on the wall opposite the vanity mirror. Amenities include hair dryers, irons (with boards), newspaper delivery, and 24-hour room service. Concierge rooms are available, with prime views of the stork-to-wildebeest menagerie.

The primary form of recreation here is spying on the roving impalas, Thompson's gazelles, giraffes, and flamingos from every possible vantage point all day and night. In addition to the floor-to-ceiling window in the cavernous lobby, a rock outcropping one story down from the lobby juts out over the savanna to permit bird's-eye views of the animals, and indoor viewing areas line the halls on every level of the U-shaped resort. The resort's enormous pool, sun deck, and two whirlpools have great animal-viewing potential (due to a strategically placed watering hole). The pool area is surrounded by restaurants. Zahanati Health Club rounds out the resort's recreation options.

Where to eat: Boma—Flavors of Africa (gumbo-to-peanut-soup global fusion cuisine, in an African market setting), Jiko—The Cooking Place (menu dominated by lighter cuisine and items from the wood-burning ovens); and The Mara (casual on-the-go grazing).

Where to drink: Victoria Falls (mezzanine lounge with African drums as tables); Cape Town Lounge and Wine Bar (near Jiko); Uzima Springs Pool Bar.

VITAL STATISTICS: Animal Kingdom Lodge enjoys enviable proximity to the Animal Kingdom and Blizzard Beach; Disney-MGM Studios is also nearby. Animal Kingdom Lodge; 2901 Osceola Parkway; Box 10000; Bay Lake, FL 32830-1000; 407-938-3000.

Transportation: Buses to the Magic Kingdom, Epcot, the Disney-MGM Studios, Animal Kingdom, Blizzard Beach, and the TTC. From the TTC, buses to Typhoon Lagoon and Downtown Disney.

Rates: Standard rooms without savanna views run $199 in value season, $230 regular, and $275 peak; standard rooms with savanna views are $265 value, $295 regular, and $340 peak; concierge rooms with savanna views begin at $380 in value season, $435 regular, and $510 peak. Suites start at $600. A $25 per diem charge applies for each extra adult (beyond two) sharing a room.

BoardWalk Inn & Villas

This fetching resort and entertainment complex recaptures an ephemeral (if not fictional) period in eastern-seaboard history. It has all the charm of a close-knit shore village awash in sun-bleached pastels. The name comes from the 48-foot-wide boardwalk out back, where you'll find a lively piano club, a swinging dance hall, and a major-league sports bar, not to mention a bakery and a brewpub. When hunger calls, you can sit down to a seafood dinner or buy a slice of pizza from a restaurant window. For dessert, try a caramel apple from the sweetshop or cotton candy from a vendor. Located lakefront directly opposite the Yacht and Beach Club, BoardWalk completes this seaside community in exceedingly romantic fashion. The BoardWalk Inn (a 372-room deluxe hotel) and BoardWalk Villas (520 villas styled in the tradition of family vacation cottages) share a lobby. Filled with antique miniatures of early boardwalk amusement rides, the lobby fronts an inviting porch with rocking chairs. A sweeping staircase leads to the resort's main recreation area as well as to the restaurants, shops, and clubs of the BoardWalk entertainment district.

BIG DRAWS: Intimate charm, an entertainment zone right out back, and a walkway to Epcot's International Gateway.

WORTH NOTING: Guestrooms at the BoardWalk Inn are comparable in size to those at Disney's other deluxe properties and offer two queen-size beds plus a child's daybed. Decorative touches include curtains imprinted with images and inscriptions from old postcards, and French doors that open to private patios or balconies. Two-story suites feature a master-bedroom loft (with king-size bed and adjoining bath with whirlpool tub), a living room with a wet bar, and a private garden enclosed in a white picket fence. Single-story concierge rooms are similarly appointed (no gardens, alas).

The BoardWalk Villas is a Disney Vacation Club resort (see page 55 for club details); because its accommodations are equipped with either a kitchenette or a full kitchen, it falls into Disney's Home Away from Home category. Villas, decorated in the eclectic fashion of seaside cottages, feature balconies (or patios) and carousel-print curtains. Studios offer a queen-size bed and a double sleeper sofa, plus a wet bar with microwave, coffeemaker, and small

---

Coming Soon: Disney's Pop Century Resort

The 20th Century is unfolding anew in the form of an expansive Disney value resort. Located near the Caribbean Beach resort, the nostalgic property will take its design and price cues from the All-Star resorts. When the three-story yo-yo and other American pop-culture icons are in place, guests will wander down memory lane, revisiting a different decade in each section of the resort. The first phase of time travel begins in late 2002, when Disney's Pop Century Resort's 2,880 rooms (the '50s through the '90s) open.

BoardWalk Tips

■ Take advantage of the resort's romantic assets—surrey rides and sunset cocktails on the waterfront.

■ For a quick bite in the morning, head to the Belle Vue Room. Continental breakfast is served at the bar.

■ Big games attract a big crowd at the ESPN Club, so get there early.

■ In the evening, catch a bus to the BoardWalk from the TTC.

A Closer Look

Read (yes, *read*) the curtains, which were created using imprints of vintage postcards. During construction, a carpenter noticed one from 1933, written by his uncle to his aunt before they were married. They still live at the address on the postcard.

refrigerator. Larger villas (with one, two, or three bedrooms) have a dining room, fully equipped kitchen, laundry facilities, whirlpool tub, and VCR. They also have a king-size bed in the master bedroom, a spacious living room with a queen sleeper sofa, and two queen-size beds or a queen-size bed and double sleeper sofa in any additional bedrooms.

Both properties have 24-hour room service. Room amenities include hair dryers, irons (with boards), and—at the Inn—newspaper delivery. A conference center provides access to business services. Guests have exclusive use of the amusement park-themed pool, two quiet pools, and three whirlpools. Recreational options include fishing excursions, two clay tennis courts, a health club (massages by appointment), a jogging trail, and croquet. Bikes, pedaldriven carts, fishing poles, and inner tubes may be rented; a poolside library rents books and videos.

Where to eat: Big River Grille & Brewing Works (microbrews, pub food); BoardWalk Bakery (baked goods, sandwiches); ESPN Club (all-American sports bar, ballpark menu); Flying Fish Cafe (creative American, steak, and seafood); Seashore Sweets' (saltwater taffy and ice cream); and Spoodles (Mediterranean).

Where to drink: Atlantic Dance (a Big Band ballroom); the Belle Vue Room (cocktails and cognac flights); Jellyrolls (dueling pianos); ESPN Club; and Leaping Horse Libations (poolside refreshments).

VITAL STATISTICS: BoardWalk guests have enviable access to Epcot, Disney-MGM Studios, and Fantasia Gardens Miniature Golf complex. BoardWalk; 2101 N. Epcot Resorts Blvd.; Box 10000; Lake Buena Vista, FL 32830-1000; 407-939-5100; fax 407-939-5150.

Transportation: Boat or walkway to Epcot's International Gateway entrance. Boat or walkway to the Disney-MGM Studios. Buses to the Magic Kingdom, Animal Kingdom, Typhoon Lagoon, Blizzard Beach, Downtown Disney, and Coronado Springs.

Rates: At the Inn, standard rooms start at $279 in value season, $309 regular, and $364 peak; concierge rooms begin at $405 value, $460 regular, and $520 peak; and suites begin at $535. A $25 per diem charge applies for each extra adult (beyond two) sharing a room. At the Villas, studios start at $279 value, $309 regular, and $364 peak; one-bedroom villas begin at $375 value, $415 regular, and $480 peak; two-bedroom villas start at $520 value, $670 regular, and $844 peak; and three-bedroom villas start at $1,275.

Contemporary

First impressions might suggest that the enormous A-frame tower of this legendary resort is simply a 15-story concrete tent that's been pitched here, a stone's throw from Space Mountain, for the benefit of the monorail trains regularly schussing through it. And the Contemporary is certainly defined by a futuristic sophistication. But there's more to the Contemporary—namely, artistic reverie that plays out in bold decor, from the sleek lobby to the quirky guestroom furnishings; three eateries, including the critically acclaimed California Grill; and terrific views of the Magic Kingdom or Bay Lake, particularly from rooms in the resort's tower (the higher, the better).

BIG DRAWS: Location. Monorail service. Ideally suited for serious tennis players.

WORTH NOTING: Guestrooms here are larger than at any other WDW resort hotel; most feature two queen-size beds plus a daybed (a king-size bed may be requested). Amenities at the 1,030-room resort include 24-hour room service. Concierge services are available to suite guests and those on the 12th floor. On the basis of its top-notch tennis facility alone, the Contemporary would be a recreational hub, but it also boasts a recently renovated pool area (with a free-form pool, quiet pool, and two whirlpools), a boat rental marina, a parasailing program, basketball and sand volleyball courts, a jogging trail, and a health club (massages by appointment). Waterskiing and fishing excursions may be arranged. Note that the Contemporary's theming and recently refurbished rooms do not exude an especially cozy ambience and rarely come off as romantic.

Where to eat: California Grill (West Coast cuisine and a 15th-floor Magic Kingdom vista); Chef Mickey's (breakfast and dinner character buffets); Concourse Steakhouse (casual for its genre); and Food and Fun Center (24-hour snacks).

Contemporary Tips

■ Caffeine cravers can get a fix at Contemporary Grounds (specialty coffees served).

■ Rooms in the resort's garden buildings generally do not yield notable views, which is why the rates are lower than in the tower.

■ Tennis players will do well to stay in the north wing because of its proximity to the resort's six lighted courts. Be sure to inquire about the resort's tennis clinics.

■ The marina is chock-full of choices for sailors, from Water Mouse boats and sailboats to Searaiders, which are faster than the Water Mouse boats and unavailable to the under-18 crowd.

■ Tower guests have convenient access to business services at the convention center. Guests staying in the south wing are close to the pool and marina areas.

Grand Floridian Tips

■ For maximum quiet and a striking panorama, request a lagoon-view room.

■ You can watch the fireworks over Cinderella Castle from the beach with little or no company.

■ Consider a honeymoon room for your second honeymoon.

■ Indulge in a treatment (or two) at the spa after a long day in the parks.

■ Book a special dinner at Victoria & Albert's way in advance.

■ Note that the resort is surprisingly popular with families, despite its posh surroundings.

■ For predinner drinks, opt for Cítricos lounge, the lounge at Narcoossee's, or cocktail service in the lobby.

■ Ask at Guest Services about sailing the Seven Seas on a private yacht. See page 179 for details.

Where to drink: California Grill Lounge (emphasis on wine and panoramic views); Contemporary Grounds (lobby coffee bar); Outer Rim (comfy alcove overlooking Bay Lake); and Sand Bar (poolside refreshments).

VITAL STATISTICS: The Contemporary, which has the Magic Kingdom virtually in its front yard and Bay Lake out back, is the only hotel with a walkway—and one of three on the monorail line—to that park. Monorail links extend the resort's neighborhood to the Polynesian and the Grand Floridian, and provide convenient commutes to Epcot. Contemporary; 4600 N. World Dr.; Box 10000; Lake Buena Vista, FL 32830-1000; 407-824-1000; fax 407-824-3539.

Transportation: A monorail resort. Walkway or monorail to the Magic Kingdom. Monorail to the TTC; from there, monorail or bus to Epcot, and buses to Typhoon Lagoon and Downtown Disney. Buses to the Disney-MGM Studios, Animal Kingdom, and Blizzard Beach. Boats to Fort Wilderness and River Country.

Rates: Standard rooms start at $224 in value season, $244 regular, and $284 peak; tower rooms begin at $320 value, $355 regular, and $410 peak; suites start at $280. A $25 per diem charge applies for each extra adult (beyond two) sharing a room.

Grand Floridian Resort & Spa

This romantic slice of Victorian confectionery, a quick hop (and a world apart) from the Magic Kingdom, recalls the opulent hotels that beckoned high society to Florida at the turn of the century. The Grand Floridian's central building and five guest buildings—snow-white structures laced with verandas and turrets, and topped with gabled roofs of red shingle—sprawl over 40 manicured acres of Seven Seas Lagoon shorefront. Not an eyeful lacks for towering palms, stunning lake views, or exquisite rose gardens. The resort's magnificent lobby—Victoriana in excelsis—features immense chandeliers, stained-glass skylights, and live piano and orchestra music that might inspire spontaneous dancing. Recently refurbished guestrooms exude bygone elegance, with old-fashioned armoires, marble-topped sinks, and room service delivered atop lace cloths.

BIG DRAWS: The height of luxury with a view of Cinderella Castle. Great for honeymoons or an escape to a kinder, gentler era. And the monorail stops here, too.

WORTH NOTING: Standard accommodations at this 900-room resort are larger than those at most deluxe hotels in the World and include two queen-size beds plus a daybed; many rooms have terraces. Amenities include hair dryers, special toiletries, bathrobes, mini-bars, nightly turndown, 24-hour room service, and newspaper delivery. Concierge rooms and suites are located on the upper floors of the main building and in guest building 6. The resort offers some of the best restaurants on property, including Victoria & Albert's. Traditional afternoon tea is served in the Garden View lounge. The Electrical Water Pageant and the Magic Kingdom fireworks can be seen from most lagoon-view rooms. A convention center offers access to business services. Boats may be rented, and fishing excursions may be arranged. Two clay tennis courts and volleyball equipment are available. The Grand Floridian Spa & Health Club is among WDW's most complete fitness facilities. The vast swimming pool and rosebush-ringed whirlpool are open 24 hours, with quiet hours in effect at night. A white-sand beach offers respite from the pool din.

Where to eat: Cítricos (south of France); Gasparilla Grill & Games (24-hour snacks); Grand Floridian Cafe (all-day Floridian fare); Narcoossee's (seafood served waterside); 1900 Park Fare (character buffet breakfast and dinner); and Victoria & Albert's (seven-course dinners).

Where to drink: Cítricos lounge (international wines and citrus martinis); Garden View (cocktails and afternoon tea); Mizner's (classic cocktails); Narcoossee's (wines overlooking the lagoon); and Summerhouse (beachside refreshments).

VITAL STATISTICS: The Grand Floridian's prime Seven Seas Lagoon locale allows for fast access to the Magic Kingdom. Proximity to the Palm and Magnolia links please golfers. The monorail stretches the hotel's neighborhood beyond the adjacent Polynesian resort to include the Contemporary resort and provides for easy commutes to Epcot. Grand Floridian; 4401 Floridian Way; Box 10000; Lake Buena Vista, FL 32830-1000; 407-824-3000; fax 407-824-3186.

Transportation: A monorail resort (platform is on the hotel's second floor). Monorail or boat to the Magic Kingdom. Monorail to the TTC to connect with the monorail to Epcot, and buses to Typhoon Lagoon and Downtown Disney.

Made-to-Order Surprises

Flowers, custom gift baskets, and champagne can be delivered to any WDW resort (and some off-property hotels) by calling 407-827-3505 before or during your visit. For an additional fee, Disney personal shoppers will further scour the World to track down favorite character merchandise and other special-request items.

Polynesian Tips

■ For a taste of tropical tradition, catch the Torch Lighting Ceremony, held on weekend nights at 6 P.M. in the main lobby.

■ Tahiti is a good choice for its relative seclusion and Magic Kingdom views (request a lagoonside room).

■ For a better view, hit the Seven Seas Lagoon on a private fireworks cruise. See page 179 for details.

■ Tucked down below Sunset Point, in front of Tahiti, is a beach that many guests don't realize is there.

■ Couples can celebrate a special occasion with a moonlit dinner on the beach. Call Room Service for more information.

■ The Grand Floridian Spa & Health Club is a short walk away.

Buses to Blizzard Beach, the Disney-MGM Studios, and Animal Kingdom. Water launch to the Polynesian resort.

Rates: Standard rooms start at $314 in value season, $359 regular, and $414 peak; concierge rooms begin at $435 value, $490 regular, and $560 peak; and suites start at $810. A $25 per diem charge applies to each extra adult (beyond two) sharing a room.

Polynesian

This resort echoes the romance and beauty of the South Pacific with enchanting realism. Polynesian music is piped throughout the lushly landscaped grounds, which feature white-sand beaches with hammocks, tiki torches that burn nightly, and sufficient flowers to perfume the air. Sprawled amid tropical gardens arc 11 two- and three-story village longhouses, all named for Pacific islands, where 847 guestrooms are located. But the Polynesian's centerpiece and primary mood setter is unquestionably the Great Ceremonial House, which (in addition to the usual front desk, shops, and restaurants) contains a huge, three-story-high garden that all but consumes the atrium lobby.

BIG DRAWS: A breathtaking, you-are-there South Seas ambience makes the Polynesian exceptionally romantic and helps to explain the resort's busy wedding calendar. Plus, the convenience of monorail service.

WORTH NOTING: Standard guestrooms, comparable in size to those at the Contemporary, are roomy and feature two queen-size beds plus a daybed. Those in Tokelau, Tahiti, and Rapa Nui are slightly larger. Rooms were thoroughly refurbished recently; decor includes vibrant bedspreads, ti leaf-shaped mirrors, bamboo accents, and woven reed canopies draped over and behind the beds. All third-floor rooms (and second-floor rooms in the Tonga, Tokelau, Tahiti, and Rapa Nui buildings) have balconies. Room service is offered until midnight. A concierge lounge with a choice view of the Magic Kingdom is a comfy retreat for guests in Hawaii and all-suite Tonga, the resort's most luxurious accommodations. In addition to the themed pool, there is a second, more removed, pool. Near Tokelau, a grassy knoll known as Sunset Point, offers a hammock. The resort boasts three white-sand beaches and great vantage points on Magic Kingdom fireworks and the Electrical Water Pageant. Boats may be rented, and fishing excursions may be arranged, and a 1¼-mile trail invites jogging around the tropical grounds.

Where to eat: Captain Cook's Snack Company (24-hour grazing); Kona Cafe (Asian-influenced casual fare and adjoining coffee bar); and 'Ohana (character breakfast and family-style Pacific Rim dinners featuring grilled meats).

Where to drink: Barefoot Bar (poolside refreshments) and Tambu lounge (tropical drinks and setting, plus samplers from 'Ohana restaurant next door).

VITAL STATISTICS: The Polynesian is located on the shore of Seven Seas Lagoon, directly opposite the Magic Kingdom, and offers both an enviable view and fast access via monorail to the park. Monorail links extend the resort's neighborhood beyond the adjacent Grand Floridian to include the Contemporary and provide for convenient commutes to Epcot. Golfers appreciate having the Palm and Magnolia courses nearby. Polynesian; 1600 South Seas Dr.; Box 10000; Lake Buena Vista, FL 32830-1000; 407-824-2000; fax 407-824-3174.

Transportation: A monorail resort (platform on second floor of the Great Ceremonial House). Water launches to the Magic Kingdom and the Grand Floridian. Monorail to the Magic Kingdom and the TTC. From the TTC, monorail or bus to Epcot, and buses to Typhoon Lagoon and Downtown Disney. Buses to the Disney-MGM Studios, Animal Kingdom, and Blizzard Beach. (**Note:** The TTC is within walking distance.)

Rates: Standard rooms start at $289 in value season, $324 regular, and $379 peak; concierge rooms begin at $445 value, $490 regular, and $560 peak; suites start at $465. A $25 per diem charge applies to each extra adult (beyond two) sharing a room.

Swan & Dolphin

The motto for these whimsical resorts might be "expect the unexpected." Certainly, noted architect Michael Graves designed these postmodern bookends with entertainment in mind. At the Dolphin, a 27-story triangular tower is flanked by buildings that are topped by two 56-foot-tall dolphin statues and covered in a mural of banana leaves. Guestrooms with such decorative touches as cabana-like doors do not preclude access to a first-rate fitness center or a showroom with Cartier gems. It's more of the same playful luxury next door at the Swan, which carves its own distinctive silhouette with 46-foot namesake statues perched atop its 12-story central building, and facades accented with turquoise waves. The Swan has 758 rooms, about half as many as the Dolphin, and its furnishings tend toward bird lamps and pineapple-stenciled headboards.

Special Room Requests

All WDW resorts offer rooms equipped for guests with disabilities, as well as nonsmoking rooms. For more detailed information, inquire with Central Reservations (407-934-7639). For more specifics related to travelers with disabilities, see the "Customized Tips" section of the *Planning Ahead* chapter.

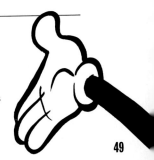

Swan & Dolphin Tips

- Request a corner room with a king-size bed at the Dolphin, and if it's available, you'll get two balconies for the price of one.

- Both the Swan and Dolphin feature large convention centers. If you're visiting for pleasure, check the name-badge quotient before you book.

- Swan and Dolphin guests may elect to pay $5 per day to receive a morning paper, in-room coffee, free local calls, and use of the Dolphin's health club for the length of their stay.

- Four tennis courts (located at the Dolphin) are kept lighted all night.

- Light sleepers should note that some rooms are steps from Board-Walk's Jellyrolls and Atlantic Dance clubs.

BIG DRAWS: Luxury in a lighthearted wrapper. Exceptional facilities. And you can walk to Epcot and BoardWalk.

WORTH NOTING: The Swan (managed by Westin) and the Dolphin (operated by Sheraton) are the only two WDW hotels whose value season extends through the summer months. Guests staying at either of the two hotels have access to all 17 restaurants and lounges, recreational activities, and may charge any meals and activities enjoyed at the sister hotel to their room tab. Such charging privileges do not extend beyond the two hotels. Guestrooms at the Swan and Dolphin are comparable to those at Disney's other deluxe resorts. Whereas standard rooms at the Dolphin feature two double beds, queen-size beds are the rule at the Swan (king-size beds are available at both). Room amenities at both hotels include stocked mini-bars and 24-hour room service, plus nightly turndown at the Swan, and coffeemakers, hair dryers, and irons with boards at the Dolphin. Club-level rooms at the Dolphin are located in the resort's tower; at the Swan they are on the top two floors of the hotel's main building. Both hotels boast several luxurious presidential suites. In addition to a white-sand beach with a volleyball net and boat rentals, the resorts share an enviable lap pool, a sprawling grotto pool with waterfalls, a small rectangular pool, and several whirlpools. Fireworks from Epcot's IllumiNations: Reflections of Earth are visible from both hotels.

Where to eat: At the Swan: Garden Grove Cafe (greenhouse setting with Gulliver-themed dinner) and Palio (Italian bistro). At the Dolphin: Coral Cafe (casual all-day dining); Dolphin Fountain (ice cream parlor); Shula's Steakhouse (steak and seafood); Juan & Only's (authentic Southwestern fare); and Tubbi's (cafeteria with 24-hour convenience store).

Where to drink: At the Swan: Kimonos (cocktail lounge with sushi bar); Lobby Court (coffees, occasional cigar menu); and Splash Grill (poolside). At the Dolphin: Cabana Bar & Grill (poolside); Copa Banana (tropical spot with a big-screen TV); Shula's Steakhouse (cozy lounge adjacent to dining area); and Juan's lounge (sangria, specialty margaritas).

VITAL STATISTICS: The Swan and Dolphin offer easy access to Epcot, the Disney-MGM Studios, BoardWalk, and the Fantasia Gardens Miniature Golf complex. Located side by side on the shore of Crescent Lake, a virtual stone's throw from Epcot's World Showcase, the hotels are flanked by BoardWalk on one side and the Yacht and Beach Club on the other. Walt Disney World Swan; 1200 Epcot Resorts Blvd.; Box 10000; Lake Buena Vista, FL 32830-1000; 407-934-3000; fax 407-934-4499. Walt Disney World Dolphin; 1500 Epcot Resorts Blvd.; Box 10000; Lake Buena Vista, FL 32830-1000; 407-934-4000; fax 407-934-4099.

Transportation: Boat or walkway to Epcot's International Gateway entrance. Boat or walkway to the Disney-MGM Studios. Buses to the Magic Kingdom, Animal Kingdom, Typhoon Lagoon, Blizzard Beach, and Downtown Disney.

Rates: At the Swan and Dolphin, standard rooms begin at $310 in value season and $350 peak, and club-level rooms are $460 value and $490 peak. For suite prices, call 800-227-1500. A $25 per diem charge applies for each extra adult (beyond two) sharing a room. Call 800-227-1500 to make reservations or visit *www.swandolphin.com.*

Wilderness Lodge & Villas

Rustic romance infuses every inspired detail of this resort, patterned after the grand National Park Service lodges of the early 1900s. Hidden away on an isolated shore of Bay Lake, Wilderness Lodge is surrounded by towering pine forests that provide a drumroll of sorts along the winding road leading to the timbered hotel. The soaring atrium lobby kindles the spirit of the great American West with hand-painted teepee chandeliers, an imposing pair of totem poles, a bubbling hot spring, and an 82-foot-tall fireplace whose layered stones actually replicate the Grand Canyon's strata. And as if Bay Lake weren't a sufficiently beautiful backdrop, the resort's natural landscape is supplemented by a roaring waterfall, a swimming area surrounded by boulders and wildflowers, and a steaming geothermic meadow complete with geyser. The guestrooms at the Lodge are located in two wings that

extend back from the lobby to the lakefront, forming a U-shaped frame around the inner courtyard. The adjacent Villas at Wilderness Lodge, styled after the railroad hotels of the late 1800s, are slated to open in early 2001. They extend the resort's neighborhood with 181 villas. The units are further distinguished by a red-brick roof and a five-story central tower. The Lodge and Villas share a lobby and a covered walkway connects the resorts.

BIG DRAWS: Luxury. Undeniable romance. The bottom line: a truly extraordinary setting at a considerable value to guests.

Wilderness Lodge Tips

- Daily tours offer a closer look at the resort's architecture or its restaurants.

- Courtyard and lake-view rooms are especially romantic, with audio accompaniment that includes waterfalls gushing and brooks babbling. Woods views provide quiet.

- The Lodge's junior suites are a good value, given their spaciousness. Honeymooners should request room 7084 for its fireworks views and whirlpool tub.

- Some rooms come with a queen-size bed and a bunk bed instead of two queen-size beds. Be sure to make your preference known.

WORTH NOTING: While all 728 Wilderness Lodge guestrooms have balconies or patios, quarters here are slightly more compact than those at Disney's other deluxe resorts, and feature two queen-size beds. Colorful quilted bedspreads, buffalo lamps, and armoires etched with mountain scenes maintain the theme. The Villas at Wilderness Lodge is a Disney Vacation Club resort (see page 55 for club details); accommodations are equipped with either a wet bar or a full kitchen, and thus fall under Disney's Home Away from Home category. Studios and larger villas with one or two bedrooms feature balconies (or patios). Villa guests enjoy full access to the Lodge next door and vice versa.

At the Lodge and Villas, room service is available for breakfast and dinner. The four corridors ringing the lobby provide access to porches overlooking the courtyard and contain cozy nooks with sofas and tucked-away fireplaces. Fire Rock Geyser spouts off 180-foot water plumes at the top of every hour from 7 A.M. until 10 P.M. A quiet pool, whirlpool, and Sturdy Branches health club are located in the villa section. Both resorts share a beach that fronts the lake. Guided fishing excursions can be arranged. Boats and bicycles may be rented, and there is a three-quarter-mile path for biking and jogging that leads to Fort Wilderness.

Where to eat: Artist Point (Pacific Northwest cuisine); Roaring Fork (snacks); and Whispering Canyon Cafe (family-style dining).

Where to drink: Territory Lounge (western motif) and Trout Pass (poolside).

VITAL STATISTICS: Wilderness Lodge and Villas; 801 and 901 W. Timberline Dr.; Box 10000; Lake Buena Vista, FL 32830-1000; 407-824-3200; fax 407-824-3232.

Transportation: Boat launch to the Magic Kingdom and Contemporary. Buses to Epcot, the Disney-MGM Studios, Animal Kingdom, Blizzard Beach, and the TTC. From the TTC, buses to Typhoon Lagoon and Downtown Disney. Walkway to Fort Wilderness and River Country.

Rates: At the Lodge, standard rooms begin at $189 in value season, $219 regular, and $265 peak; suites start at $620. Honeymoon rooms (with whirlpool tub) start at $250. A $25 per diem charge applies for each extra adult (beyond two) sharing a room (at the Lodge only). At the Villas, studios start at $264 value, $294 regular, and $349 peak; one-bedroom villas begin at $360 value, $400 regular, and $465 peak; two-bedroom villas start at $509 value, $625 regular, and $755 peak.

Yacht & Beach Club

This inspired duo conjures such a heady vision of turn-of-the-century Nantucket and Martha's Vineyard, you'd swear you smelled salt in the air. Certainly, architect Robert A. M. Stern's two-part evocation of the grand old seaside hotels has the gulls fooled. The Yacht and Beach Club stretch along a picturesque shoreline complete with white-sand beach, swimming lagoon, lighthouse, and marina. As the five-story beige clapboard structure of the Yacht Club gives way to the sky-blue Beach Club (the two are connected), the interior motif shifts from seriously nautical to seashore whimsical. The Yacht Club has a rich, exclusive feel to it—there's a stunning globe anchoring the lobby, and polished brass abounds. Next door at the Beach Club, beach umbrellas act as pillars, and clambakes are a nightly occurrence.

BIG DRAWS: Gracious accommodations. Compelling theming. Exceptional swimming area. Some of the World's finest restaurants and lounges. Enviable access to Epcot and the Disney-MGM Studios.

WORTH NOTING: There are 621 guestrooms at the Yacht Club and 572 rooms at the Beach Club. All are comparable in size to those at Disney's other deluxe resorts; as a rule, they feature two queen-size beds and a daybed (king-size beds are available). At the Yacht Club, rooms maintain the nautical theme with such touches as brass-trimmed bathroom mirrors patterned after portholes; most rooms have good-size balconies. At the Beach Club, guestrooms keep the seashore motif with the likes of cabana-style striped curtains. Amenities at both resorts include mini-bars, an iron and board, a hair dryer, newspaper delivery, and 24-hour room service. Only the Yacht Club offers concierge rooms.

A three-acre mini water park called Stormalong Bay earns the Yacht and Beach Club bragging rights to the World's best resort swimming area; the sprawling, sandy-bottomed pool, open only to hotel guests, includes sections with jets, swirling current loops, and slides (traditional whirlpools also stand by). Each resort also has a smaller quiet pool and whirlpool, so removed you must seek them out. The Ship Shape health club is among the most extensive fitness centers at a WDW property. Boat rentals and two tennis courts are offered, fishing excursions can be arranged, and volleyball and croquet equipment is available.

Resort Primer

- Reservationists cannot guarantee a room location or view, so arrive early to request the best selection.

- Rooms on the upper floors afford the most privacy.

- Adjoining rooms and king-size beds can usually be requested but are not assured.

- Concierge rooms, in addition to extra service, generally include continental breakfast and afternoon snacks.

Yacht & Beach Club Tips

■ The stunning views belong strictly to those with lakeside rooms.

■ At both resorts, it's a lengthy walk to the lobby from the outermost reaches of guest wings.

■ At the Beach Club, second- and fourth-floor rooms have balconies; balconies on the fourth floor are slightly larger.

■ Balconies at the Yacht Club are bigger than those at the Beach Club, which are standing room only.

■ Inquire at the Yacht Club's Guest Services desk about the free weekly garden tours.

■ Take a ride on a Criss-Craft speedboat. See page 179 for details.

■ There are hideaway tables for two in the Ale and Compass lounge in the lobby area of the Yacht Club.

Where to eat: At the Beach Club: Cape May Cafe (character breakfasts and clambake buffets). At the Yacht Club: Yacht Club Galley (all-day casual) and Yachtsman Steakhouse. Shared by both hotels is the Beaches & Cream Soda Shop (a classic soda fountain).

Where to drink: At the Beach Club: Martha's Vineyard (cloud nine for wine lovers) and Rip Tide (lobby niche). At the Yacht Club: Ale and Compass (cozy lobby nook) and Crew's Cup (well-heeled beer emporium). For poolside refreshments and snacks, there's Hurricane Hanna's Grill.

VITAL STATISTICS: The Yacht and Beach Club enjoy extraordinary proximity to Epcot, Disney-MGM Studios, BoardWalk, and the Fantasia Gardens Miniature Golf complex. Located side by side on a shore of Crescent Lake that offers a footpath to Epcot's International Gateway entrance, these sister resorts are joined lakeside by the BoardWalk, Swan, and Dolphin. Yacht Club; 1700 Epcot Resorts Blvd.; Box 10000; Lake Buena Vista, FL 32830-1000; 407-934-7000; fax 407-934-3450. Beach Club; 1800 Epcot Resorts Blvd.; Box 10000; Lake Buena Vista, FL 32830-1000; 407-934-8000; fax 407-934-3850.

Transportation: Boats or walkway to Epcot's International Gateway entrance near the France pavilion. Boats or walkway to the Disney-MGM Studios. Buses to the Magic Kingdom, Animal Kingdom, Typhoon Lagoon, Blizzard Beach, and Downtown Disney.

Rates: Standard rooms at the Yacht and Beach Club resorts begin at $279 in value season, $309 regular, and $364 peak; concierge rooms at the Yacht Club start at $405 value, $460 regular, and $520 peak; Yacht Club suites start at $490 and Beach Club suites start at $465. A $25 per diem charge applies to each extra adult (beyond two) sharing a room.

Home Away From Home
Disney's Old Key West Resort

Pastel-hued clapboard guesthouses with tin roofs and white picket fences set the cheerful tone of this Key Westerly retreat. Here, unassuming luxury dovetails with an intimate, laid-back atmosphere to create the look and feel of a friendly resort community. A sprawling village, it is bounded by the wooded fairways of the Lake Buena Vista golf links, and anchored at its center by a lighthouse that overlooks the main swimming area and moonlights as a sauna. A picturesque waterway called the Trumbo Canal flows from the heart of the resort, eventually uniting with Lake Buena Vista. Spacious accommodations equipped with kitchens may set this resort apart, but what gives the place cachet is its warmth. Every doorstep in its two- and three-story guest buildings is fronted with a mat that reads WELCOME HOME.

BIG DRAWS: Spacious accommodations, ideal for long stays. Homey and soothing environs. Value for groups. Convenience of kitchens. Well located for golfers.

WORTH NOTING: This resort was the first Disney Vacation Club property (see below). It features studio accommodations and one-, two-, and three-bedroom villas. The villas have a distinctly Key West feel, and are decorated in light woods with ceiling fans and color schemes of sea-foam green and mauve. Each studio features a large bedroom with two queen-size beds; a wet bar with a microwave, coffeemaker, and small refrigerator; and a spacious bathroom. Larger villas offer a dining room, fully equipped kitchen, laundry facilities, whirlpool bathtub, and VCR. They also feature a king-size bed in the master bedroom, two queen-size beds in each additional bedroom, and a spacious living room with queen-size sofa bed. All accommodations have balconies or porches. Boats and bicycles are available for rent. Fishing excursions can be arranged. The three tennis courts tend to be quiet and accessible. The main swimming area, complete with a huge whirlpool, supplements three quiet pools. There is a small fitness center, and the resort's winding streets lend themselves well to jogging or cycling. Conch Flats Community Hall offers table tennis, board games, and video rentals.

Join the Club?

Frequent visitors who consider WDW a home away from home might consider joining the ranks of the Disney Vacation Club. For a one-time price and annual dues, members may stay at Disney's Old Key West Resort, BoardWalk Villas, The Villas at Wilderness Lodge, or at many resorts beyond WDW, including Disney's Hilton Head Island Resort, in South Carolina, and, just two hours from WDW, Disney's Vero Beach Resort (see page 58). They can also opt for the Disney Cruise Line or another WDW resort. Built-in flexibility (in timing and room size) improves on traditional time-share plans. For more information, visit *www.dvcmagic.com*.

Old Key West Tips

■ For a waterfront setting that's pleasantly removed from the main recreation area, request a villa in the Turtle Shack vicinity. Numbers 43 and 44 are good, given their water views and close proximity to the pool, snack bar, tennis court, and bus stop alike.

■ Celebrate your birthday with a bang on a private fireworks cruise. See page 179 for details.

■ It's possible to have a whole Key lime pie delivered to your room.

■ All accommodations but the studios feature whirlpool bathtubs.

■ One-bedroom villas yield more than twice the space of a studio for a relatively small jump in cost.

Where to eat: Good's Food to Go (poolside snacks) and Olivia's Cafe (casual all-day dining with Key West flourishes). Grills and picnic tables are available. Pizza delivery from Dixie Landings is offered until midnight. Conch Flats General Store stocks groceries.

Where to drink: Gurgling Suitcase (tiny spirited pub) and Turtle Shack (poolside refreshments).

VITAL STATISTICS: This resort is well located for golfers. It also enjoys easy access to Downtown Disney and good proximity to Epcot and Disney-MGM Studios. Disney's Old Key West Resort; 1510 N. Cove Rd.; Box 10000; Lake Buena Vista, FL 32830-1000; 407-827-7700; fax 407-827-7710.

Transportation: Buses to Epcot, the Magic Kingdom, the Disney-MGM Studios, Animal Kingdom, Typhoon Lagoon, Blizzard Beach, and Downtown Disney. Boats to Downtown Disney.

Rates: Studios are $244 in value season, $269 regular, and $309 peak; one-bedroom villas are $330 value, $365 regular, and $420 peak; two-bedrooms are $459 value, $525 regular, and $635 peak; and three-bedrooms start at $955 value, $1,050 regular, and $1,170 peak.

Fort Wilderness Resort & Campground

No fewer than 700 acres of woodland just hopping with rabbits combine with WDW's largest lake to provide the foundation for Fort Wilderness, a retreat that relies on the great outdoors for atmosphere. A place that's as much about recreation as low-key lodging, it is brimming with inspiration for nature walks, fishing, and canoeing. Shaded campsites are arranged on 28 loops, linked by thoroughfares. While some of the 784 sites are designated for tents, most are devoted to RV camping; hundreds of spots sport air-conditioned Wilderness Cabins, comfortable units that are comparable to well-equipped trailer homes.

BIG DRAWS: Natural setting. Value. And recreation galore.

WORTH NOTING: Most loops have at least one air-conditioned comfort station equipped with restrooms, telephones, showers, laundry facilities, and an ice machine. Campsites range in length from 25 to 65 feet. All sites offer a charcoal grill, picnic table, and a 30/50-amp electrical outlet. Most include sanitary-disposal connections, and nearly half have cable television hook-ups. Wilderness Cabins are separated from other campsites. They feature rustic decor and a

deck with a picnic table; amenities include a hair dryer, and an iron (with a board). Each Wilderness Cabin is air-conditioned and offers daily maid service as well as a fully equipped eat-in kitchen, a living room with a TV and VCR, and a full bathroom. Pets are welcome at designated campsites ($3 per day). Pet loops are not wired for cable. Recreational options include swimming, boating, tennis, and biking. Guided fishing excursions may be arranged. The Hoop-Dee-Doo Musical Revue dinner show is presented nightly (see *Dining & Entertainment*).

Where to eat: Most guests cook their own meals (supplies are sold at Meadow Trading Post and Settlement Trading Post), but there's also Trail's End Buffet (home-style dining).

Where to drink: Crockett's Tavern (cocktail service).

VITAL STATISTICS: Fort Wilderness occupies Bay Lake's southern shore. It offers ready access to the Magic Kingdom and closely borders the Osprey Ridge and Eagle Pines golf courses. Fort Wilderness; 4510 N. Fort Wilderness Trail; Box 10000; Lake Buena Vista, FL 32830-1000; 407-824-2900; fax 407-824-3508.

Transportation: Electric golf carts and bikes can be rented to supplement the internal bus system that links the campsites and recreation areas (buses circulate at 20-minute intervals). Boats to the Magic Kingdom and Contemporary. Buses from Settlement Depot to Blizzard Beach and Animal Kingdom, and from the visitor parking lot to the TTC. From the TTC, monorails service the Magic Kingdom, Epcot, and the Contemporary, Polynesian, and Grand Floridian resorts.

Fort Wilderness Tips

■ Bikes and electric carts are, sudden rains aside, the preferred means for getting around.

■ A car is the quickest way to get to other parts of the World from this resort.

■ Views of Magic Kingdom fireworks and the Electrical Water Pageant are readily available.

■ Tent campers should request loop 1500 or 2000 for quiet; RV campers will find greater privacy on loops 1600 through 1900 (pets welcome).

A Great Beach Add-on

A stay at Disney's Vero Beach Resort—an oceanfront Disney Vacation Club property just two hours away by car—combines nicely with a WDW vacation. The resort's homey comforts are similar to those at Disney's Old Key West Resort (described on page 55).

Among its assets are pristine beaches and proximity to manatee retreats and sunken ships fit for dive trips (this is the Treasure Coast, after all). A tropical tangle separates the resort from the beach. Packages that combine a Vero Beach trip with a WDW visit are available. For more information, call 800-359-8000.

Rates: Preferred sites with full hookups, including water, electricity, sewage, and cable TV, are $47 in value season, $62 regular, and $70 peak; sites with full hookups minus the cable TV are $39 value, $57 regular, and $65 peak; sites with electricity hookups only are $34 value, $47 regular, and $55 peak. There is a limit of ten persons per campsite, and a $2 per diem charge applies to each extra adult (beyond two) sharing a site. Rates for Wilderness Cabins are $219 value, $254 regular, and $279 peak. Maximum occupancy is six, and there is a $5 per diem charge that applies to each extra adult (beyond two) sharing a unit.

The Villas at the Disney Institute

This community of villas, stretching from the Lake Buena Vista golf course to the shores of the lake itself, meshes rustic charm with casual comforts. Spread over a lightly wooded and canal-crossed expanse, the peaceful resort offers few hints of its Disney parentage. Among the five types of accommodations are high-rise treehouses set in the woods, skylight-blessed fairway villas, and cedar-sided all-suite bungalows.

BIG DRAWS: Rustic and relaxing environs. Golf close by. Great spa. Convenient access to Downtown Disney.

WORTH NOTING: The only accommodations without full kitchens are the Bungalows, each of which features a living area, a bedroom with two queen-size beds, a balcony (or patio), a wet bar with a microwave, coffeemaker, and a small refrigerator. Townhouses are either one-bedroom (with a queen-size bed in the loft bedroom and a sleeper sofa in the living room) or two-bedroom (with a queen-size bed in the loft bedroom, two twins in the second bedroom, and a queen sleeper sofa in the living room). The roomy Fairway Villas have cathedral ceilings and offer a queen-size bed in one bedroom, two double beds in the other, and a pull-down bed or a sleeper sofa in the living room. The Tree-house Villas—secluded accommodations—offer three bedrooms, two bathrooms, and a utility room in two-story octagonal houses on stilts. The Grand Vista Homes are luxurious villas whose amenities include refrigerators and nightly turndown. Lodging for guests with disabilities is available. Note that the decor in The Villas at the Disney Institute is on the drab side for a Disney accommodation.

Bungalows and Townhouses are largely reserved for guests participating in group and corporate retreat programs. With the exception of its spa and expansive health club, the Disney Institute no longer offers instructional and enrichment programs to the general public. However, the exceptional spa/fitness center here is still open to all WDW resort guests. For more information on The Spa at the Disney Institute, turn to page 182. Guests at the Villas enjoy a smorgasbord of recreational diversions, including the nearby golf course; six swimming pools; a whirlpool; a jogging trail; four clay tennis courts; fishing excursions; and boat, bike, and golf-cart rentals.

Where to eat: At press time, the restaurants at the Disney Institute were scheduled for drastic changes. Call 407-WDW-DINE for details. Groceries may be ordered for room delivery (407-827-4147). Downtown Disney restaurants are located nearby.

Where to drink: When it comes to imbibing, there are opportunities aplenty at nearby Downtown Disney.

VITAL STATISTICS: The Villas at the Disney Institute, located on the northern shore of Lake Buena Vista, have unsurpassed proximity to the Lake Buena Vista golf links and Downtown Disney. Epcot, Typhoon Lagoon. Disney-MGM Studios are also nearby. The Villas at the Disney Institute; 1960 N. Magnolia Way; Box 10000; Lake Buena Vista, FL 32830-1000; 407-827-1100; fax 407-934-2741.

Transportation: Buses to the Magic Kingdom, Epcot, the Disney-MGM Studios, Animal Kingdom, Typhoon Lagoon, Blizzard Beach, and Downtown Disney. Paved paths to the Downtown Disney Marketplace and West Side.

Rates: Bungalows are $209 in value season, $239 regular, and $259 peak; one-bedroom Townhouses are $254 value, $274 regular, and $294 peak; two-bedroom Townhouses are $359 value, $394 regular, and $414 peak; Treehouse Villas are $379 value, $404 regular, and $424 peak; Fairway Villas are $419 value, $454 regular, and $474 peak; and Grand Vista Homes begin at $1,100.

The Villas at the Disney Institute Tips

■ Guests can easily reach Downtown Disney by golf cart and, in the case of the nearest villas (Townhouses 1–40), by foot.

■ The resort's crisscrossing pathways (ideal for jogging) can be confusing to navigate. Also note that most walkways are dimly lit at night.

■ If it's space you're after, the two-bedroom Townhouses have about 50 percent more footage than the Treehouse Villas—and cost less.

■ The Spa at the Disney Institute—also one of the best fitness centers in the World—offers a comprehensive lineup of state-of-the-art Cybex equipment. It's a veritable warehouse of shape-up gear.

■ Unless you're a night owl, Townhouses are too close to the din of Pleasure Island for comfort.

Caribbean Beach Tips

- Aruba is a good choice for seclusion and for proximity to Old Port Royale (they're linked by bridge).

- For honeymoon-style isolation, request a room in Trinidad South. Located just off the main loop, its buildings and beach are especially removed.

- Martinique tends to be the liveliest village.

- The 1.4-mile promenade circling Barefoot Bay is ideal for biking and jogging. Bikes and boats may be rented. A special length-of-stay option is available for boat renters.

- Families flock here so plan on encountering plenty of children.

Moderate
Caribbean Beach

In this colorful evocation of the Caribbean, the spirit of the islands is rendered via an immense lake ringed by beaches and villages representing Barbados, Martinique, Trinidad, Jamaica, and Aruba. Each village is marked by clusters of two-story guest buildings that transport you to the Caribbean with cool pastel facades, white railings, and vivid metallic roofs. The separate Custom House reception building resembles one you might encounter at a tropical resort. Lush landscaping adds to the ambience. Old Port Royale, which houses the resort's eateries and shops, and opens out to its main recreation area and themed pool, takes cues from an island market.

BIG DRAWS: Excellent value. Cheery environs with a convincingly Caribbean feel.

WORTH NOTING: The resort has a total of 2,112 rooms. Slightly larger than those at Disney's other moderately priced resorts, they feature two double beds (king-size beds are available) and soft-hued decor. Amenities include an in-room coffeemaker. Room service, which ventures a touch beyond pizza, is offered from 4 P.M. until midnight. The resort's 45-acre centerpiece, Barefoot Bay, is larger than World Showcase Lagoon. Villages are sprawled around it in a way that can make travel between some guest areas cumbersome despite footbridges and "local" buses. The resort's sole whirlpool is nestled into its bustling themed pool. Each village offers its own beach, quiet pool, and array of courtyards.

Where to eat: Captain's Tavern (for hearty American fare with limited Caribbean influence) and a food court featuring six counter-service options.

Where to drink: Banana Cabana (poolside refreshments) and the above-mentioned Captain's Tavern (beer, wine, and cocktails).

VITAL STATISTICS: Caribbean Beach is off on its own but well situated for pursuits other than the Magic Kingdom, with Epcot, the Disney-MGM Studios, and Blizzard Beach close at hand, on one side, and Typhoon Lagoon and Downtown Disney nearby, on the other. Caribbean Beach; 900 Cayman Way; Box 10000; Lake Buena Vista, FL 32830-1000; 407-934-3400; fax 407-934-3288.

Transportation: Buses stop at each village en route to the Magic Kingdom, Epcot, the Disney-MGM Studios, Animal Kingdom, Typhoon Lagoon, Blizzard Beach, and Downtown Disney.

Rates: Rooms begin at $129 in value season, $149 in regular season, and $174 during peak periods. A $15 per diem charge applies for each extra adult (beyond two) sharing a room.

Coronado Springs

The architecture of this sprawling resort gives its nod to Mexico and the American Southwest, with brightly tinted buildings accented by tile roofs, soaring columns, and arched entryways. Three clusters of regionally themed guest buildings rim the 15-acre Lago Dorado lagoon. The terra-cotta Casitas occupy a citylike landscape that segues into rural surroundings. Here, pueblo-style Ranchos invite guests to dwell among cacti adjacent to a dry streambed. In the resort's third section, the scenery shifts once more, with rocky beaches, hammocks, and festive Cabanas filling the horizon. Guestrooms in the three areas are similarly appointed, with brilliant yellow, scarlet, or deep-blue accents. Walkways around the lagoon lead from guest-room areas to the main recreation zone (dominated by a five-story Mayan pyramid) and the central building that holds the resort's temporal treasures: an intricately tiled rotunda lobby, two eateries, a lounge, and a gift shop carrying Mexican handicrafts.

BIG DRAWS: A standout among the moderates for its health club, suites, and business hotel perks.

WORTH NOTING: Guestrooms at this 1,921-room resort are smaller than those at Disney's deluxe hotels. Decor reveals Mexican and Southwestern influences, and reflects the style of each guest area. Standard rooms feature two double beds

Coronado Springs Tips

■ A ten-percent gratuity is automatically added to all dine-in purchases made at the Pepper Market food court.

■ January, May, September, and October are popular convention months. Most groups are housed in the Casitas area, near the convention facilities, and a separate check-in area is provided.

■ The Ranchos are nearest the pool area; the Casitas are closer to the main building, convention center, and health club; and the Cabanas are convenient to both.

■ There's a lot of ground to cover between the central building and some guestrooms. If you want a room near the hub, make sure to make your preference known when you make the reservation.

Dixie Landings Tips

■ For optimal atmosphere and minimal walking, request a room in Magnolia Bend's Oak Manor, or lodge number 18 or 27 in the resort's Alligator Bayou section.

■ Mansion rooms exude honeymoon-style elegance and seclusion.

■ Elevators are available in the resort's Magnolia Bend section only.

■ The Sassagoula River Cruise is a pleasant outing *and* a convenient means of transportation.

■ Try Cotton Co-Op's southern snacks (consider the spicy Cajun Hot Nuts).

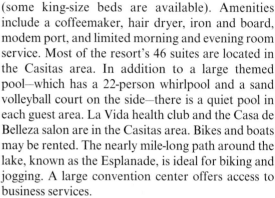

(some king-size beds are available). Amenities include a coffeemaker, hair dryer, iron and board, modem port, and limited morning and evening room service. Most of the resort's 46 suites are located in the Casitas area. In addition to a large themed pool—which has a 22-person whirlpool and a sand volleyball court on the side—there is a quiet pool in each guest area. La Vida health club and the Casa de Belleza salon are in the Casitas area. Bikes and boats may be rented. The nearly mile-long path around the lake, known as the Esplanade, is ideal for biking and jogging. A large convention center offers access to business services.

Where to eat: Maya Grill (Southwestern flavors) and the Pepper Market (food court resembling an outdoor market).

Where to drink: Francisco's (lounge with Mexican snacks) and Siesta's (pool bar).

VITAL STATISTICS: Located near Animal Kingdom and Blizzard Beach. Coronado Springs; 1000 W. Buena Vista Dr.; Box 10000; Lake Buena Vista, FL 32830-1000; 407-939-1000; fax 407-939-0425.

Transportation: Buses stop at each guest area en route to the Magic Kingdom, Epcot, the Disney-MGM Studios, Animal Kingdom, Typhoon Lagoon, Blizzard Beach, Downtown Disney, and BoardWalk.

Rates: Rooms begin at $129 in value season, $149 regular, and $174 peak; suites start at $258. A $15 per diem charge applies for each extra adult (beyond two) sharing a room.

Dixie Landings

Southern hospitality takes two forms at this 2,048-room resort: pillared mansions with groomed lawns and *Gone with the Wind* elegance and, farther upriver, rustic homes with tin roofs and rough-hewn bayou charm that are tucked among trees and bushes. Guestrooms located in the three-story Magnolia Bend mansions and the two-story Alligator Bayou lodges are similarly appointed. The man-made Sassagoula River winds through the heart of the resort, curling around its main recreation area like a moat. Bridges link guest lodgings with this area and the steamship-style building that house the resort's eateries, gift shop, and check-in facilities.

BIG DRAWS: Excellent value. An exceedingly lovely natural setting.

WORTH NOTING: Rooms are smaller than those at Disney's deluxe hotels, but pleasantly inviting. Each features two double beds (some king-size beds and trundle beds are available). This is a large, sprawling resort with twice as many rooms as its sister resort, Port Orleans; some accommodations are a bit removed from the central building or the nearest bus stop. Room service delivers pizza and supplements from 4 P.M. to midnight. Bikes and boats may be rented. The resort's extensive pathways are well suited for joggers, and a carriage path leads to Port Orleans. Five quiet pools (open 24 hours, provided they stay quiet) are sprinkled around the Bayou and Mansion guest areas. A whirlpool is located near the main pool. Catch-and-release fishing excursions are offered, as is a stocked, secluded fishing hole (cane poles available). Guests may use the themed pool at Port Orleans in addition to the one here.

Where to eat: Boatwright's Dining Hall (casual restaurant specializing in southern cuisine) and Colonel's Cotton Mill (sprawling food court).

Where to drink: Cotton Co-Op (fireplace and evening entertainment) and Muddy Rivers (poolside refreshments).

VITAL STATISTICS: Dixie Landings is located on a bank of the Sassagoula River and offers hassle-free commutes to Downtown Disney, not to mention its sister resort, Port Orleans (reachable by boat or carriage path). Epcot and the Disney-MGM Studios are close at hand, as are three of WDW's 18-hole golf courses. Dixie Landings; 1251 Dixie Dr.; Box 10000; Lake Buena Vista, FL 32830-1000; 407-934-6000; fax 407-934-5777.

Transportation: Buses stop at guest areas en route to the Magic Kingdom, Epcot, the Disney-MGM Studios, Animal Kingdom, Typhoon Lagoon, Blizzard Beach, and Downtown Disney. Water launches, known as the Sassagoula River Cruise, travel to Port Orleans and Downtown Disney.

Rates: Rooms begin at $129 in value season, $149 regular, and $174 peak. A $15 per diem charge applies for each extra adult (beyond two) sharing a room.

Port Orleans

New Orleans' historic French Quarter is evoked in this resort's prim row house-style guest buildings, which are wrapped in ornate wrought-iron railings and set amid romantic gardens, quiet courtyards, and tree-lined city blocks. Old-fashioned lampposts add to the ambience, as do signs denoting such streets as Rue D'Baga and Café Au Lait Way. The resort is entered via Port Orleans Square, an airy atrium with adjoining one-story buildings that house the hotel's front desk, gift shop, and arcade on one side, and its restaurant, lounge complete with a scat club, and food court on the other. (Follow the French horn chandeliers to the Mardi Gras mural to check in.) Guestrooms are located in seven three-story buildings, which are set on either side of the central thoroughfare that begins just beyond Port Orleans Square and ends at the resort's large themed pool. The whole enclave is set alongside a stand-in Mississippi known as the Sassagoula River. This is the sister resort of neighboring Dixie Landings.

Port Orleans Tips

- This is too pretty a place to wake up to a view of the parking lot, so consider reserving a room overlooking the gardens or splurge on riverscape digs. Note that pool views can spoil the ambience.

- Of the buildings with riverfront rooms, number 1 is nicely isolated. Buildings 2 and 5 are close to the pool area.

- The boat to Downtown Disney is often quicker than the bus.

- Experience Port Orleans' romantic atmosphere via a bike ride along the river.

- Don't miss the fresh beignets (a true taste of the Big Easy), whose aroma regularly wafts through the food court.

- Although there is no quiet pool, the whirlpool in the main pool area is set off in a courtyard by vine-covered arches.

BIG DRAWS: A terrific bang for the buck. The truly charming environs rank among Disney's most memorable. Easily the least sprawling and most manageable of the moderately priced resorts.

WORTH NOTING: The pretty, homey rooms are a bit smaller than those at Disney's more expensive hotels but are perfectly comfortable. Each of the 1,008 rooms features two double beds; some king-size beds are available. The vast food court and the hearty fare at Bonfamille's Cafe earn repeat guests. Room service is limited to pizza, wings, and ice cream (4 P.M. to midnight). A Dixieland band often entertains in the main courtyard; a street artist is available for portraits. A carriage path—ideal for jogging, strolling, and biking—wends alongside the river to Port Orleans' sister resort, Dixie Landings, less than a mile upriver. Bikes and boats may be rented. A large whirlpool is centrally located. In addition to the fantasy swimming pool here, Port Orleans guests are permitted use of Dixie Landings' themed pool; they can also take advantage of its secluded fishing hole (catch-and-release only). Guided fishing trips depart from the resort daily; reservations must be made 24 hours in advance. The Sassagoula River Cruise is a pleasant outing, and also a convenient mode of transportation.

Where to eat: Bonfamille's Cafe (a dining room with Creole cooking and French Quarter style) and Sassagoula Floatworks & Food Factory (food court with Mardi Gras ambience and inexpensive fare).

Where to drink: Mardi Grogs (poolside refreshments) and Scat Cat's Club (for specialty drinks and evening entertainment).

VITAL STATISTICS: Port Orleans enjoys special access to Downtown Disney via the Sassagoula River Cruise, which also links it with Dixie Landings, its sister resort upriver. It's close to Epcot, the Disney-MGM Studios, and three 18-hole golf courses as well. Port Orleans; 2201 Orleans Dr.; Box 10000; Lake Buena Vista, FL 32830-1000; 407-934-5000; fax 407-934-5353.

Transportation: Buses to the Magic Kingdom, Epcot, the Disney-MGM Studios, Animal Kingdom, Typhoon Lagoon, Blizzard Beach, and Downtown Disney. Water launches to Dixie Landings and Downtown Disney.

Rates: Rooms begin at $129 in value season, $149 regular, and $174 peak. A $15 per diem charge applies for each extra adult (beyond two) sharing a room.

Value

All-Star Movies, All-Star Music, & All-Star Sports Resorts

Bright in a manner normally reserved for toy packaging, these fun-loving resorts exist at the intersection of entertainment architecture and pop art. Picture a landscape in which three-story football helmets, cowboy boots, and dalmatians are the norm, and you have an idea of the oversize sense of whimsy that governs the All-Star Movies, All-Star Music, and All-Star Sports resorts. Identical in all but their telltale preoccupations, each has its own utterly felicitous central check-in building, complete with food court, and its own pair of signature swimming pools. Each features ten guest buildings that are divided into five distinct (movies, music, or sports) themes and 1,920 thematically correct rooms. Sports fans have a larger-than-Shaquille O'Neal *raison d'être* in the

All-Star Stats

■ The jukeboxes at the rock 'n' roll guest building could hold 4,000 compact discs, enough music for 135 days.

■ It would take more than nine million tennis balls to fill one of the tennis cans holding court at All-Star Sports.

■ Not coincidentally, there are no fewer than 101 spotted puppies on and about the *101 Dalmatians* buildings.

All-Star Resorts Tips

■ These resorts attract families with small children in droves. All-Star Music tends to have a higher ratio of adults to children.

■ For maximum quiet, request a third-floor room in a building away from the food court or main pool action (at All-Star Music, it's Broadway or country; at All-Star Sports, tennis or basketball; at All-Star Movies, *The Love Bug* or *The Mighty Ducks*).

■ Reservations are required for luggage assistance upon checkout; call the night before.

■ All-Star guests can rent boats at any of the other WDW resorts.

■ Unless you plan to drive everywhere, request a room near the lobby (i.e., bus stop).

All-Star Sports resort's homages to basketball, baseball, football, tennis, and surfing. The All-Star Music resort makes equally exaggerated overtures to calypso, jazz, Broadway, rock, and country music. The All-Star Movies resort makes outlandish reprises of *101 Dalmatians*, *The Mighty Ducks*, *Fantasia*, *The Love Bug*, and *Toy Story*.

BIG DRAW: All the advantages of staying on WDW turf at a fraction of the cost of its other resorts.

WORTH NOTING: Requests for specific sport, music, or movie motifs cannot be guaranteed, but are likely to be met, considering the resorts' enormous capacity (384 rooms per theme, five themes per resort). Rooms are, not surprisingly, the smallest of those at any WDW resort. While spare, they're perfectly adequate, if perhaps a tad lacking in drawer space. In all rooms except those equipped for travelers with disabilities, there's sufficient space under the beds to stash a suitcase. Themes are maintained with a great deal more subtlety—bedspreads, curtains, light fixtures—in guestrooms than on the startling grounds. Rooms with king-size beds are available on request, as are additional amenities such as down pillows and hair dryers. Onsite recreation is limited to arcades and two whimsically designed pools at each resort. Pizza delivery, plus beer and wine, is available until midnight.

Where to eat: Each hotel has a vast, themed food court: All-Star Sports (End Zone); All-Star Music (Intermission); All-Star Movies (World Premiere).

Where to drink: At All-Star Sports: Team Spirits pool bar. At All-Star Music: Singing Spirits pool bar. At All-Star Movies: Silver Screen Spirits pool bar.

VITAL STATISTICS: All-Star resorts have excellent proximity to Disney's Animal Kingdom and Blizzard Beach; Epcot and Disney-MGM Studios are also close at hand. All-Star Movies; 1991 W. Buena Vista Dr.; Box 10000; Lake Buena Vista, FL 32830-1000; 407-939-7000; fax 407-939-7111. All-Star Music; 1801 W. Buena Vista Dr.; Box 10000; Lake Buena Vista, FL 32830-1000; 407-939-6000; fax 407-939-7222. All-Star Sports; 1701 W. Buena Vista Dr.; Box 10000; Lake Buena Vista, FL 32830-1000; 407-939-5000; fax 407-939-7333.

Transportation: Buses to the Magic Kingdom, Epcot, the Disney-MGM Studios, Animal Kingdom, Typhoon Lagoon, Blizzard Beach, and Downtown Disney.

Rates: Rooms begin at $77 in value season, $99 regular, and $104 peak. A $10 per diem charge applies to each extra adult (beyond two) sharing a room.

Disney Cruise Line

The first thing to understand about the Disney Cruise Line's seamless one-week vacations, which can pair a WDW resort stay with a cruise: *Disney Magic* and its sister ship, *Disney Wonder,* are *not* floating Fantasylands.

The 1,750-passenger ships are casually elegant, designed to recapture the majesty of early ocean liners. They're equipped to satisfy even the most savvy of cruisers, with a mix of traditional seafaring diversions, classic Disney touches, and an occasional quirky surprise (such as a restaurant whose decor changes from strictly black and white to total Technicolor during your meal). Recreation areas are designed to lure families and adults *sans* kids to altogether different parts of the ship. Each ship even has a pool and a restaurant earmarked for adults only.

Lest anyone forget who owns these vessels, Disney characters crop up from stem to stern. A bronze statue of Mickey as helmsman greets arriving guests on the *Disney Magic* and a life-size statue of Goofy hangs over the stern (he's painting the ship, not suffering from seasickness). Characters of the flesh-and-fur variety are also on hand to mix, mingle, and otherwise assist the captain.

By day, fun in the sun alternates with lunch, indoor distractions, and catnaps. When the sun goes down, the focus shifts to dining and hitting the deck that's home to a Pleasure Island-like cluster of adults-only party spots.

Disney Cruise Line land-sea vacations begin with a stay at WDW and finish up with a voyage on the *Disney Wonder*. After transferring to Port Canaveral, guests embark on a three- or four-night cruise to the Bahamas. (Seven-night Caribbean cruise-only packages to the U.S. Virgin Islands take place aboard the *Disney Magic*.) En route to Castaway Cay, Disney's private isle, the ships make a stop in busy Nassau or Freeport. How nice it is that only Disney can call at Castaway Cay.

Land Ho!

Each voyage on the Disney Cruise Line includes a day-long stop at Castaway Cay, Disney's charted, yet private, isle. With all the perks of a tropical paradise, an afternoon at Castaway Cay is sure to cure even the most severe cases of Gilligan envy. Disney has allowed the island to retain its natural beauty while accommodating a variety of activities, including volleyball, snorkeling, biking, and hiking. The 1,000-acre Bahamian island features a mile-long stretch of secluded sand reserved for adult sun worshippers, as well as those seeking private open-air massages in cabanas overlooking the ocean. There's also a restaurant, bar, and more for Bahama mamas and papas to explore.

Disney Cruise Line Tips

- Resort IDs can be used to charge drinks, mini-bar snacks, and salon services, as well as gratuities for servers and cabin crew.

- Palo, the adults-only dining room, is the only restaurant that accepts reservations. Book it as soon as possible, once you're onboard.

- Unlike a trip around World Showcase, in which you merely *feel* as if you've left the country, on a Disney Cruise Line vacation you really do. Pack a passport (or birth certificate).

BIG DRAWS: The ultimate surf-and-turf experience, Disney-style. Private island rendezvous. Adults, teens, and tots are unlikely to step on one another's toes.

WORTH NOTING: Each room has a safe, TV, hair dryer, small refrigerator, and telephone with "land line." Facilities include three pools, a sports deck, and the Vista Spa & Salon. In addition to nightclub-style entertainment, the ship boasts adult-oriented enrichment programs, deck parties, and two theaters: Buena Vista Theater shows movies (first-run and classic Disney films); the Walt Disney Theater hosts an original musical production each evening. (Consult the cruise director for details.)

Where to eat: On the *Disney Magic*, Animator's Palate (room undergoes spectral metamorphosis), Parrot Cay (Caribbean), Lumière's (continental, casually elegant), and Palo (Italian fare, romantic, reserved for adults). Topsider Buffet is a casual daytime spot—kids rule dinner hour. On the *Disney Wonder*, Triton's replaces Lumière's, and Beach Blanket Buffet replaces Topsider Buffet. To avoid the kiddies, request the second dinner seating.

Where to drink: On the *Disney Magic*, The Promenade Lounge (elegant bar), ESPN Skybox (spirited sports bar), Beat Street, where you'll find Offbeat (comedy club), Rockin' Bar D (live band and deejay), and Sessions (piano bar). The *Disney Wonder* has comparable options, including a trio of clubs in Route 66 (Barrel of Laughs, Wavebands, and Cadillac's).

VITAL STATISTICS: Shipboard accommodations on the *Disney Magic* and the *Disney Wonder* are about 25 percent roomier than cabins on most other ships. Rooms have a queen-size bed or two twin-size beds. A majority are outside staterooms with a bath and a half; almost half have private verandas.

Transportation: For a fee, motor coaches transport guests to Port Canaveral, the embarkation point. There's usually no second check-in. Most resort keys open respective staterooms (not so for Swan and Dolphin guests). Upon returning to Port Canaveral, guests are taken to Orlando International Airport.

Rates: Twelve stateroom categories correspond to comparable rooms at WDW resorts. Moderate resorts yield inside staterooms; deluxe net ocean views. Value rates for a seven-day, land-sea vacation begin at $829 per person, based on double occupancy. Price includes stateroom and WDW resort accommodations, unlimited park admission, and shipboard meals and recreation. (Seven-day, sea-only packages start at $829.) Packages including airfare and ground transfers are available. For more information or to plan a cruise, contact a travel agent, call 800-511-1333, or visit *www.disneycruise.com*.

Resorts on Hotel Plaza Boulevard

The three properties described below occupy a unique position among non-Disney accommodations because they, along with four other hotels (Best Western Lake Buena Vista, Courtyard by Marriott, DoubleTree Guest Suites, and Grosvenor), are located inside the boundaries of Walt Disney World, within close proximity of Downtown Disney.

While convenient location is the chief advantage of staying at one of the resorts along Hotel Plaza Boulevard, other privileges include easy access to all five Disney golf courses, priority seating at select WDW restaurants and dinner shows, preferred seating at Planet Hollywood before 5 P.M. (no small perk, given the waits), and a 20 percent discount on Pleasure Island admission when you presented a dinner receipt from one of the hotels' restaurants for the same evening.

All the hotels have Disney gift shops, as well as free Disney Channel, ESPN, and a WDW informational channel for in-room viewing. They also sell park (and other) tickets, including the "E-Ride" pass, and provide their own free bus service to the Magic Kingdom, Epcot, the Disney-MGM Studios, Animal Kingdom, Typhoon Lagoon, Blizzard Beach, and Downtown Disney. Six of the hotels have car-rental desks. Rooms can be booked through the individual hotels or through WDW Central Reservations (407-934-7639).

Hilton

Set on 23 well-groomed acres, the Hilton has a colorful aqua and peach facade and an air of laid-back gentility. Two large aquariums back the reception desk in the spacious lobby, where the plants are changed seasonally. After an $8 million renovation, the 814 newly refurbished guestrooms are tastefully decorated in mauve, peach, and earth tones.

BIG DRAWS: Located across the road from the Downtown Disney Marketplace. Pool areas with adult appeal. Free transportation to all Disney golf courses.

WORTH NOTING: All guestrooms feature mini-bars, voice mail, and modem ports; corner rooms have balconies. A well-equipped health club, two heated swimming pools, and two whirlpools surrounded by palms and pines are definite pluses, along with upscale shops for men and women and 24-hour room service.

Where to eat: Finn's Grill (Key West setting with oyster bar, steak and seafood dinners, and a seafood buffet with cooked-to-order pasta on Saturday); Benihana Japanese steak house and sushi bar; Covington Mill (all-day dining

Hilton Tips

■ Rooms with the best views overlook the pools or the fountain at the hotel's entrance.

■ For easy access to the pool, request a ground-floor room.

Royal Plaza Tips

■ There are separate gamerooms for adults and for kids, and no one under 16 is allowed in the large fitness room.

■ The enormous king rooms feature baths with separate glass-enclosed showers.

■ The Burt Reynolds, Barbara Mandrell, and Sports suites are accessorized with pertinent memorabilia.

in a New England setting); and Mainstreet Market (gourmet deli, ice cream counter, and country store).

Where to drink: Rum Largo Pool Bar & Cafe (for tropical concoctions); John T's Sports Bar; and Mugs (for wines by the glass and specialty coffees).

VITAL STATISTICS: Located right across the road from the Downtown Disney Marketplace. Hilton; 1751 Hotel Plaza Blvd.; Lake Buena Vista, FL 32830; 407-827-4000 or 800-782-4414; fax 407-827-3890; *www.hilton-wdwv.com.*

Transportation: Regularly scheduled complimentary bus transport is offered to the Walt Disney World theme parks.

Rates: Rooms are $160 to $345, and suites are $359 to $1,500, depending on the season.

Royal Plaza

Totally transformed after a two-year renovation and as accommodating as its pineapple motif intimates, the Royal Plaza is the only smaller hotel on Hotel Plaza Boulevard with real adult appeal. Besides an outstanding pool area surrounded by lanai rooms, there are four lighted tennis courts. Forgot your poolside reading? Borrow a novel from the lending library.

BIG DRAWS: An impressive renovation; and a great pool area with large outdoor whirlpool and live musical entertainment; adult ambience.

WORTH NOTING: The 394 rooms, including 22 suites, are divided between a 17-story main tower with a glass-enclosed elevator scaling the facade and two-story lanai wings. Each guestroom has a pleasant sitting area set off by shuttered partitions, as well as a desk, dresser, double armoire, bath with marble counter and oversize tub, ceiling fan, safe, and mini-bar. Other amenities include hair dryers, a coffeemaker, and video rental.

Where to eat: Giraffe Grill; Marketessen (for snacks).
Where to drink: Giraffe Grill and Sips (poolside bar).

VITAL STATISTICS: A half mile from the Downtown Disney Marketplace. Royal Plaza; Box 22203; 1905 Hotel Plaza Blvd.; Lake Buena Vista, FL 32830; 407-828-2828 or 800-248-7890; fax 407-827-6338; *www.royalplaza.com.*

Transportation: Regularly scheduled complimentary bus transport is provided to the WDW theme parks.

Rates: Guestrooms are $109 to $179 for up to five guests; suites range from $209 to $699.

Wyndham Palace Resort & Spa

The largest of the resorts along Hotel Plaza Boulevard (its entrance is on Buena Vista Drive), the Wyndham Palace is actually a cluster of towers, one of them 27 stories high. The grounds are lushly landscaped, with shaded walkways; inside, the decor is elegant. The reception area offers several cozy sitting nooks that invite lingering, and the Island Suite building has secluded courtyards. Many of the 1,014 rooms and suites offer a private patio or balcony, complete with a view of Epcot's Spaceship Earth.

BIG DRAWS: A European-style spa (see page 183) that rivals the one in the Grand Floridian; popular night spots; and numerous sports and recreational options.

WORTH NOTING: All guestrooms have ceiling fans, two phones (one bedside, one on the desk), voice mail, and 24-hour room service. Four rooms feature whirlpool tubs. One- and two-bedroom suites are available. For recreation, there's a vast fitness center, a luxurious spa, a sand volleyball court, three pools, three lighted tennis courts, and two lakeside gazebos.

Where to eat: Arthur's 27 (rooftop restaurant with a continental menu); the Outback restaurant (specializing in fresh seafood and Black Angus beef; not part of the chain bearing the same name); Watercress Cafe and Pastry Shop (24-hour counter service, baked goods, and deli items); and the Court-yard Mini-Market (for snacks and smoothies in a quiet outdoor setting).

Where to drink: The Laughing Kookaburra Good Time Bar (spirited spot known for live musical entertainment); and Top of the Palace (quiet lounge with a stunning view and live entertainment Wednesday through Saturday).

VITAL STATISTICS: The resort is located right across the road from the Downtown Disney Marketplace. Wyndham Palace Resort & Spa; 1900 Buena Vista Dr.; Lake Buena Vista, FL 32830; 407-827-2727 or 877-999-3223; fax 407-827-6034; www.wyndham.com.

Transportation: Regularly scheduled complimentary bus transport to the WDW theme parks is provided.

Rates: Rooms range from $129 to $269; rates for suites are $229 to $529.

Wyndham Palace Tips

■ The Top of the Palace lounge provides a good view of Epcot's fireworks, serves desserts and many wines by the glass, and offers a free glass of champagne at sunset.

■ Arthur's 27 rooftop restaurant is popular among visitors as well as Orlando residents.

■ For the allergy-prone, 65 rooms feature filtered air and water.

Beyond the World

When adult visitors to Walt Disney World consider staying somewhere off-property, it may be because they think that Mickey only knows the kid-pleasing side of the hotel business (not so). Or they may be unaware that Disney has some reasonably priced accommodations, namely the All-Star resorts. But no matter what your style or budget, when it comes to deciphering the myriad options beyond WDW's hotels, the main difficulty lies in sorting out the best from all the rest.

We've simplified matters by highlighting our top choices for adults—from luxury to economy. For ease of comparison, this listing places the off-site properties into Disney resort categories consistent with their rate scales and accommodation types: namely, Deluxe, Moderate, Value, and Home Away from Home (used to distinguish all-suite and villa-type lodging options).

Grand Cypress Tips

■ Choose the Hyatt Regency for pizzazz, the Villas of Grand Cypress for solitude.

■ Sunday brunch at the Hyatt Regency's La Coquina is legendary.

■ On the Rocks bar, tucked in the grotto beside the pool, and the outdoor adults-only whirlpool are perfect for a romantic rendezvous.

Deluxe

Grand Cypress

The eye-catching 750-room Hyatt Regency Grand Cypress is this destination resort's 18-story centerpiece, while the secluded Villas of Grand Cypress largely remain a secret. The resort's recreation roster boasts a health club, 45 holes of Jack Nicklaus-designed golf courses (including one 18-hole and three 9-hole layouts); tennis courts; a 21-acre lake with rental boats; a 45-acre nature preserve; fitness and jogging trails; racquetball and volleyball courts; horseback riding; and a waterfall-laden pool area.

BIG DRAWS: Style, service, terrific restaurants, great golf, and a large free-form swimming pool.

WORTH NOTING: A million-dollar art collection graces the resort's public areas and landscaped grounds (walking tours are available), and there's a wedding gazebo. Guestroom decor at the Hyatt is traditional, with a mint-and-rose color scheme. Many of the Mediterranean-style Villas, which face the fairways, have fireplaces and whirlpools; the club suites are smaller but have spacious bedrooms and baths. The Villas enclave has its own pool. The on-site golf academy, equestrian center, and tennis club (with a dozen courts) offer numerous activities.

Where to eat: At the Hyatt Regency: Hemingway's (seafood, steak, and game); Cascade (plenty of healthful entrées and a sinfully exquisite Key lime pie); La Coquina (contemporary cuisine); and the White Horse Saloon (steak). At the Villas: the Black Swan (sophisticated but noisy); the casual Fairways restaurant; and a poolside snack bar.

Where to drink: At the Hyatt Regency: Trellises (atrium piano bar); Hurricane Bar (Key West-style); the White Horse Saloon (country entertainment); and On the Rocks (poolside refreshments).

VITAL STATISTICS: The resort is the next-door neighbor to the hotels lining Hotel Plaza Boulevard. Hyatt Regency Grand Cypress; One Grand Cypress Blvd.; Orlando, FL 32836; 407-239-1234 or 800-554-9288; fax 407-239-3800. Villas of Grand Cypress; One N. Jacaranda Blvd.; Orlando, FL 32836; 407-239-4700 or 800-835-7377; fax 407-239-7219; *www.hyattgrandcypress.com.*

Transportation: The Hyatt Regency offers free shuttle service to the Disney theme parks; there is continuous transport between the Villas and the hotel.

Rates: At the Hyatt Regency, guestrooms are $205 to $540, and suites start at $695. At the Villas, club suites are $295 to $440; one-bedroom villas are $395 to $540; two-bedroom units are $570 to $860; and three-bedroom units are $845 to $1,280.

Peabody Orlando

The only sister property to the famed Peabody in Memphis, this imposing 891-room luxury tower with the duck logo is International Drive's most luxurious hotel. Recreational facilities include a vast heated pool, four lighted tennis courts, and a health club with personal trainers and 17 Nautilus stations.

BIG DRAWS: Elegance. Gracious service. First-rate dining accommodations.

WORTH NOTING: Luxuriously appointed guestrooms feature mini-bars, hair dryers, a small TV in the bathroom, nightly turndown service, data-port hookup, in-room movies and video games, 24-hour room service, and daily newspaper delivery.

Where to eat: Dux (the elegant signature restaurant, where the menu is creative and *no duck* is served); Capriccio (northern Italian cuisine and mesquite-grilled specialties in an exhibition kitchen; Sunday champagne brunch); and the B-Line Diner (a 1950s-style diner that's open 24 hours). High tea is served weekdays in the lobby and is a terrific value (less than $10).

Peabody Orlando Tips

■ The famous Peabody ducks ceremoniously parade from a private elevator into the three-story atrium lobby, down a red carpet, and into a marble water fountain daily at 11 A.M., then reverse the drill at 5 P.M.

■ Substantially reduced rates for seniors make the resort a superb value for guests 50 and older.

DoubleTree Orlando Maingate Tips

■ This place is ideal if you want to be near the action but not always in the thick of it.

■ If you're traveling with another couple or a group of friends, you'll feel comfortable, not cramped, here.

■ Don't pass up the opportunity to visit nearby Celebration.

Where to drink: Four bars, including The Lobby Bar, for nightly live entertainment and daily duck drills.

VITAL STATISTICS: The Peabody is directly across from the Orange County Convention Center and a short drive from Orlando's Official Visitor Information Center. The Peabody Orlando; 9801 International Dr.; Orlando, FL 32819; 407-352-4000 or 800-732-2639; fax 407-351-0073; *www.peabody-orlando.com*.

Transportation: The hotel's whimsical Double-Ducker bus provides regular shuttle service to the four Disney theme parks for $6 round-trip.

Rates: Rooms are $330 to $420, or $125 for guests 50 and older; suites run $550 to $1,500.

Home Away From Home
DoubleTree Guest Suites Orlando Maingate

This secluded, wooded enclave has 150 bi-level one-, two-, and three-bedroom villas that sleep four, six, or eight people. The complex has a fitness room, two lighted tennis courts, a basketball court, a large swimming pool, and a whirlpool. A mini-golf course is next door.

BIG DRAWS: Spacious accommodations. Easy-going ambience. Great location near WDW, though you'd hardly know it.

WORTH NOTING: Each unit feels like a small apartment, with a tiled entry, a patio, two baths, a living/dining area with an atrium ceiling, a full kitchen, ceiling fans, two TVs, and ample lighting throughout. There's also a sitting area with a desk and sofa bed. Although an iron (with board), a clothes basket, and toiletries are provided, daily maid service reminds you you're in a hotel.

Where to eat: A small dining room on the premises serves breakfast, lunch, and dinner; many eateries are nearby in Kissimmee and Celebration.

Where to drink: In the lobby bar.

VITAL STATISTICS: This property is situated five miles east of Walt Disney World and five miles west of Celebration, the town that Disney founded in 1997. DoubleTree Guest Suites Orlando Maingate; 4787 W. Irlo Bronson Memorial Hwy. (road marker 12); Kissimmee, FL 34746; 407-397-0555 or 800-222-8733; fax 407-397-0553; *www.doubletreehotels.com*.

Transportation: Complimentary shuttle service four times a day to Disney's Transportation and Ticket Center.

Rates: One- and two-bedroom villas are $119 to $189; three-bedroom units are $159 to $229.

Summerfield Suites by Wyndham

This five-story, 150-unit property with a tile roof and elegant lobby adds another dimension to the all-suite theme: a 24-hour convenience store with microwavable entrées and movie rentals. Other amenities include an exercise room, a heated pool and deck, a whirlpool, and a complimentary continental breakfast buffet (with hot selections for a small charge).

BIG DRAWS: Relatively spacious one- and two-bedroom suites (the latter can accommodate two couples traveling together).

WORTH NOTING: The bedrooms and living rooms feature all new furnishings down to the mattresses, plus tropical colors, including startlingly pink walls. In addition to a fully outfitted kitchen, each unit is equipped with a VCR, an iron and board, a desk in each bedroom, voice mail, and computer hookups. There is no restaurant on the premises, only a lobby bar and a pretty breakfast room, but plenty of eateries are located within walking distance. As a special service, the hotel will deliver groceries to your room by 6:30 P.M. if you leave a completed form with the front desk early in the morning.

VITAL STATISTICS: Summerfield Suites is at the south end of International Drive, opposite the Mercado Mediterranean shopping, dining, and entertainment complex, and is convenient to the Disney theme parks and to downtown Orlando. Summerfield Suites International; 8480 International Dr.; Orlando, FL 32819; 407-352-2400 or 800-830-4964; fax 407-352-4631; *www.summerfield-orlando.com.*

   Transportation: Shuttle service to the Disney theme parks is not available from this location.

   Rates: One-bedroom units, which sleep four, range from $119 to $249; two-bedroom units, which sleep six, are $159 to $289; and two-bedroom trio units, which sleep eight, are $179 to $319.

Summerfield Suites Tips

■ The Summerfield Suites in Lake Buena Vista offers complimentary shuttle service to Walt Disney World and is closer to the parks, but the International Drive location, listed here, is more adult-oriented.

■ During your stay, make it a point to dine or have drinks at nearby Bahama Breeze (8849 International Drive, 407-248-2499), one of the area's best and most popular casual restaurants.

■ Discounted rates as low as $79 are usually available in the spring and fall.

■ When the main parking lot is full, spaces are almost always available behind the hotel, near the meeting facilities.

Country Hearth Inn Tips

■ Sit on the veranda in the afternoon, cocktail in hand, and rock away all your cares.

■ Skip Sunday brunch here and splurge on the one at the Peabody hotel, instead.

Moderate
Clarion Plaza

This invitingly adult 810-unit hotel has tastefully decorated public areas and guestrooms, plus an impressive heated pool complete with a waterfall-embellished whirlpool.

BIG DRAWS: A business hotel by design, the property has reasonable rates, lively ambience, and spacious rooms that make it popular with leisure travelers.

WORTH NOTING: The spacious guestrooms and suites have pale wood furniture, teal carpeting, new comforters, artwork, and window treatments. Amenities include safes, hair dryers, irons and boards, and separate vanity areas; guest laundries are available.

Where to eat: Jack's Place (with caricature sketches à la Manhattan's legendary Sardi's, for seafood and steak dinners, and formidable desserts); Cafe Matisse (buffets and à la carte items for breakfast, lunch, and dinner); Rossini's Pizza (calzones and more); and Lite Bite (24-hour bakery and deli).

Where to drink: In the lobby bar and at the Backstage nightclub (music nightly until 2 A.M.; no cover).

VITAL STATISTICS: Located on International Drive adjacent to the Orange County Convention Center and near Orlando's Official Visitor Information Center. Clarion Plaza; 9700 International Dr.; Orlando, FL 32819-8144; 407-996-9700 or 800-627-8258; fax 407-996-9112; *www.clarionplaza.com.*

Transportation: Shuttle service from the hotel to the four Disney theme parks costs $10 round-trip per person; reservations are needed.

Rates: Standard rooms are $189 to $209; suites, which sleep four to eight people, are $275 to $868. Lower rates are almost always available.

Value
Country Hearth Inn

This two-story, gingerbread house-style property with rocking chairs on the porch and homey touches throughout is the closest you'll come to finding quaint accommodations on International Drive. The well-tended, landscaped grounds include a good-size (but unheated) pool, a lush courtyard, and a gazebo.

BIG DRAWS: Charming ambience and reasonable prices.

WORTH NOTING: The hotel's 150 guestrooms feature pine furniture, colorful drapes and bedspreads, French doors, and verandas. Most have two queen-size beds. Hardwood floors, a patterned tin ceiling, and chandeliers grace the lobby. Room service and movie rental are available.

Where to eat: Country Parlor (complimentary continental breakfast, à la carte dinner, and Sunday brunch).

Where to drink: The hotel's Front Porch lounge.

VITAL STATISTICS: The inn is across from the Convention Center (but set back from the road). Country Hearth Inn; 9861 International Dr.; Orlando, FL 32819; 407-352-0008 or 800-447-1890; fax 407-352-5449; *www.countryhearth.com.*

Transportation: Hotel shuttles run to and from the four Disney theme parks daily and cost $11 round-trip.

Rates: Prices range from $79 to $149.

PerriHouse Bed & Breakfast Inn

This ranch-style house, in a country setting next door to the Hyatt Regency Grand Cypress equestrian center, has eight rooms with private entrances, plus a separate three bedroom, three bathroom farmhouse for larger groups. Menus from area restaurants are available for guests to peruse.

BIG DRAWS: Tranquillity. Twenty-four-hour use of the whirlpool and small pool. Concierge service. Accommodating hosts who respect guests' privacy.

WORTH NOTING: Each well-appointed guestroom has a king- or queen-size bed (one room has two queens), a table and chairs, a TV, a telephone (local calls are free), and two robes. The central library features a "Florida fireplace" with fake flames, couches, books, games, gift items, a bird-sighting journal as well as a preponderance of other bird-related decor. There is a guest laundry ($4 charge). No scheduled transportation is available to the Walt Disney World theme parks.

Where to eat: Breakfast in the dining area, on the patio, or in the cottages.

Where to drink: Store libations in the guest refrigerator, or head to the Hyatt.

VITAL STATISTICS: Less than two miles from Downtown Disney, the B&B is convenient to all the WDW parks and other area attractions. PerriHouse Bed & Breakfast Inn; 10417 Centurion Court; Box 22005; Lake Buena Vista, FL 32830; 407-876-4830 or 800-780-4830; fax 407-345-1508; *www.perrihouse.com.*

Rates: Rooms are $89 to $139, including a help-yourself continental breakfast; cottages are $199 to $499.

PerriHouse Bed & Breakfast Tips

- The owners supply binoculars for bird-watching guests.
- Three-, five-, and seven-day packages are available.

Spectacular fireworks come with the territory at Walt Disney World.

Theme Parks: The Big Four

To experience Walt Disney World's quartet of major theme parks without children is tantamount to celebrating a major holiday without the complication of traffic or in-laws. It's positively liberating.

Let the Magic Kingdom runneth over with strollers and too-tired toddlers. As adults free to roam the Magic Kingdom, Epcot, Disney-MGM Studios, and Animal Kingdom on our own terms, we need not be concerned with such things. We are a minority (read: non-school-age individuals under no obligation whatsoever to facilitate the entertainment of any maturity-challenged person within 47 square miles) in one of those rare settings in which the minority holds all the advantages.

If we sometimes feel a bit conspicuous touring the parks as unaccompanied adults, it's because we're flaunting the inherent freedom. We're taking advantage of the fact that we're among friends who readily agree that a shaded bench, a nap in a hammock, or a soak in the whirlpool back at the resort would really hit the spot right now. We are free to buzz through the Magic Kingdom at a clip no character-conscious family could maintain, or meander through Epcot's World Showcase pavilions at what might be called escargot pace. All the while we're taking advantage of time-saving techniques like Disney's new Fastpass, which allows walk-on access to several popular attractions in all four theme parks. (See page 81 for details.)

When we see people consumed by a self-imposed game of tag that obliges them to touch each and every attraction, we wish we could somehow interrupt the game and remind them that they are on vacation.

The Mouse Is Spoken For

Walt Disney himself supplied the voice for Mickey Mouse from 1928 to 1946.

The immense array of experiences that constitutes Walt Disney World has a way of inspiring a desire to "collect them all." This is only natural. But by being more selective and pausing to say, "You know, Mickey, as much as I appreciate all the entertainment you've lined up, I just don't have time to do everything," you'll wind up with a much more enjoyable and satisfying experience.

Each park has stuff on its shelves that we want in our shopping cart. It's easy to rationalize visiting all four; they're specialty stores, after all, and the Magic Kingdom may have such essentials as Splash Mountain and Pirates of the Caribbean, but it doesn't sell Cranium Command or that 3-D movie we like so much, Honey, I Shrunk the Audience. For these, we have to go to Epcot. Many of our favorites can be found here, but we can't get The Twilight Zone Tower of Terror or Rock 'n' Roller Coaster; these are only at Disney-MGM Studios. And such novelties as Kilimanjaro Safaris, Kali River Rapids, and Dinosaur are Animal Kingdom exclusives.

That's okay. We like to immerse ourselves in the inspiring atmospheres that make these parks so distinct. When we're at the Magic Kingdom, we take one look at Cinderella Castle and cease to function as adults. Suddenly, we are in the amusement business, with only ourselves to please. In any case, we've never had even the slightest problem entertaining ourselves in the Magic Kingdom.

In Epcot, it's easy to retain our adult sensibilities, since its point is to be something other than an amusement park (although there's certainly plenty of funny business going on in, say, Ellen's Energy Adventure). The highly conceptual, experiential environs of Future World nudge our curiosity, engage our interest, and heighten our awareness. For a

Unless otherwise noted, all phone numbers are in the area code 407.

change of pace, we move on to the Magic Snackdom, better known as World Showcase. Granted, there is much more to this part of Epcot than snacks from around the world. One day, we got so caught up watching drummers in Japan, we almost let seagulls take our soft pretzels from Germany.

At the Disney-MGM Studios, we can't help but savor the relaxed atmosphere of this starry-eyed tribute to 1940s Hollywood. The place has such a sophisticated air, a cozy nostalgia, a plucky sense of fun.

Entering the epic realm of Disney's Animal Kingdom makes us feel like avid adventurers bound for distant lands and bygone eras. We are momentarily persuaded that we've traveled to Africa on safari, to prehistoric times for a *tête à tête* with dinosaurs, and to Asia for a rousing ride on the rapids through a rain forest under siege. The place brings out the wildebeest in us without fail.

We believe the parks are best explored in a certain order, especially your first time out. Starting with the least character-intensive theme parks lets you ease into Disney gradually, so that by the time Mickey Mouse appears in butter form at your dinner table, you've been conditioned to expect it.

Devote day one to Animal Kingdom so you're not champing at the bit. Preempt the fantasy zones with a day at Epcot and you'll sooner appreciate it on its own merit. Follow your day at Epcot with a day at the Disney-MGM Studios. This works well for two reasons: Enchantment is a great chaser for enlightenment, and it ups the character presence without overwhelming. If you're raring to meet Mickey or eager for a closer look at Cinderella Castle, spend your fourth day exploring the Magic Kingdom. (In this chapter, the parks are presented in the order they were created: Magic Kingdom, 1971; Epcot, 1982; Disney-MGM Studios, 1989; and Animal Kingdom, 1998.) After you've toured each park, spend remaining days exploring other compelling corners of the World and revisiting favorite attractions—preferably between soaks in a soothing whirlpool.

Save Time In Line

Want to waltz onto an attraction without waiting in line? By using Disney's complimentary Fastpass system, at selected attractions in all four theme parks, you can do just that. How's it work? Slip your admission pass into the machine. It will spit out your ticket along with a timed voucher. Come back at any point within the voucher's time frame and you'll bypass the long wait (a.k.a. "the stand-by line"). Consult the Touring Priorities in the margins of this chapter for a roster of Fastpass attractions and check each park's guidemap for a current list of attractions that feature this time-saving service.

The Magic Kingdom is usually open from 9 A.M. to 7 P.M.; park hours are extended during holiday periods and summer months. Call 407-939-4636 for up-to-the-minute details. One-day park admission is $48.76 for adults (see *Planning Ahead* for ticket options). Prices are subject to change.

MAGIC KINGDOM

As once-upon-a-timish and happily-ever-afteresque a place as exists, the Magic Kingdom is sure proof that you can judge a park by its largest icon (in this case, Cinderella Castle). While it is the most character-intensive and certainly the strongest kid magnet of all the parks, flying elephants couldn't keep us away.

What puts the Magic Kingdom on the adult map? For starters, it's manageable. Most of the essentials here are easily traversed in a day. High on the list of imperatives is Disney's own mountain range—Space Mountain, Splash Mountain, and Big Thunder Mountain Railroad—an undeniably thrilling threesome of rides. What it lacks in fine cuisine and opportunities to imbibe, it more than makes up for in magic. Disney has made a real art of coaxing folks into a state of wonderment that seldom occurs in adulthood, and this park represents that art taken to its highest level. It's a rare adult who doesn't fall under the spell of the Magic Kingdom's ballroom of waltzing apparitions, its heavy-breathing ode to an alien encounter, or its convincing den of leering pirates. For nostalgic whimsy, there are kiddie rides such as Peter Pan's Flight that don't aspire to recapture the magic of childhood so much as to momentarily revive it. The SpectroMagic parade is also bound to reacquaint you with your inner child. This spectacle of fiber-optic delight showcases 600,000 miniature bulbs that light in wild changing patterns, and move in perfect concert with sound effects and a musical score. The parade, which is due to return to the park in early 2001, is absolutely illuminating.

Of course, a gazillion children can have a way of getting on anyone's nerves after a while, so some strategies are in order. First, master the art of noticing children only when they are being cute. To keep the "magic barometer" from falling, take advantage of less crowded evening hours, and weave in and out of major traffic zones (Fantasyland and Frontierland are generally the most congested areas). Seek refuge in the quiet nooks described in the margins of this chapter and in such havens as The Hall of Presidents; for a bigger break, indulge in a leisurely lunch at one of the resorts that are easily accessible via monorail.

GUIDING PRINCIPLES: Know thy touring priorities. Know thy path of least resistance. These commandments are the basis for any enjoyable theme park visit—but they take on even greater importance for adults venturing through the Magic Kingdom. Of course, you can't exactly determine your priorities without first knowing your turf. Therefore, the section that follows is designed to offer a telling preview for first-time visitors and a timely review for returnees. Structured as a counterclockwise walking tour through the seven themed "lands" that make up the park, it provides a geographical orientation to the Magic Kingdom while taking a critical inventory of the attractions as they

relate to adults. Land by land, it highlights the adult essentials, points out redeeming and unfortunate characteristics of the nonessentials, and flags the newest additions. For the sake of easy reference, we've also included a Touring Priorities list ranking the park's best adult bets. To learn the most efficient touring strategies, consult the Hot Tips in the margins of this section and the flexible tour plan provided in the *Planning Ahead* chapter.

For information on how to get to the Magic Kingdom, see the "Getting Around" section of the *Planning Ahead* chapter. For the goods on Magic Kingdom shops worth exploring, see the "Shopping" section of the *Diversions* chapter. And, finally, to find out about the park's best bets for dining, see the book's evaluative "Restaurant Guide" in the *Dining & Entertainment* chapter.

GETTING ORIENTED: Go through the turnstiles, pass an area with rental lockers, and you're in Town Square, the cul-de-sac at the foot of Main Street. From here look straight out to the park's most-recognizable landmark, Cinderella Castle. It's at the opposite end of Main Street behind an area known as the the Hub, or Central Plaza. On the left before the Hub is the main **Tip Board**, an information board listing current waiting times for the park's most popular attractions. (A second Tip Board in the Magic Kingdom can be found in Tomorrowland.)

Along for the E-Ride

Ever dream of roaming the Magic Kingdom after hours? Sure you have! Now, Walt Disney World resort guests have the opportunity to do just that, and with little company. On select E-Ride Nights (call 407-939-4636 for details) you can tour the park for several hours after it closes to the public. Tickets cost $10, and must be purchased at a WDW resort. What's open? The most popular attractions, of course. On our last visit, we practically had the park to ourselves.

HOT TIPS

■ On Monday, Thursday, and Saturday, guests staying at WDW resorts may enter the Magic Kingdom up to 1½ hours prior to the official opening time and get an early crack at Space Mountain and all Fantasyland attractions. Early-entry days and attractions are subject to change.

■ Not coincidentally, Monday, Thursday, and Saturday tend to be the most crowded days at the Magic Kingdom.

■ The afternoon or evening parade is a golden opportunity to take advantage of shorter lines at the most popular attractions.

It's helpful to think of the layout of the Magic Kingdom as a tree. Main Street, U.S.A., is the trunk; the other six themed areas—Adventureland, Fantasyland, Frontierland, Liberty Square, Mickey's Toontown Fair, and Tomorrowland—dangle at the ends of the tree's gnarled boughs (actually bridges). The first bridge on your left leads to Adventureland; the second, to Liberty Square and Frontierland; the pathway straight ahead passes through Cinderella Castle on its way to the heart of Fantasyland; another bridge passes to the right of the castle to enter Fantasyland nearest Mickey's Toontown Fair and Tomorrowland; and the bridge on your immediate right leads directly to Tomorrowland. The lands are also linked via a broad footpath that wends its way behind the castle.

A Walking Tour

L et's begin our tour in **Town Square**, which is important as the location of **City Hall**, where a person can make all manner of inquiries and arrangements (no, you can't get married here). Even if you don't need to pick up a guidemap, make priority seating arrangements, exchange foreign currency, or check the lost and found, stop by to play Q&A with the informed folks behind the counter. Note that the local ATMs are under the train station, near the lockers.

The archway we walked under to get here is actually the foundation of the **Walt Disney World Railroad** depot. A 1928 steam engine that once carted sugarcane across the Yucatán now hauls freight (largely first-time visitors, train buffs, and homesick commuters) on a 20-minute loop around the Magic Kingdom. It's a fine way—albeit not always the fastest—to get to Frontierland and Mickey's Toontown Fair if you don't want to walk.

Onward.

Main Street, U.S.A.

M ain Street is notable as the tidy strip of storefronts where adults first gawk at, then feel compelled to photograph, Cinderella Castle. While there's no shame in it, don't be so distracted that you overlook the street's early 1900's charm. Amusements here are decidedly low-key. For grooming as entertainment, there's the old-fashioned Harmony Barber Shop (tucked behind the Emporium), where the Dapper Dans sometimes accompany a haircut. By all means, check out their sweet four-part harmonies. Main Street stays open a half hour after the rest of the park has closed, although the shops (see "Shopping" in the *Diversions* chapter for details) tend to be less crowded in the early afternoon.

MAIN STREET, U.S.A.
- 1 Main Street Vehicles
- 2 Walt Disney World Railroad
- 3 Main Street Exposition Hall

ADVENTURELAND
- 4 Jungle Cruise
- 5 Pirates of the Caribbean
- 6 Swiss Family Treehouse
- 7 The Enchanted Tiki Room—Under New Management
- 8 The Magic Carpets of Aladdin

FRONTIERLAND
- 9 Big Thunder Mountain Railroad
- 10 Country Bear Jamboree
- 11 Frontierland Shootin' Arcade
- 12 Splash Mountain
- 13 Tom Sawyer Island
- 14 Diamond Horseshoe Saloon Revue
- 15 Walt Disney World Railroad Station

LIBERTY SQUARE
- 16 The Hall of Presidents
- 17 The Haunted Mansion
- 18 Liberty Belle Riverboat

FANTASYLAND
- 19 Cinderella's Golden Carousel
- 20 Dumbo the Flying Elephant
- 21 It's a Small World
- 22 Mad Tea Party
- 23 The Many Adventures of Winnie the Pooh
- 24 Peter Pan's Flight
- 25 Legend of the Lion King
- 26 Snow White's Scary Adventures
- 27 Ariel's Grotto

MICKEY'S TOONTOWN FAIR
- 28 Donald's Boat
- 29 Mickey's Country House
- 30 Minnie's Country House
- 31 Toontown Hall of Fame
- 32 The Barnstormer
- 33 Walt Disney World Railroad Station

TOMORROWLAND
- 34 Astro Orbiter
- 35 Buzz Lightyear's Space Ranger Spin
- 36 The ExtraTERRORestrial Alien Encounter
- 37 Tomorrowland Indy Speedway
- 38 Space Mountain
- 39 The Timekeeper
- 40 Walt Disney's Carousel of Progress
- 41 Tomorrowland Transit Authority

·········· Parade Route

N ←

Touring Priorities

DON'T MISS

•CONTINUED ON NEXT PAGE

Tomorrowland

Futuristic in a way that would likely go right over Buck Rogers' head, Tomorrowland is a city of the future that never was. Because it's home base for two of the park's most popular attractions—Space Mountain and Alien Encounter—Tomorrowland is best visited first thing after the gates open.

Space Mountain, a must-do for all but those who categorically avoid the fast stuff, is one to head for straightaway as Fastpasses may run out before day's end. Once the stand-by line reaches outside this white structure at the far side of Tomorrowland, it generally doesn't ease up until evening. To gauge whether Space Mountain is for you, consider how you feel about roller coasters. This one rockets through a space-age sheath of darkness, shooting stars, and flashing lights. It's a fast and furious ride with spectacular special effects—an absolute must for the adventurous, and an unforgettable adventure for the suddenly courageous. Space Mountain is also a turbulent ride so passengers must be in good health and free from heart conditions, back and neck problems, and other physical limitations (such as pregnancy), as the posted signs warn. If you've just eaten, wait. If you decide you'd rather observe the rockets' red glare going only seven miles per hour, the **Tomorrowland Transit Authority** offers a preview to Space Mountain and other attractions on a track that's strictly horizontal. The train is boarded in the heart of Tomorrowland near **Astro Orbiter** (an elevated ride with rockets that's primarily for kids but good fun for adults; it seems to go faster the lower you fly in your Buck Rogers-mobile).

The scariest thing ever to hit the Magic Kingdom, **The ExtraTERRORestrial Alien Encounter** even has scary lines. It's not a motion ride but rather an intense 20-minute experience born of an interplanetary travel demo gone awry. The story: A company from another planet has developed something called a teleporter that's capable of beaming people between planets, and is treating you to a demonstration via live broadcast. You are seated in a dimly lit room, with one of these teleporters occupying center stage, when unsettling events begin to occur. A restraint is lowered over your shoulders. The chairman of the corporation volunteers to come to Earth, but an alien arrives in his place. There is an explosion. Suddenly, it is completely dark and you hear screams and groans, feel panting on the nape of your neck, and are sprayed with what in this context seems to be alien slime. The verdict: Special effects *are* the experience. Although this attraction is more suspenseful and unsettling than terrifying, if you scare easily or are simply good at playing along, you'll get some chills up your spine.

Just across from Alien Encounter, **The Timekeeper** is another Tomorrowland attraction that warrants your attention, only this one's a hoot, not a holler. A good bet for early in the day because it's a standing engagement, The Timekeeper is an

arresting 20-minute Circle-Vision 360 film amusingly hosted by Audio-Animatronic characters. Basically, a wacky robot, who could leave the attraction and *be* Robin Williams, sends his buddy, a flying robot camera named 9-Eye, back in time on assignment to transmit photos of all she sees for our enjoyment. At the 1900 Paris Exposition, she bumps into H. G. Wells and Jules Verne, one of whom hitches a ride to the future. If you're a *Cheers* fan, you'll probably recognize 9-Eye's voice as that of Rhea Perlman. As for old-fashioned actors, the sort with no Audio-Animatronic stand-ins, you'll see Jeremy Irons playing the role of H. G. Wells and Michel Piccoli as Jules Verne. The bottom line: Pass only if you've been there (to Innsbruck, Austria, say) and done that (bobsledded down a 1,200-meter run at 60 miles per hour).

Right next to The Timekeeper is **Buzz Lightyear's Space Ranger Spin**, where *Toy Story*'s Mr. Infinity and Beyond solicits your assistance in cuffing the universe's most insidious battery hoarder. The 4½-minute journey is part video game, part shooting gallery, thanks to your spaceship's spin-control joystick and laser guns (how else to combat the likes of Rock'em Sock'em Robot?).

At **Walt Disney's Carousel of Progress**, the stage stays put and you rotate around it during the 20-minute show. The attraction fulfills its promise as a

•CONTINUED FROM PREVIOUS PAGE

DON'T OVERLOOK

Walt Disney World Railroad; Legend of the Lion King**; Liberty Belle Riverboat; Carousel of Progress; Mickey's Toontown Fair; Mad Tea Party; Tomorrowland Transit Authority; The Hall of Presidents; Tomorrowland Indy Speedway; Diamond Horseshoe Saloon Revue**; The Many Adventures of Winnie the Pooh*; Astro Orbiter; The Time-keeper; The Enchanted Tiki Room—Under New Management

DON'T KNOCK YOURSELF OUT

Cinderella's Golden Carrousel; Swiss Family Treehouse; Snow White's Scary Adventures; Dumbo the Flying Elephant; Tom Sawyer Island; The Magic Carpets of Aladdin

* Fastpass attraction as of press time. Consult your guidemap for new additions.

** Pay close attention to performance schedules.

Quiet Nooks

- Rose garden on the right as you face Cinderella Castle

- Cinderella Wishing Well, near the castle on a pathway to Tomorrowland

- Walt Disney World Railroad

- Harmony Barber Shop

- Shaded tables behind the shops in Liberty Square

- Liberty Belle Riverboat

- Rocking chairs on the front porches of Frontierland and Liberty Square shops

- Aunt Polly's Dockside Inn on Tom Sawyer Island

- Anywhere but Fantasyland and Toontown

warm and fuzzy portrayal of how electricity has altered our lives. Its last scene offers a lighthearted glimpse of life in the not too distant future. Don't be dismayed by crowds; this place swallows them whole. Heading north toward Fantasyland, you pass Space Mountain and come upon the rather low-octane **Tomorrowland Indy Speedway**.

Mickey's Toontown Fair

This tiny blip between Tomorrowland and Fantasyland is the park's newest land. When you visit the area with interactive environs akin to Disneyland's Toontown, you'll find an old-fashioned county fair in progress. The cuteness is in the details (Mickey's ear-bearing crops, Minnie as the local Martha Stewart). Don't miss your chance to tour the homes of Mickey and Minnie. At **Mickey's Country House**, take a peek in the kitchen but watch out—he's in the process of remodeling. Attractions are primarily for kids, but it's still fun to wander. For one-stop character meeting, the **Toontown Hall of Fame** can't be beat. And if you're looking to take some baby steps before venturing onto Space Mountain, **The Barnstormer at Goofy's Wiseacre Farm** may be just your speed. This coaster with mini-twists and turns is quick and painless.

Fantasyland

The danger to the adult entering this, the cheeriest, most magical, and most nostalgic corner of the Magic Kingdom, is that there's a very fine line between rubbing elbows with Cinderella, Peter Pan, and Snow White and being caught in a child thicket. The optimum way to take in Fantasyland is to visit just before and during the daily 3 P.M. parade or in the evening when the parks are open late. Because there is nothing adult about Fantasyland—whimsy is the name of the game.

That said, certain attractions are so artfully executed that they transcend the kiddie genre. Of these, **It's a Small World**—a ten-minute boat ride through the happiest, busiest, and most diversely populated dollhouse on the planet—is surely the most elaborate. Much more subtle is **Peter Pan's Flight**, an alluring sprinkle of pixie dust in which you can—and do—fly for three minutes above absolutely delightful scenes of Captain Hook and nighttime London in a pirate ship built for two. **Legend of the Lion King**, a 25-minute stage show based on the animated film *The Lion King*, is a knockout mix of puppetry, film clips, and special effects that kids adore but fail to appreciate.

Then there are the purely nostalgic attractions, worth your time only if you're hankering to relive a certain story or amusement ride from your past. Have a thing for carousels in general or **Cinderella's Golden Carrousel** in particular? Go for it. Think you'd get a huge kick out of squeezing your group into an oversize teacup and spinning yourselves silly? Get to the **Mad Tea Party**. Don't skip **Dumbo the Flying Elephant** if you'll regret it later, but at the same time, don't expect to be wowed by a straightforward kiddie attraction such as **Snow White's Scary Adventures**. Although it has more happy

moments than it did in the old days, the twisting journey still feels like a trip through a witch-filled fun house. **The Many Adventures of Winnie the Pooh** (which replaced Mr. Toad's Wild Ride) is a sweetly tempting honey jar of a journey through the Hundred Acre Wood.

Whatever you do, don't miss the gorgeous mosaic murals beneath the open archway of **Cinderella Castle**. No less than a million well-placed pieces of Italian glass tell the whole tale, ugly stepsisters, glass slipper, and all.

Liberty Square

Tucked between Fantasyland and Frontierland, this comparatively small area tends to be relatively peaceful. Brick and clapboard buildings carry the theme—Colonial America—as does the Liberty Tree, a 130-something oak hung with 13 lanterns to recall the original Colonies.

Though Liberty Square has just a few attractions, it still takes more than an hour to see them all. **The Hall of Presidents** merits attention not just as a well-delivered 20-minute dose of patriotism in which Abraham Lincoln and Bill Clinton speak, but as a chance to observe all chief executives of our country in action. The shifting, swaying, and nodding begins the moment the curtain rises on the impeccably dressed group of Audio-Animatronic figures. The pace is slow, but just right for an air-conditioned theater with comfy seats. Don't be intimidated by a big line—this is a *big* theater. The **Liberty Belle Riverboat**—a large, paddle wheel-driven steamboat that makes 17-minute loops around Tom Sawyer Island—is a pleasant distraction, especially on a steamy afternoon. Don't ask what **The Haunted Mansion** is doing in Liberty Square. Just note that it's a not-to-be-missed eight-minute experience overrun with clever special effects and ghoulish delights (your typical ballroom of waltzing ghosts, door knockers that knock by themselves, and spirited graveyards).

Entertainment

The character-laden floats in Disney's Magical Moments Parade take over Main Street daily at 3 P.M. Also, the Dapper Dans periodically pop onto Main Street to serenade guests with their four-part harmonies.

When the park is open late, the spectacular Fantasy in the Sky fireworks (200 shells released in seven minutes) is presented nightly. And the dazzling SpectroMagic light parade, which replaces The Main Street Electrical Parade in spring 2001, wends its luminous fiber-optic way down Main Street nightly. (The best vantage point is the railroad platform; if there are two performances, the later one is usually less crowded.)

Check a park guidemap for the schedule.

Frontierland

This land conjures something of the Old West, with a little country charm—and even an ATM near the Diamond Horseshoe Saloon—thrown in for good measure. Although there's more to Frontierland than mountains, it is most notable as the home to two of the Magic Kingdom's most addictive thrills—Splash Mountain and Big Thunder Mountain Railroad.

The first thing to know about **Splash Mountain** is that it's okay to feel anxious just watching the log boats plunge down this ride's big drop—you're looking at the steepest flume in the world (although it appears to be a straight drop, it's actually 52 feet down at a 45-degree angle). Even so, this water-bound ride themed to Disney's *Song of the South* is tamer than it looks from the ground. Steep plunge aside, there are just three smaller dips during the 11-minute trip. If you're like us, the first time around you'll be way too nervous about when "it" is going to happen to fully appreciate the delightful humor, enormously appealing characters, and uplifting "Zip-A-Dee-Doo-Dah" ambience. But coax yourself into riding once and you'll be hooked. If you prefer to get splashed, not drenched, sit in the back of the log. Onlookers should note that a water cannon takes aim at the observation bridge without warning. A note on timing: Both Splash Mountain and Big Thunder Mountain Railroad tend to draw big crowds all day; your best bet is to shoot for early morning or evening.

Think of **Big Thunder Mountain Railroad** as a thrilling ride on the mild side. As roller coasters go, this one's exciting as much for the surrounding scenery your runaway mine train races past—bats, goats, a flooded mining town—as for the ride itself. Big Thunder Mountain Railroad is not nearly so fast or turbulent as Space Mountain, and nothing in its four-minute series of reverberating swoops and jerky turns comes close to Splash Mountain's intimidating plunge. For a bigger thrill, ride it after dark, when you can't see what lies ahead even from the first car.

But Frontierland's appeal extends beyond its two high-profile attractions. The **Country Bear Jamboree**, a 16-minute musical variety show put on by 20 impossibly corny Audio-Animatronic bears, is a fine attraction to hit when you're feeling a little punchy. If your schedule can accommodate an entire hour's worth of song, dancing, and hokeyness, the **Diamond Horseshoe Saloon Revue** delivers. While **Tom Sawyer Island**, a short raft ride away, provides a nice break from the more structured parts of the park, it tends to attract lots of kids.

Adventureland

In 2001, Adventureland will be transformed into the marketplace of *Aladdin*'s Agrabah. Along with this facelift comes a new Dumbo-style ride coined **The Magic Carpets of Aladdin**, on which riders pilot mystical flying carpets. Among this land's other attractions are the immensely popular Pirates of the Caribbean and Jungle Cruise, best visited during the early morning and evening.

The Enchanted Tiki Room—Under New Management is a recent revamp worthy of a traffic-stopping whistle. The nine-minute affair still showcases Disney's earliest Audio-Animatronic figures but adds plucky new company to the chirping, chattering birds of yore. *Aladdin*'s Iago and *The Lion King*'s Zazu push the limits of caged-bird choreography. Remember **Pirates of the Caribbean** as an elaborate, engaging, not-to-be-missed boat ride in which you watch pirates attack and raid a Caribbean village. A classic attraction, it provides plenty of leering, jeering examples of how wonderfully, frighteningly realistic Disney's Audio-Animatronics can be. Note that the ten-minute Pirates of the Caribbean ride includes a small dip and some loud cannon blasts.

The **Jungle Cruise** is a very popular attraction that transports passengers on a steamy ten-minute boat trip through the Nile Valley and the Amazon rain forest. Although the flora is quite beautiful, the lines for this ride can be prohibitively long so consider using Fastpass to save some time. Finally, if you feel up to climbing some serious stairs, **Swiss Family Treehouse** is a fascinating replica of the Robinsons' ingenious perch that's worth the effort, even though the tree itself is a product of the prop department's imagination.

Snacker's Guide

For a healthy bite, visit the Liberty Square Market in Liberty Square for fresh fruit and baked potatoes, Auntie Gravity's Galactic Goodies in Tomorrowland for fruit smoothies and juices, or Aloha Isle in Adventureland for pineapple spears.

For a sweet treat, seek out cookies at the Main Street Bake Shop; jumbo rice crispie treats, fudge, and peanut brittle at the Main Street Confectionery; cinnamon pretzels at a cart in Fantasyland; or caramel corn at Sleepy Hollow in Liberty Square.

For a frozen refresher, try the pineapple whip at Aloha Isle in Adventureland, or choose a flavor at the Plaza Ice Cream Parlor on Main Street.

For a savory pick-me-up, head for the Egg Roll Wagon in Adventureland, the Turkey Leg Wagon in Frontierland and Tomorrowland, or the cappuccino cart right outside Tony's Town Square restaurant at the foot of Main Street, U.S.A.

EPCOT

Epcot's hours are staggered. Whereas Future World opens at 9 A.M., World Showcase comes to life at 11 A.M. Both areas of the park close at 9 P.M. Epcot's hours are extended during holidays and the summer months; call 407-939-4636 for up-to-the-minute details. One-day park admission is $48.76 for adults (see *Planning Ahead* for ticket options). Prices are subject to change.

Think of Epcot as an extraordinary balancing act. This park is huge—about three times the size of the Magic Kingdom—and it performs two rather ambitious feats simultaneously. While the part of Epcot known as Future World offers a multifaceted look at what lies ahead for humankind, its alter ego, World Showcase, transports guests (at least in spirit) to many different countries. This division of labor works well, and it certainly keeps things interesting here. While the more serious-minded Future World is striving to spark the imagination, illuminate the technological future, and heighten environmental awareness, lively World Showcase is serving forth Oktoberfest, traditional English pub grub, and panoramic views of France, China, and Canada. As Future World is ushering visitors into an ultramodern greenhouse that showcases NASA experiments, World Showcase is escorting others along a calm river deep in the heart of Mexico and over a stormy Norwegian sea. Together, the two entities stimulate guests to discover new things about people, places, and, indeed, their own curiosity.

If Epcot boasts a tremendous following among legal voters, it's because it has more of the things adults appreciate: live entertainment; quiet gardens; beer, wine, and frozen drinks; tasteful shops and galleries; international cuisine; sophisticated restaurants; and specialty coffees—and that's just the supplementary stuff. Epcot also woos the older crowd by making Mickey a little more scarce and by splicing enrichment of one form or another into the greater part of its amusements. It appeals to adults on a purely aesthetic level as well: World Showcase, wrapped around a vast lagoon, has a commanding natural and architectural beauty that changes with each border crossing. And Future World more than holds its own with the massive, gleaming silver geosphere of Spaceship Earth. Not surprisingly, we've met a number of Walt Disney World regulars who spend their entire vacations here at Epcot.

Epcot has its die-hard Future World fans and its World Showcase fanatics, but most visitors list favorite pavilions on both sides of the lagoon. Recent renovations and additions to Epcot make this especially true today. Disney has made smart changes in Epcot's entertainment mix that have lightened up Future World, livened up World Showcase, and in the process, earned the park a fresh crop of admirers—both young and old.

We'll describe the attractions later so that we might first present The Official Six Things We Bet You Didn't Know You Could Do at Epcot List: (1) You can get some terrific gardening tips. (2) You can simultaneously break a sweat and split the 100th annual Rose Bowl Parade right down the middle. (Pedaling against the tide, and seemingly catching floats, bands, horses, and majorettes quite by surprise, we got a Wonder Cycle up to 15½ miles per hour.) (3) You can experience the British Invasion. Or at least swear you did, when you hear this cheeky band playing Beatles tunes. (4) You can watch a butterfly open its wings for the first time. If you want, you can be nibbling on a freshly picked sprig of spearmint while that beautiful orange-barred sulphur butterfly decides when to flee the hatching box. (5) You can send a picture postcard of yourself anywhere in the world via e-mail. (6) You can get an impromptu lesson in belly dancing from an obliging Moroccan dancer.

The most important thing to know about Epcot is that it is no small undertaking. Even the choosiest visitor will need two full days to cover the park effectively at a comfortable pace.

Since Future World and World Showcase keep different hours, strategically minded guests will do well to follow our lead. In the name of efficiency,

Hidden Mickey

Take a close look at the mural in the loading area of Norway's Maelstrom ride. One of the Vikings is wearing Mouse ears!

HOT TIPS

■ On Tuesday and Friday, guests staying at WDW resorts may enter Epcot up to 1½ hours before the official opening time and get an early crack at select Future World pavilions, usually Spaceship Earth, Test Track, and Wonders of Life. Early-entry days and attractions are subject to change.

■ Not coincidentally, Tuesday and Friday tend to be the most crowded days at Epcot.

■ Not a morning person? Head to crowd-free World Showcase (opening at 11 A.M.) while everyone else is in Future World.

we say: Take in a few key Future World pavilions during the hours before World Showcase opens. Explore World Showcase during the early afternoon, when Future World is most congested. Return to Future World to explore a few more pavilions during the relatively uncongested hours of late afternoon and early evening. Finally, revisit World Showcase during pleasant evening hours to experience the beauty of the park at twilight, as well as Illumi-Nations: Reflections of Earth.

GUIDING PRINCIPLES: The following section is designed to offer a telling preview for first-time visitors and a timely update for returnees. Structured as a guided walking tour through the themed pavilions of Future World and the countries of World Showcase, it provides a geographical orientation to the layout of the park. Running commentary takes stock of all pavilions (and the attractions located therein) and their place in the adult world, highlighting the essentials, pointing out the redeeming qualities of less compelling attractions, and noting recent additions and renovations to Epcot.

For at-a-glance cues, the Touring Priorities list in the margin ranks the park's best adult bets. **Note:** This book's evaluations of attractions are based on the quality of the experience and the entertainment value for an adult with average interest in the topic, but if you have a serious fascination with the subject at hand—gardening or farming, say—you should find the attraction and the pavilion (in this case, the "Behind the Seeds" tour in The Land) all the more satisfying.

To learn the most efficient strategies for exploring Epcot, look to the Hot Tips in the margins of this section, and the flexible touring plans provided in the *Planning Ahead* chapter. For information about getting to Epcot via Walt Disney World transportation or car, consult the "Getting Around" section of the *Planning Ahead* chapter. For tips and recommendations on dining at Epcot, refer to the "Restaurant Guide" in the *Dining & Entertainment* chapter.

GETTING ORIENTED: It's helpful to think of Epcot as the park with the hourglass figure. In this conception, the gleaming silver ball of Spaceship Earth is the head and northernmost point; the other Future World pavilions, arranged on either side of Spaceship Earth in southward arches, form the outline of Epcot's "upper body"; and the promenade of World Showcase pavilions connects to Future World at Epcot's "waist" and, tracing the lines of a long, full skirt, wraps around World Showcase Lagoon. The American Adventure pavilion,

WORLD SHOWCASE

MOROCCO

FRANCE

JAPAN

THE AMERICAN ADVENTURE

INTERNATIONAL GATEWAY

ITALY

UNITED KINGDOM

GERMANY

CANADA

FUTURE WORLD

WORLD SHOWCASE LAGOON

IMAGINATION!

THE LAND

SHOWCASE PLAZA

INNOVENTIONS WEST

THE LIVING SEAS

CHINA

NORWAY

INNOVENTIONS EAST

SPACESHIP EARTH

To Buses

MEXICO

TEST TRACK

Entrance Plaza

WONDERS OF LIFE

UNIVERSE OF ENERGY

N

Touring Priorities

•CONTINUED ON NEXT PAGE

located due south of Spaceship Earth along the bottom hem of the World Showcase skirt, effectively serves as the foot of Epcot.

Visitors should come prepared to do a great deal of walking, as the World Showcase Promenade itself is 1.2 miles around. Avid walkers and the health-conscious will be interested to know that a person typically covers more than two miles in one full day of touring Epcot. Don't be dismayed, though; Epcot is equipped with plenty of resting spots (see the margins of this section for tips to the whereabouts of said nooks), as well as a key foot-saving alternative. Water taxis link Showcase Plaza at the foot of Future World with Germany and Morocco, located at the farthest corners of World Showcase. Many seniors who choose to tour the smaller theme parks on foot rent a wheelchair or a self-driven Electric Convenience Vehicle (ECV) here at Epcot.

A Walking Tour

Our tour begins at the main entrance. This is where you take care of logistics while the gleaming ball of Spaceship Earth offers a 16-million-pound hint (to you and, on a clear day, to airplane passengers flying along either Florida coast) as to the precise direction of Future World. Epcot's monorail station is right outside the gates here, as is an ATM (located on the far left just before you enter the park). On the far right side of the entranceway, also outside the gates, you can exchange currency, make a phone call, and pick up any cumbersome purchases you arranged to have forwarded here during your visit. **Note:** If you need to use any of these services mid-visit, have your hand stamped upon exiting the turnstiles so that you may re-enter the park. Lost and Found is in the Guest Relations lobby at Innoventions East. As you close in on the big ball, remember that there are still more services in its shadows. If you'd like your image engraved on a one-inch square tile for the striking Leave a Legacy tribute to Walt Disney World guests, this is the place to stop for information. (For $35, you may have your picture taken and added to the monument. If you'd like some company, it costs $38 for a tile for two.) If you need a storage locker, pass around Spaceship Earth's right side. Otherwise, keep left. This course will lead you past the stroller and wheelchair rentals.

If you haven't made dining plans, stop by Guest Relations next to Spaceship Earth to make priority seating arrangements or hold your horses until you get to the eatery of your choice. Otherwise, focus on the center of Innoventions Plaza, where you'll find the **Tip Board**, an electronic information board listing current waiting times for popular attractions.

Future World

You know you're in Future World when you see a thunderous fountain that acts like it owns the place, something resembling an oversize golf ball that would require a club roughly the size of the Empire State Building, kaleidoscopic fiber-optic patterns in the walkway, abstract gardens that could pass for modern art, and freewheeling water fountains that do swan dives and geyser imitations.

This highly conceptual land makes a striking first impression, and no wonder—it's awash in the sort of grand music that might trumpet the credits of an Academy Award-winning film. And it wears its sleek architecture and futuristic landscaping like a power suit. The eight themed pavilions that make up Future World collectively document humanity's progress in this world and offer intriguing visions of our technological fate. Such broad concerns as communications, health, and the environment serve as springboards for the attractions, which make stimulating experiences of topics that commonly make boring conversation.

If you haven't paid a visit here in the past few years, you'll notice that an ongoing tweaking spree has invigorated Future World. Like a well-inked wad of Silly Putty that's been balled up and rolled out anew, the pavilion celebrating imagination has morphed into a whole new mind-bending experience. Test Track, a ride on the wild side of automobile testing, has finally put Epcot in a novel spot: atop the thrill seeker's "Must Do" list. And Innoventions has been rerouted as a futuristic roadtrip. Proof that Epcot's self-improvement kick is no passing phase: A new space-themed pavilion is currently on Disney's launching pad.

A reminder: This tour is designed to provide a sense of place, not a recommended plan of attack. Future World pavilions are described here as you would encounter them geographically, beginning with Spaceship Earth, the park's northernmost pavilion. Innoventions, which cradles the west (right, as you face World Showcase) and east (left) sides of the central plaza, is next, followed by a counterclockwise exploration of the remaining pavilions, from The Living Seas in the northwestern corner of Future World southward to The Land and Imagination!, and across the central plaza to the eastern flank of pavilions, beginning with Wonders of Life and Universe of Energy.

•CONTINUED FROM PREVIOUS PAGE

DON'T OVERLOOK

Innoventions; Spaceship Earth; Journey Into Your Imagination; China**; Mexico; Italy; Morocco; Germany; United Kingdom; *Circle of Life* in the Land

DON'T KNOCK YOURSELF OUT

Food Rocks in The Land; El Río del Tiempo boat ride in Mexico

* Fastpass attraction as of press time. Consult your guidemap for new additions.

** Pay close attention to performance schedules.

Entertainment

Epcot's entertainment slate is ever-changing. So pick up a guidemap at Guest Relations (or elsewhere in the park) and consult it often.

In Future World, acrobats and a trash-can percussive unit dressed in custodial wear are popular head-turners.

The Fountain of Nations erupts into a computer-choreographed water ballet every 15 minutes.

At the Wonders of Life pavilion, catch the AnaComical Players, an improvisational theater troupe that relies on audience participation.

•CONTINUED ON NEXT PAGE

Spaceship Earth

This 180-foot-tall "geosphere" sticks out like a wayward planet come to roost. You may be interested to learn that the silver exterior comes from layers of anodized aluminum and polyethylene, and is composed of 954 triangular panels, not all of equal size or shape (although it takes a keen eye to discern any differences). Or maybe you'd rather hear how the gleaming exterior funnels every raindrop that hits it into World Showcase Lagoon.

Although the sight of its outer layer is an experience all its own, Spaceship Earth is visually arresting to the core. The **Spaceship Earth** ride inside the geosphere winds past exquisitely detailed scenes, neatly tracing the evolution of human communication using Audio-Animatronic figures that here, in their element, seem more natural than many sitcom actors. In 14 minutes you've gone from CroMagnon grunts all the way to the fabled information superhighway. Narration by Jeremy Irons adds an element of drama. The finale provides a hip, forward-looking finish for Spaceship Earth; take away the lasers and it would still be the ride's biggest head-turner. This attraction—your worst bet first thing in the morning—is least crowded during the hours just prior to park closing.

Outside, in the Global Neighborhood, you can dabble in interactive activities.

Innoventions

Think of the latest incarnation of Innoventions as a trip down future lane. Disney recast this huge showcase of technological goodies, all 100,000 square feet of it, as entertaining rest stops and sophisticated scenery along a very important piece of pavement: The Road to Tomorrow. But please, leave your gas-guzzler in the parking lot—pedestrians (and occasionally electric cars) rule on this engaging excuse for a freeway. If The Road to Tomorrow is frequently congested, it's because Innoventions is a bright labyrinth of activity that hot rods and Sunday drivers alike find difficult to pass through quickly. Well-marked exits ensure that you won't miss a single turnoff (hands-on exhibit), even if you're looking at your handy, dandy road map upside down. That's right, there's a road map.

Hold the map upright, and you'll see that Innoventions is still housed in two structures, still presented by major manufacturers such as IBM, AT&T, Motorola, Honeywell, Xerox, Lutron, and General Motors. The building known as Innoventions East is largely devoted to the kinds of products and gadgets that could one day rise up and outfinesse Martha Stewart; Innoventions West hails more from the Bill Gates school of cool. But the two segments of The Road to Tomorrow thematically twist and turn far too frequently to be strictly categorized.

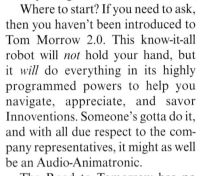

Where to start? If you need to ask, then you haven't been introduced to Tom Morrow 2.0. This know-it-all robot will *not* hold your hand, but it *will* do everything in its highly programmed powers to help you navigate, appreciate, and savor Innoventions. Someone's gotta do it, and with all due respect to the company representatives, it might as well be an Audio-Animatronic.

The Road to Tomorrow has no scenic overlooks to speak of. But as sure as you're wearing sneakers, you'll be pulling over like a vista-gorging tourist on Hawaii's Hana Highway. Instead of succumbing to idyllic picnic spots, you'll be lured by Disney Online's invitation to send a video e-mail or picture postcard to a friend or to communicate via music or paintbrush strokes with someone at a decidedly different latitude. Rather than being wooed by waterfalls, you'll be drawn to the machinations of Xerox. Unless, of course, you long ago tired of experimenting with such things as digitally erasable paper, nearly instantaneous language translation, and virtual staples and stickers. Although a genetically engineered forest may not sound as seductive as swaying palms, it's perhaps best to reserve judgment until you've eyed 30,000 trees in a petri dish and planted a virtual tree at The Magical Forest.

•*CONTINUED FROM PREVIOUS PAGE*

In addition, each World Showcase pavilion has a cast of performers, any of whom could be appearing during your visit. Among the possibilities: bagpipe players in Canada, a mop-top band playing tribute to the British Invasion in the United Kingdom, belly dancers in Morocco, drummers in Japan, singers in Italy, oompah musicians in Germany, acrobats in China, and a mariachi band in Mexico. The American Adventure features the Voices of Liberty a cappella group and stage shows at America Gardens Theatre.

Epcot's IllumiNations: Reflections of Earth all but sets fire to the senses in its dramatic, hypnotic simulation of our planet's evolution. This nightly finale starts off with a bang and ends on an even more explosive note. Stand somewhere (anywhere) along the promenade and prepare to be moved.

Tapestry of Nations, a parade incorporating giant, colorful puppets and mesmerizing music, is worth a look if it's on the schedule during your visit.

A Flash from the Future?

Other compelling off-ramps lead you to realms of sensory overload. It's difficult to say "ho hum, boring" with any conviction when you're knocking around with wireless video phones (merci, Motorola) and experiencing the apotheosis of home theater (bravo, Lutron).

Strange but true: The Radiological Society of North America's demo of medical imaging advances is perhaps the most clever exhibit of all. It's not just people's perceptions of the world that have progressed from flat to curved and finally to three dimensional. Taking a cue from Christopher Columbus, radiologists have similarly expanded their viewpoint of the human body. The history of radiological exploration becomes all the more fascinating when projections transform the floor and walls of the theater into enveloping seas of X rays and progressively more detailed cross-sections of MRIs, CAT scans, and PET nuclear medicine scans. Best of all, the prognosis looks good.

The keys to an enjoyable Innoventions experience:
- Adjust your touring plans if you need to, but be sure to visit when you're feeling fresh—this is no place for a zombie.
- Take advantage of the fact that this pavilion is split between two buildings; check out the one on the east side of the plaza in the morning and explore the one on the west side in the evening.
- Give the exhibits some time. If you breeze through, you'll miss a lot.
- If you're skeptical or curious about something, ask the question.

The Living Seas

The Caribbean is not as far away as you think. If you want to catch a wave, some mammoth lettuce-munching manatees, and a richly stocked coral reef environment (pop.: 2,000) that even a scuba diver would find extraordinary, look no further. This pavilion, dedicated to the study of oceanography and ocean ecology, ranks among Epcot's most inspired areas. During the toasty summer months, it's particularly refreshing to ogle The Living Seas' pièce de résistance, a 5.7-million-gallon tank in which a simulated Caribbean Sea and man-made reef support a glorious array of life, including sharks, dolphins, sea turtles, rays, and crustaceans.

There are two paths to this not-to-be-missed underwater vista, where in addition to colorful sea life you can observe one-person submarines and divers conducting marine experiments. If you're certified in scuba diving or want a little Dolphin 101, take the behind-the-scenes route. For details, heed the tips at the bottom of page 107.

To immerse yourself thoroughly without getting wet, take the **Caribbean Coral Reef Ride**. This three-pronged journey features a waterlogged film, a simulated descent to the ocean floor (the elevator-like capsules actually plunge only an inch), and a quick taxi through an underwater viewing tunnel to the main event, **Sea Base Alpha**. Here, you can linger all you like in front of enormous eight-inch-thick windows to the undersea world (be on the lookout for moray eels, barracuda, and puffers). Exhibits offer insight into marine research methods, additional display tanks, and—unless you encounter those endangered, impossibly animated sea barges known as manatees frequently in your travels—compelling reasons to stick around awhile.

Of course, no seafaring adventure is complete without the opportunity to shout "Land ho!" so it's only right that The Land is the next pavilion.

The Land

This popular six-acre plot, surpassed in size only by Innoventions (or the manatees at The Living Seas), explores themes related to food and farming while planting seeds of environmental consciousness. Underneath this pavilion's dramatic skylighted roof, you'll find a well-balanced slate of attractions, a bountiful food court, and a lazy Susan of a restaurant, the Garden Grill, which rotates *very* slowly past several of the ecosystems featured in the pavilion's boat ride. All things considered, The Land merits two green thumbs up as the purveyor of one of Future World's strongest lineups.

The **Living with the Land** boat ride is a beautifully informative 13½-minute journey that escorts you through a stormy prairie, a windswept desert, and a South American rain forest en route to experimental greenhouses and an area given over to fish farming. The dripping, squawking rain forest is so realistic, you'd need to chomp on a faux fern to convince yourself it's all plastic. The narration is an interesting commentary on the history and future of

Dolphin Alert

Behind-the-scenes tours aren't the only way to make the most of dolphin sightings on your trip through The Living Seas. Daily demonstrations are sure to enhance any visit. Since schedules vary and are posted *inside* the pavilion only, check at Guest Relations for details so you can time your visit accordingly. Or stop by during feeding time (usually around 10 A.M., though this is subject to change).

A Healthy Crop

If you're eating your vegetables (and fruits) at the Garden Grill, Coral Reef, or Sunshine Season Food Fair, odds are good that you're sharing in The Land pavilion's bounty. Some 30 tons of produce are harvested each year from The Land's greenhouses. Talk about fresh local ingredients!

agriculture. The impressive greenhouses show futuristic technology at work on real crops (many of which are served here at Epcot), with NASA experiments and cucumbers in desert training among the highlights. This popular attraction is best visited in the morning or during the hours just prior to park closing. If you're an avid gardener or Living with the Land has you thoroughly intrigued, we heartily recommend **Behind The Seeds** (for details on this behind-the-scenes tour, see page 107).

The Circle of Life is an entertaining ecological fable featuring Timon and Pumbaa, the wisenheimer meerkat-warthog duo from the Disney film *The Lion King*, as developers, and Simba as the environmentally sensitive lion. The 20-minute film includes stunning nature footage.

Remember **Food Rocks**—a so-called musical tribute to good nutrition that turns out to be a nutrition-oriented salute to great music—as a satisfying snack. This 15-minute concert performed by Audio-Animatronic lip-synchers is Disney showing its sense of humor. Among the reasons you'll be a groupie: Pita Gabriel singing "I wanna be your high fiber," and The Refrigerator Police's arresting refrain, "Every bite you take, every egg you break" (guess who is a milk carton with dark sunglasses?). It's usually possible to get into the next show. But wander around the muraled pre-show area and you'll learn a lot—like what Ethiopian goats have to do with coffee.

Imagination!

While you'd think that glass buildings would leave very little to the imagination, the glass pyramids that house the Imagination! pavilion have quite the opposite effect. If necessity is truly the mother of invention, then this is where she resides, playing with minds as if they were Play Doh, pushing a philosophy that might be called patent or perish. Fronted by fountains that seem to have agendas of their own, this pavilion is one of Future World's most inspired.

Ever-curious about what it feels like to be an inventor with those little light bulbs always appearing above your head, you enter the **Journey Into Your Imagination** attraction, and discover that you have stumbled upon an open house hosted by the Imagination Institute. Before you can fasten your thinking cap, you've become somewhat of a test subject for a project called The Imagination Scanner. During your visit, you are put through a set of illusory experiments designed to challenge your perception skills—or at least mess with your head. And don't forget to stop by **Image Works: Kodak "What If" Labs**, an interactive area that will challenge your perceptions.

But the attraction at the Imagination! pavilion that earns the most exuberant high five is **Honey, I Shrunk the Audience**. If you have time to visit only a few attractions at Epcot, this spectacle of a 3-D movie should be high on your list. The 25-minute film is so riddled with sensational special effects that the audience is consistently reduced to a shrieking, squirming, giggling mass. The experience is not rough, but the effects *are* heightened with a little bit of suspense, so we'll say no more. Crowds are least congested in the morning.

Coming Attraction

Your ticket to space exploration is on the horizon at Epcot: It comes in the form of a brand-new pavilion with an outer space theme, slated to replace the old Horizons attraction in the not-too-distant future. Mission: Space, rocketing toward Future World with an E.T.A. of 2003, promises to deliver an intense deep-space training experience. In lieu of an actual blast-off, guests will be shot into orbit via a motion simulator—not unlike the ones real astronauts use. Former NASA advisors and astronauts are working with Disney Imagineers to lend authenticity to this thrill ride. Let the countdown begin.

Cool Down

Need to quench your thirst after making the rounds of Future World? Try a quick sampling of drinks from around the globe at Ice Station Cool next to Innoventions. On a hot summer day, you'll happily enter the tunnel (where the temperature is a very cool 32 degrees) that leads to a room full of self-serve soda machines. Grab a complimentary cup and sip away at flavored drinks made by The Coca Cola Company for countries the world over. Mix flavors at your own risk. A great pit stop when you need to cool off.

Test Track

Behind this pavilion's steely doors lies the fastest ride at Walt Disney World. In this supercharged introduction to the world of automobile testing, the ride's computer-controlled vehicles barrel up steep hills, zip down straightaways, squeak around heavily banked hairpin turns, and slam on the brakes. **Test Track** is much more than a thrilling ride: It's a realistic run-through of tests performed on real cars at real facilities, known as proving grounds.

As you walk through the plant you see everything from the all-important seat-squirming test to the crucial trials endured by air bags, tires, and the human interface clan (our courageous crash-prone counterparts) to ensure our safety. Then you hop into a six-person vehicle, fasten your seat belt, and—making note that you've got a video display, but no steering wheel or brake pedal—prepare for an exciting five-minute road trip. As the sporty open-top cars traverse the nearly one-mile track, you experience a rough-and-tumble suspension workout, become indebted to antilock brakes, narrowly avoid a crash, and whiz outside and around the pavilion at speeds up to 65 miles per hour. Incredible insight into cars is a given; you'll also gain respect for the complex systems contained

therein. On the way out, be sure to stop and check out the smarty-pants car demo and the automotive boutique.

Test Track is an altogether different experience by day and by night (you can guess which is more intense). If it's raining, we suggest you turn your face to the sky and ask yourself this question: Would I enjoy zooming down a highway in a convertible with the top down right about now?

For the least intimidating crowds, grab a Fastpass or try to visit in the evening while everyone else is viewing IllumiNations: Reflections of Earth. **Note:** Since this is something of a rough attraction, riders must be free from heart conditions, back and neck problems, and other physical limitations.

Wonders of Life

While the 72-foot-tall-steel DNA molecule certainly marks the territory of this mostly whimsical pavilion devoted to health and fitness concerns, the sculpture also provides a visual reminder of the uniqueness of this area of Future World. Wonders of Life gets credit for having introduced three elements to Epcot—the first true thrill ride, a health-food bar, and (believe it or not) exercise equipment.

First, the pavilion's main attraction: **Body Wars**, a frenetic five-minute trip through the human body in a flight simulator. This ride could be the fraternal twin of Star Tours, the rocky ride through space located at the Disney-MGM Studios, but for a couple of things. It is a year older and a few notches rougher than its Studios counterpart. The premise of Body Wars is that you are along for the ride on a routine medical probe to remove a splinter (from the inside) when things get out of hand. Before you know it, you're barreling through regions such as the human lungs, heart, and brain. Body Wars is a tremendously exciting journey, both visually and physically, that rates among Epcot's biggest thrills, but it is also a turbulent ride with a lot of very herky-jerky movements.

Note that if you're especially squeamish, you may find the visual content too much in this context. If you are pregnant, you should not venture onto this ride. You should also bypass Body Wars if you've eaten recently, have a back problem or heart condition, are susceptible to motion sickness, or have other physical limitations. While crowds flock to this attraction, it is generally least

Hidden Mickey

If you look very, very closely, you can spot Mickey in the mural above the entrance to Body Wars at the Wonders of Life pavilion.

Like Child's Play

As Walt Disney once said, "Laughter is no enemy to learning." And so it is that Epcot's Future World is blessed with dozens of attractions that make great fun of enlightenment. For entertainment that is so whimsical you're barely conscious of any information intake, consider the following amusements:

■ Cranium Command at Wonders of Life

■ Body Wars at Wonders of Life

■ Food Rocks at The Land

■ Living with the Land at The Land

■ Ellen's Energy Adventure at Universe of Energy

■ Caribbean Coral Reef Ride at The Living Seas

■ Innoventions East and West

■ The Global Neighborhood near the exit of Spaceship Earth

congested first thing in the morning and during the hours just prior to park closing.

Another Wonders of Life attraction that merits not-to-be-missed status is **Cranium Command**, an utterly tame, utterly delightful 17-minute journey into the mind of a 12-year-old boy. This is an attraction so good, Billy Crystal would have a tough time making it funnier. Here's the setup: The commander of a specialized corps of brain pilots is issuing assignments, and our pal Buzzy must pilot an adolescent boy. The show follows a day in this boy's life, with Buzzy calling the shots. Celebrity cameos include George Wendt (Norm from *Cheers*) manning the stomach, Dana Carvey and Kevin Nealon (playing Hans and Franz of *Saturday Night Live* fame) as the heart, and comedian Bobcat Goldthwait as the adrenal gland.

For some more mind-bending fun, explore the challenges of the Sensory Funhouse, located just outside Cranium Command. And don't neglect the stable of Wonder Cycles, computerized stationary bicycles that let you pedal (headlong into traffic) through the Rose Bowl Parade and Disneyland. Hey, when will that opportunity present itself again?

Universe of Energy

Behind this mirrored facade lies a pavilion on a serious power trip (it draws some of its electricity from photovoltaic cells mounted on the roof). Universe of Energy has always been notable for its lifelike dinosaurs, some of Disney's largest Audio-Animatronic animals. But since its update, the show here also boasts some familiar faces and fetches a few nominations for Best Comedy in an Epcot Pavilion.

The pavilion is given over entirely to a 45-minute presentation that explores the origins of fossil fuels and muses about alternative energy sources. **Ellen's Energy Adventure** is powered by Ellen's sudden yen for knowledge about such things—largely so that she can beat her know-it-all college roommate Judy should they ever land on their favorite game show together. Bill Nye, the Science Guy, offers to educate Ellen, and just happens to have some rather extensive visual aids handy. As Bill lectures Ellen, arresting visuals are shown on a series of huge screens. (Look for a cameo by a caveman you'd swear was a famous sitcom actor.)

When Bill insists they travel back 220 million years to seek greater knowledge, the seating area rotates and splits into six vehicles that then move into the clammy air of the primeval world. Here, you encounter erupting volcanoes, an eerie fog, and prehistoric creatures locked in combat, rearing up suddenly from a tide pool, and gazing down at you like vultures. You also come upon an Audio-Animatronic Ellen, desperately attempting to reason with a snakelike dinosaur. She makes it out of the forest in one piece, and hits the big time on her game show, if only in her dreams. (For those playing along at home, the category is ENERGY; the answer, THE ONE ENERGY SOURCE WE'LL NEVER EXHAUST. We won't give away the question.) This pavilion is best visited in the late afternoon. A large group is let into the theater every 17 minutes, so don't let the crowd scare you, but if the line extends beyond the marquee, try again later.

Future World Unplugged

Insight into the inner workings of Epcot is easier to come by than you might think. The passwords in Future World:

■ **Behind The Seeds:** Continuous one-hour greenhouse tours at The Land ($6) cover much the same terrain as the Living with the Land boat ride, but in a more intimate fashion. Tours are offered throughout the day, starting at 10:30 A.M. Same-day reservations may be made as soon as the pavilion opens at 9 A.M. For information, call 407-WDW-TOUR (939-8687).

■ **DiveQuest:** In addition to offering an informal introduction to marine research and conservation, this 2½-hour program ($140) invites certified scuba divers to suit up for a 30- to 40-minute dive in The Living Seas aquarium. For details, call 407-WDW-TOUR (939-8687).

■ **Dolphins in Depth:** The same $140 buys you 30 minutes in the water with the dolphins at The Living Seas and a videotape to prove it. Call 407-WDW-TOUR (939-8687) for details on this 3½-hour experience.

Leave Future World by walking through Innoventions Plaza and past the fountain that aspires to be Niagara Falls (in an odd case of confused identity or perhaps an attempt at foreshadowing, it's called the Fountain of Nations). As you head south over the walkway that leads to World Showcase, be sure to look to each side: On the right, a spontaneously erupting fountain is delivering a merciless soaking (mostly to children); on the left, note the ATM, and farther down, the resident flock of flamingos that is bathing in the canal. Welcome to the flip side of Future World.

World Showcase

Think of World Showcase as a handful of gourmet jelly beans, the sort so flavorful, they make your taste buds believe you're actually putting away strawberry cheesecake, champagne punch, and chocolate pudding. You know they're just jelly beans, of course, but you pretend, fully savoring the essence of that piña colada. In the same way, World Showcase cajoles your senses into accepting its international pavilions at face value, enveloping you in such delectable representations of Germany, Japan, Mexico, and more, that you are content to play along.

This parade of nations, a cultural thoroughfare wrapped around a lagoon the size of 85 football fields, is marked by dramatic mood swings. The atmosphere changes markedly with each border crossing, going from positively romantic to utterly serene, toe-tappingly upbeat, patriotic, festive, wistfully Old World, or cheerfully relaxed in a matter of yards.

Of course, the World Showcase pavilions are not simply outstanding mood pieces but occasions to get uniquely acquainted with the people, history, and beauty of the world's nations. Each pavilion has a strong, unmistakable sense of place that announces itself with painstakingly re-created landmarks and faithful landscaping that ensures bougainvillea in Mexico and lotus blossoms in China. Each contributes culinary specialties from the apple-tart-to-ice-cream smorgasbord that makes World Showcase one of the hottest meal tickets in Walt Disney World.

To transport yourself totally, try to supplement the smattering of attractions—panoramic films, theater and dinner shows, boat rides, and the nightly not-to-be-missed fireworks extravaganza—with the legions of less structured pursuits. Start by trying to catch at least one street performance per country. So frequent it's practically ongoing (check your guidemap for exact times), this feast of live entertainment encompasses everything from mariachi bands to acrobats, belly dancing, and bagpipes, and it makes a great accompaniment to a mobile wine tasting. Take time, too, to chitchat with the "locals" in each village (nearly all of whom claim the represented country as their homeland) and to talk with visiting artisans as they demonstrate their crafts. To personalize your journey even more, make a mission of snacking, drinking, shopping, gallery-hopping, or even benchwarming your way around the World. For adults, these relaxing activities are the very essence of a visit to World Showcase.

Structurally, World Showcase is perhaps the most user-friendly area of Walt Disney World's theme parks. You may get tired walking along the 1.2-mile promenade that leads past all pavilions as it encircles the lagoon, but you won't lose your sense of direction. While locations of countries here don't correspond at all to their placement on the planet, the landscape offers a wealth of Eiffel Tower-like clues that *almost* preclude use of a map. Because World Showcase is less attraction-driven (6 of the 12 pavilions have no attractions, per se), it requires less strategic maneuvering.

International Gateway

Think of this second entrance as Epcot's back door. The turnstiles here provide a direct "in" to World Showcase, depositing guests between the France and United Kingdom pavilions. Because the International Gateway is connected via walkway to the Yacht and Beach Club, BoardWalk, Swan, and Dolphin resorts, guests at these lodgings have exceptional access to Epcot. (Water launches also make the trip.) Be aware that:

■ Wheelchairs are available for rent at this entrance.

■ Nothing in World Showcase opens until 11 A.M., so guests arriving earlier must walk to Future World at the opposite end of the park.

■ If you plan ahead, you can make a quick exit from here, after IllumiNations: Reflections of Earth.

Snacking Around the World

When your stomach's growling, every World Showcase country has a little something to satisfy your craving. Here's an inkling of what we have (happily) sampled.

Near the Canadian border, it's "beaver tail" pastries from a cart. In the United Kingdom, we like the fish, chips, and baked potatoes outside the Rose & Crown Pub.

•CONTINUED ON NEXT PAGE

If World Showcase came with instructions, the handy booklet might say:

■ Touring is a clockwise or counterclockwise proposition that's best begun (as soon as this part of Epcot opens) on an empty stomach.

■ Shops are optimally saved for the afternoon, when the throngs from Future World have descended, lengthening lines for movies, rides, and shows.

■ The movies at Canada, France, and China are often better appreciated when spaced out over two days.

■ IllumiNations: Reflections of Earth is the biggest entertainment draw in all of Epcot. The nightly spectacle of fireworks, lasers, and music is visible from most any point around World Showcase.

Moving along, this tour describes World Showcase pavilions in the order they're encountered when walking counterclockwise around the lagoon.

Canada

I n a marked departure from the real world, a refreshment stand poised a good 50 yards before the border makes it possible to arrive in Canada with Molson in hand. This large pavilion—which merits kudos as the site of an outstanding panoramic film, an "underground" steak house, interesting shops, and the coolest spot in World Showcase—covers an impressive amount of territory in its bid to capture the distinctive beauty and cultural diversity of the Western Hemisphere's largest nation. An artful ode to the Indians of Canada's Northwest (towering totem poles and a trading post) leads to an architectural tribute to French Canada (the Hôtel du Canada here is a hybrid of Ottawa's Château Laurier and Quebec's Château Frontenac).

From here, follow the sounds of rushing water to find the cooling sprays of a miniaturized Niagara Falls that's tucked neatly into the face of a Canadian Rocky and usually blessed with a rainbow. A stunning feature film, a visual anthem of sorts appropriately called *O Canada!*, is shown in all its Circle-Vision 360 glory within the mountain itself. The 17-minute movie places you smack in the middle of most all things Canadian, including a hockey game, a flock of Canadian geese taking flight, enormous reindeer herds, and the Royal Canadian Mounted Police. It's a standing engagement, so it's best viewed early in the day when you're still fresh. Whatever you do, don't miss it. As you leave, check out the bountiful greenery inspired by the famous Butchart Gardens, in Victoria, British Columbia—while not as cool as the falls, they're still a great place to claim a bench, especially when the Pipes of Nova Scotia or the Off Kilter troupe of Celtic rock musicians is performing.

United Kingdom

This cheery neighborhood, which reveals its identity via the bright-red phone booths dotting its cobblestoned streets, is a fine place for a bit of shopping or a pint of ale. What's less obvious: the knotted herb garden tucked behind the thatched-roof cottage (note the spearmint plants); the butterfly hatchery on the hill; and the courtyard at the rear of the pavilion, where you'll find a traditional English hedge maze. You may even catch the Beatlesque rock group that performs in the garden. A table at the Rose & Crown Pub is the best perspective from which to view this pavilion, because the Tudor, Georgian, and Victorian structures seem all the more real from the window of a friendly English pub.

Architectural enlightenment is a great excuse to dally in the fine shops. You can cover 300 years of building styles just by walking from the slate floor of The Tea Caddy straight through to the carpeted room with the Waterford crystal chandelier, which signals your arrival at the Neoclassical period and the shop known as The Queen's Table.

France

A footbridge from the United Kingdom leads across a picturesque canal to one of the most romantic areas of World Showcase. Petite streets and Eiffel Tower aside, you're looking at Paris during the Belle Epoque ("beautiful age") of the late 19th century. The one-time Parisian institution Les Halles is re-created here, as is a one-ninth-scale Eiffel Tower that would be infinitely more evocative were it not so obviously perched atop a building. Luxurious boutiques, bustling sidewalk cafes, and, of course, pastries that announce their presence *par avion* are among the big draws here, as is the wine-tasting counter at the nicely stocked La Maison du Vin. Beckoning, too, is one of the most peaceful spots in all of Epcot—a quiet park on the canal side of the pavilion that might have leapt off the canvas of Georges Seurat's *Sunday Afternoon on the Island of La Grande Jatte.*

But the biggest lure here is the breathtaking 18-minute film ***Impressions de France***, which puts its five 21- by 27-foot screens to terrific use in a *tour de*

•CONTINUED FROM PREVIOUS PAGE

In France, we appreciate the Boulangerie Pâtisserie's fine snacking sensibility, particularly the pastry known as the Marvelous. In Morocco, we go for the baklava. Japan's Matsu No Ma sates when we're in a sushi frame of mind. The American Adventure's Liberty Inn provides—what else?— apple pie, french fries, and ice cream. La Bottega Italiana stands by with scrumptious Italian specialties. Germany comes through with killer soft pretzels, potato salad, and bratwurst at Sommerfest. China steps up with egg rolls at the Lotus Blossom Cafe. Norway (specifically Kringla Bakeri og Kafe) satisfies sweet and savory instincts, most notably with open-face sandwiches and *vaflers* (heart-shaped waffles) made on the spot and topped with fresh preserves. And Mexico doesn't disappoint with the requisite chips and salsa at the lagoonside Cantina de San Angel. In other words: No set dining plans? No problem.

Quiet Nooks

France that ranges from Alpine skiing to foothills of buttery pastries. If you know France, you'll love it; if you don't, you'll want to. The superb score, featuring French classical composers, could stand on its own. *Impressions de France* is least congested during the morning and early-evening hours. A few key words to help you communicate with the locals: Say *bonjour* (*bohn-ZHOOR*) for good day, *merci beaucoup* (*mehr-see boh-KOO*) for thank you very much, and *au revoir* (*OH re-VWAR*) for good-bye.

Morocco

This enchanting area—arguably the most meticulously crafted of all the represented nations—also happens to be the loudest World Showcase pavilion. The authenticity has something to do with the fact that nine tons of tile were handmade, hand-cut, and hand-laid by Moroccan artisans into the mosaics seen here. The prayer tower at the entrance takes after the famous Koutoubia Minaret, in Marrakesh, and sets the scene for the energetic Moroccan musicians and dancers who perform in the courtyard. The Bab Boujouloud gate, patterned after one that stands in the city of Fez, leads to the Medina (old part of the city), a tangled array of narrow passageways where basketry, leather goods, and brass items are among the wares for sale.

Walk through the bazaar, whether or not you feel like shopping, so that you can get a feel for the Medina and try out your Arabic. Hello is *salam alekoum (sah-LAHM wah-LAY-koom)*, thank you is *shokran (SHOWK-ran)*, and good-bye is *b'slama (b'-SLEM-ah)*. The Medina also brings you to the entrance of Marrakesh restaurant, notable for its North African menu, its belly dancers, and the fact that it's one of the only full-service restaurants in World Showcase where you can frequently get a table without securing priority seating. You can also savor Mediterranean-style chicken, beef, and lamb sandwiches, salads, and desserts at the more casual Tangierine Cafe. Make a point of checking out the extraordinary tile work and costumes displayed at the Gallery of Arts and History, and be on the lookout for visiting artisans demonstrating their crafts. It's interesting to note that the gardens are irrigated by an ancient working waterwheel located on the promenade. Morocco is easily toured any time of day. For a more structured look at the pavilion, sign up for a guided tour at the Morocco National Tourist Office inside. The complimentary tours last from 20 to 40 minutes and are available between noon and 7 P.M.

Japan

As quietly inviting as Morocco is vibrantly enticing, Japan is a pavilion of considerable beauty and serenity. Its most prominent landmarks are the red *torii* gate (a popular good-luck symbol), which stands close to the lagoon, and the five-tiered pagoda, created in the mold of an eighth-century shrine located in Nara. Each level of the pagoda represents one of the elements that, according to Buddhist teachings, produced everything in the universe (from bottom to top: earth, water, fire, wind, and sky).

The most compelling features of this pavilion are the entertainment (the Matsuriza drummers), the elaborate detail of its manicured gardens (note the differently patterned fences, and the bamboo "scarecrow" contraption in

the stream), and the art exhibit at the Bijutsu-kan Gallery. "Karakuri: Magical Toys of Japan" showcases the nation's playful side. Japan also claims one of the largest shops in Epcot. Housed in a structure reminiscent of a section of the Gosho Imperial Palace, which was originally constructed in Kyoto in 794 A.D., the Mitsukoshi Department Store counts bonsai trees, kimonos, dolls, tea sets, incense, jewelry, and decorative ceremonial swords among its offerings. You could spend hours just lingering over the unique merchandise. All that shopping may spark your appetite. At Teppanyaki Dining Rooms, a feast consisting of vegetables, steak, chicken, and seafood is prepared tableside by authentic Japanese chefs. This pavilion is easily toured any time of day. Good morning in Japanese is *ohayo gozaimasu (oh-hi-yoh goh-zy-ee-mahs)*, thank you is *arigato gozaimasu (ah-ree-gah-toh goh-zy-ee-mahs)*, and good evening is *konban wa (kohn-bahn wah)*.

Tired of Walking?

The *FriendShip* water taxis link Showcase Plaza at the foot of Future World with Germany and Morocco, across the lagoon at the farthest corners of World Showcase. Convenient—but keep in mind that it may be quicker to walk.

Where the Art Is

Exhibits change periodically, but here's an indication of what you can expect to see:

■ Mexico's "Reign of Glory" exhibit features pre-Columbian pieces (some are on loan from the Smithsonian).

■ Norway's tiny Stave Church Gallery contains exhibits tracing the history of the once-commonplace churches.

■ Japan's Bijutsu-kan Gallery becomes a toy chest with "Karakuri: Magical Toys of Japan."

■ Morocco's Gallery of Arts and History showcases intricate tile work and costumes.

■ China's House of Whispering Willows displays ancient Chinese art and artifacts.

The American Adventure

The centerpiece pavilion of World Showcase is so devoted to Americana, it can bring out the Norman Rockwell in you even when you're cranky. Housed in a Colonial-style manse that combines elements of Independence Hall, the Old State House in Boston, Monticello, and various structures in Colonial Williamsburg, it's dressed for the part. The 26-minute show inside—an evocative multimedia presentation about American history—is among Disney's best, both for its astonishingly detailed sets and sophisticated Audio-Animatronic figures and for its ability to rouse goose bumps from unsuspecting patriots. Ben Franklin and Mark Twain lead what's been called "a hundred-yard dash capturing the spirit of the country at specific moments in time."

A talented a cappella vocal group called the Voices of Liberty sometimes entertains in the lobby before the show begins. (So talented are these singers that they are consistently able to get most every person in the place singing "God Bless America.") The wait for The American Adventure can be long because the show itself is lengthy, so stop by for curtain times and plan accordingly. This pavilion also features a fast-food restaurant and the lagoonside **America Gardens Theatre**, where you may find some entertainment. An interesting aside: The garden alongside The American Adventure acknowledges the days before red, white, and blue by showcasing plants used traditionally by Native Americans for food and medicinal purposes.

Italy

This little Italy is defined by an abiding you-are-there ambience and meticulous authenticity that extend from the gondolas tied to striped moorings at the pavilion's very own Venetian island to the homemade (before your eyes) fettuccine and spaghetti at its popular L'Originale Alfredo di Roma Ristorante.

Look to the very top of the scaled-down Venetian campanile dominating the romantic piazza here, and you'll see an angel covered in gold leaf that was molded into a spitting image of the one atop the bell tower in the real St. Mark's Square, in Venice. The Doge's Palace here is so faithfully rendered that its facade resembles the marbled pattern of the original. Adding to the effect are tall, slender stands of Italian cypress, replicas of Venetian statues, an abundance of potted flowers, and delightfully fragrant olive and citrus trees.

This pavilion is among the most romantic and evocative areas in all of World Showcase. It has no major attractions per se, but between its memorable street

performers (such as a New Age classical music group) and the strolling musicians who play during dinner at Alfredo's, it has all the entertainment it needs. Among the shopping options is a gem of a gourmet food purveyor, called La Bottega Italiana, that also stocks fine Italian wines. This pavilion is easily visited at any time of day. When in Italy, note that good day is *buon giorno (boo-on JOR-no)*, thank you is *grazie (GRAHT-see-eh)*, and good-bye is *arrivederci (ah-ree-veh-DAIR-chee)*.

Germany

In a word: *oompah*. Arguably the most festive country in all of World Showcase, Germany is immediately recognizable by its fairy-tale architecture. To the rear of the central cobblestoned square (which is named for Saint George), you'll see a giant cuckoo clock, complete with Hummel figurines that emerge on the hour. Immediately past this clock lies the Biergarten, the vast restaurant and entertainment hall that—thanks to lively lunch and dinner shows primed with German beer, sausages, and yodelers—serves as the pinnacle of this pavilion's entertainment. For a more impromptu beer or piece of Black Forest cake, there's an outdoor counter called Sommerfest; a strolling accordionist and trio frequently usher the festive Bavarian atmosphere of the Biergarten out into the square.

Germany also scores with tempting shops, an ATM, and the Weinkeller, which offers wine-tasting opportunities. In Glas und Porzellan, it's usually possible to watch a Goebel artist demonstrating the elaborate process by which Hummel figurines are created. Outside, note the miniature 1930s German village, complete with castle, farmhouse, monastery, and even a wee commuter railroad. Germany is easily toured at any time of day. When in Germany, good day is *guten Tag (GOOT-en-tahkh)*, thank you very much is *danke schön (DAHN-kuh shurn)*, and good-bye is *auf Wiedersehen (owf VEE-der-zay-in)*.

For the Lovebirds ...

Epcot's World Showcase has some great romantic spots, namely:

- El Río del Tiempo boat ride and the San Angel Inn in Mexico
- The lovely courtyard at the rear of the United Kingdom
- Italy's piazza and gondola landing
- Every inch of France

■ **Hidden Treasures of World Showcase:** The instructor stops just short of turning pavilions inside out to illuminate their scrupulous detailing and eye-fooling design.

■ **Gardens of the World:** A horticulturist leads guests through the distinctive gardens. Discover the lengths to which Disney goes to create authentic-looking landscapes, and find out how to apply clever techniques at home.

Tours last three to five hours and cost $49 to $85 (some require Epcot admission). Schedules vary; reservations are necessary but may be made the morning of the tour. Call 407-WDW-TOUR (939-8687).

China

This at once serene and exciting pavilion is marked by a dramatic half-scale replica of Beijing's Temple of Heaven set behind stands of whistling bamboo and quiet reflecting pools, where you'll often see an egret posturing on a rock and almost always see floating lotus blossoms. Traditional Chinese music wafts over the sound system. In addition to its arresting gardens, the pavilion features the House of Whispering Willows, an exhibit of ancient Chinese art and artifacts from well-known collections that's always worth a look. Live entertainment here is invariably stirring, whether it's a demonstration by the Pu Yang Acrobats or a rare performance of the Chinese Lion Dance.

But the main reason to visit China is the Circle-Vision 360 film shown inside the Temple of Heaven, which is right up there with the extraordinary films presented at Canada and France. Basically, you stand, and *Wonders of China* whisks you on a 19-minute, blink-and-you've-missed-the-Great-Wall journey that visits Inner Mongolia, Beijing's Forbidden City, and Shanghai, and provides the most fascinating glimpses of China and its people. Pay special attention to the fleeting scene of mist-enshrouded Huangshan Mountain, if you can; the film crew and 40 laborers had to haul the 600-pound camera nearly a mile uphill for those three seconds of footage. When in China, hello is *ni hao* (*nee HOW*), thank you is *xiexie* (*shay-shay*), and good-bye is *zai jian* (*SIGH jee-ahn*).

Norway

This 11th addition to the World Showcase landscape is immediately intriguing. A curious array of buildings rings the pavilion's cobblestoned square, including a reproduction of a wooden stave church (an endangered species of sorts, with just 28 remaining in Norway) and a replica of the 14th-century Akershus Castle that still stands in Oslo's harbor. Beside a grassy-roofed, thick-logged structure, which harks back to Setesdal, there's a statue of a Norwegian running champion, living legend Grete Waitz. This Land of the Midnight Sun has added some twists to the World Showcase lineup—among them, the promise of troll encounters and Norwegian handicrafts of the hand-knit-sweater variety.

The stave church houses a gallery of artifacts recalling the history of these charming benchmarks of Norwegian culture (don't skip it, if only to see the inside of this teensy church). But Norway really scores with **Maelstrom**, a trip in dragon-headed boats through Viking territory that is good fun, if not a veritable thrill ride. An inspired and technologically sophisticated voyage that surprises you with a troll here, a backward plunge there, a sudden waterfall here, a storm there, Maelstrom doesn't throw big punches; it just keeps you guessing. The five-minute trip lets you out at a quaint Norwegian village, then finishes up with a brief film on the essence of Norway. This attraction is least crowded in the evening. If you'd like to take a more in-depth look at this pavilion or learn more about the architecture of Norway, stop at the Tourism information desk at the end of the ride. Complimentary tours are given twice daily. When in Norway, hello is *god dag* (*goo DAHG*), thank you is *takk* (*TOCK*), and good-bye is *adjø* (*ahd-YUR*).

Mexico

There's no mistaking this pavilion's identity. A wild thicket of tropical foliage leads past squawking (sometimes shrieking) macaws to a great pyramid. Inside, you wend your way through a brief but consistently engaging cultural exhibit to the main event. What you see next—a thoroughly romantic vision of a quaint Mexican village at twilight—is among the most wondrously escapist visions in World Showcase. True to form, there are stands selling colorful sombreros, baskets, pottery, and piñatas (the shop off to the left sells higher-quality Mexican handicrafts). In the rear of the plaza, note the dimly lit San Angel Inn and, behind it, the river and smoking volcano. Here, too, you'll find the embarkation point for **El Río del Tiempo**, a pleasant six-minute boat trip through Mexican history that might be described as a subdued south-of-the-border It's a Small World. If you encounter long lines early in the day, skip it, and check back later. Note, too, that the mariachi band that performs inside and outside of this imposing pavilion is quite good. When in Mexico, hello is *hola* (*OH-lah*), thank you very much is *muchas gracias* (*MOO-chahs GRAH-see-ahs*), and good-bye is *adios* (*ah-dee-OHS*).

Drinks Around the World

There's Samuel Adams lager at The American Adventure and at least one good imported excuse to bend the ol' elbow in each World Showcase country. Namely: Molson and more from the Refreshment Port in Canada; shandies, Guinness, black and tans, Tennent's, and beyond from the Rose & Crown Pub in the United Kingdom; a bottle of Kronenbourg from the Boulangerie Pâtisserie or a glass of wine from La Maison du Vin in France; Kirin beer or sake specialty drinks at Matsu No Ma, in Japan; vino from Italy can be sampled (with a pastry, of course) at La Bottega Italiana in Italy; Beck's beer and H. Schmitt Söhne wine at Germany's Sommerfest; Chinese wine and beer at the Lotus Blossom Cafe; Ringnes drafts from Kringla Bakeri og Kafe, in Norway; and what else but margaritas in Mexico's Cantina de San Angel.

DISNEY-MGM STUDIOS

Like an actress who is just right for the part, the Disney-MGM Studios is perfectly cast as the vivacious, movie-obsessed theme park that is seemingly incapable of keeping a secret. Since its 1989 debut, this park has worked hard to make the transition from entertaining sidekick to leading lady, and it has succeeded.

The Disney-MGM Studios holds its own at Walt Disney World not merely by offering ticket holders a rose-colored reminiscence of 1940s Hollywood but also by resurrecting decades of Tinseltown magic as innovative rides, stage performances and theater shows, and by baring all manner of backstage secrets. The park immerses guests in showbiz to the point that they can momentarily forget there *is* life beyond television and motion pictures.

You'd do well to think of the Studios as the adults' Magic Kingdom. The place is magical, but in a more meaningful and sophisticated way; it is marked by a whimsicality far more ageless than that which pervades the Magic Kingdom itself. Sure, it has a Beauty and the Beast stage show and a 3-D movie featuring the Muppets, but these hardly constitute a satellite Fantasyland. In fact, at times the Studios even seems to have been scripted for a mature crowd, carefully crafted with a wink of the eye by (and for) grown-ups to elicit knowing laughs and no-holds-barred nostalgia.

Certainly, The Great Movie Ride has greater meaning to an audience steeped in the films of James Cagney, Judy Garland, and Humphrey Bogart. Another case in point: the 50's Prime Time Cafe, a nostalgia-fest of a restaurant that harks back to the era of *Father Knows Best* and *I Love Lucy,* with a montage of black-and-white television clips, pot roast, Formica tables, fussbudgety moms, and vinyl sofas. It's packed with inside jokes the younger crowd just wouldn't get. Meanwhile, over at the frightful Twilight Zone Tower of Terror, any adult with an inkling of Rod Serling's legacy will appreciate Disney's superbly rendered fifth dimension, despite the approaching doom (*multiple* plummets down an elevator shaft). Even one of the Studios' most child-oriented attractions, Voyage of The Little Mermaid, packs a few lines that whoosh right over kids' heads (sea witch to love-struck mermaid about to be stripped of her voice in exchange for a pair of feet: "Don't underestimate the importance of body language.").

The Studios also speaks to adults by offering an intimate brush with Disney's creative and technical prowess, a chance to penetrate, and even take part in, the magic. The park is so brimming with behind-the-scenes glimpses that a photo of Walt himself sketching a certain fawn nets but quick glances as folks enter The Magic of Disney Animation to meet the next Mickey Mouse wannabe in its formative stages. Other tours allow you to prowl the catwalks of a television production studio, to feel the power of special effects in a catastrophe-laced demo, complete with flash flood, and to learn the gymnastic logistics behind daring film stunts. Audience participation plays a bigger part in attractions here, making experiences dynamic and uniquely personal.

While the Studios remains the most manageable of Walt Disney World's major theme parks, it has more than doubled its repertoire over the years. The most dramatic addition, the Tower of Terror, looms over the park's ostensible landmark, a specially endowed water tank commonly known as the "Earffel Tower."

HOT TIPS

■ On Wednesday and Sunday, guests staying at WDW resorts may enter the Disney-MGM Studios up to 1½ hours before the official opening time and get an early crack at selected attractions, such as Tower of Terror, The Great Movie Ride, Jim Henson's Muppet*Vision 3-D, and Star Tours. Early-entry days and attractions are subject to change.

■ Not coincidentally, Wednesday and Sunday tend to be the most crowded days here at the Studios.

The latest expansion brought the dramatic nighttime show known as Fantasmic!, Sounds Dangerous starring Drew Carey, Disney's Doug Live!, and the looping Rock 'n' Roller Coaster starring Aerosmith.

Certain attractions here, such as Beauty and the Beast—Live on Stage, sometimes open an hour or more after the curtains rise. This fact underlines the importance of pausing to align your schedule with the showtimes and crowd patterns listed on the Tip Board. The board will also alert you to any celebrities who will be making appearances during your visit. The most strategic spot to take a breather: a sofa at the Tune-In Lounge, which plants you next to the 50's Prime Time Cafe and smack in the middle of a vintage living room. Surrounded by old TV sets playing food-oriented scenes from shows of yesteryear, you'll have access to mixed drinks and appetizers (served, of course, by waiters in V-neck sweaters playing the role of "Dad").

GUIDING PRINCIPLES: The following walking tour is designed to offer a basic overview of Disney MGM-Studios for first-time visitors and a timely update for returnees. The running commentary highlights the adult essentials, pointing out redeeming qualities of less-than-vital attractions, and spotlighting recent additions to the park. The Touring Priorities list contained in this section ranks the park's best adult bets and makes note of Fastpass attractions.

The size of the Disney-MGM Studios makes it possible to experience most everything there is to see and do in a day, but only if you're efficient. For additional touring tactics, consult the Hot Tips located in the margins of this section and the flexible touring plans in the *Planning Ahead* chapter. For information on how to get to the Studios via WDW transportation or by car, see "Getting Around" in the *Planning Ahead* chapter. To find out about the unique shops and merchandise at the Disney-MGM Studios, see the "Shopping" section of the *Diversions* chapter. For restaurant recommendations, look to the "Restaurant Guide" in the *Dining & Entertainment* chapter.

GETTING ORIENTED: The Disney-MGM Studios is considerably smaller than Epcot, but somewhat difficult to navigate since it has no distinctive shape or main artery. You enter the park—and 1940s Tinseltown—via Hollywood Boulevard, a bustling shopping venue. The first major intersection you come to is Sunset Boulevard, an equally starry-eyed venue that branches off to the right of Hollywood Boulevard; this shopping and entertainment strip ends in a cul-de-sac right at the foot of the park's tallest (and spookiest) landmark, the 199-foot Tower of Terror.

Ⓐ Beauty and the Beast—
Live on Stage

Ⓑ Fantasmic!

Ⓒ The Twilight Zone
Tower of Terror

Ⓓ Rock 'n' Roller
Coaster

Ⓔ The Magic of Disney
Animation

Ⓕ Bear in the Big Blue
House—Live on Stage

Ⓖ Voyage of The Little
Mermaid

Ⓗ Backstage Pass

Ⓘ Disney-MGM Studios
Backlot Tour

Ⓙ American Film
Institute Showcase

Ⓚ Honey, I Shrunk the Kids
Movie Set Adventure

Ⓛ Disney's The Hunchback
of Notre Dame—A Musical
Adventure

Ⓜ Jim Henson's
Muppet★Vision 3-D

Ⓝ Star Tours

Ⓞ Indiana Jones Epic
Stunt Spectacular

Ⓟ Sounds Dangerous
starring Drew Carey

Ⓠ Disney's Doug Live!

Ⓡ The Great Movie Ride

·········· Parade Route

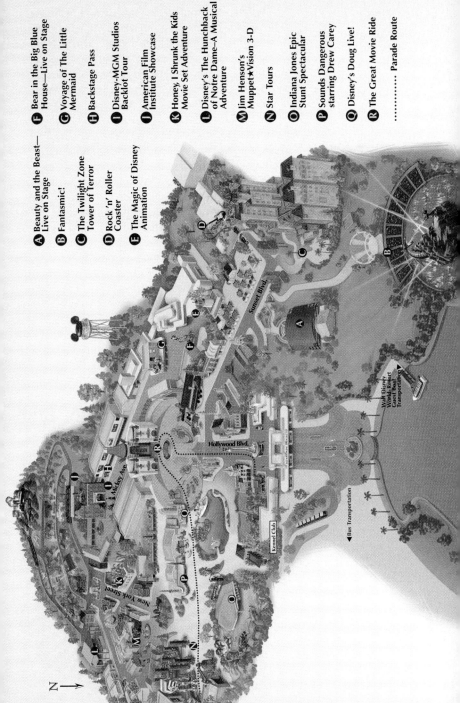

Touring Priorities

•CONTINUED ON NEXT PAGE

Hollywood Boulevard ends where The Great Movie Ride begins—at a replica of Mann's (formerly Grauman's) Chinese Theatre. This ornate building is the most centrally located landmark at the Studios, and the plaza fronting it, called Hollywood Plaza, is the site of a Hidden Mickey. (From above, garden plots in this plaza form his eyes and nose, the theater entrance is his mouth, and Echo Lake and the building that houses the Hollywood Brown Derby serve as ears.)

If you stand in Hollywood Plaza facing Disney's Chinese Theater, you'll see an archway off to your right; this leads to Mickey Avenue, an area with more of a backstage feel to it, where tours of working animation, movie, and television studios are among the attractions. If you make a left off Hollywood Boulevard and proceed clockwise past Echo Lake, you are on course for such attractions as Sounds Dangerous starring Drew Carey, Indiana Jones Epic Stunt Spectacular, and the ever-popular Star Tours. Just past Star Tours lies one last (but certainly not least) entertainment pocket. Jim Henson's Muppet*Vision 3-D theater is the main draw here, together with a realistic reproduction of a Manhattan block called New York Street (complete with skyline facade). Walk left past the skyscraper end of New York Street and you're on a quick track back to Hollywood Plaza and the Chinese Theater. Got that? Good.

A Walking Tour

Just inside the gates, you may be too distracted by the bright Art Deco looks of Hollywood Boulevard to notice a building on your left—but this is the site of Guest Relations, where you can go for information as well as first aid. Stop here or at Crossroads of the World (the gift stand smack in the center of the entrance plaza) to pick up a guidemap if you still need one. To your immediate right, check out Oscar's Super Service, which has a 1949 Chevrolet tow truck parked out front. This is one of several striking and utterly unscratched classic automobiles you'll notice along the streets of the park. (We're not sure how they got through the turnstiles.) Also remember Oscar's as the spot for lockers and wheelchair rentals; the lost and found, along with package pickup, is right next door. If you'd like to witness the taping of a television show, inquire at the production window adjacent to Oscar's to see what, if anything, is being filmed during your visit and to obtain tickets (free, and available on a first-come, first-served basis). Note that there is an ATM just outside the turnstiles here.

Hollywood Boulevard

One look at this main drag and you have a hunch you're not in Central Florida anymore. The strip oozes star quality with a Mae West sort of subtlety. Movie tunes from Hollywood's Golden Age waft through the air. Palm trees make like Fred and Ginger in the tropical breeze. Streamlined storefronts with neon and chrome Art Deco flourishes line the boulevard like would-be movie sets hoping to get noticed. Don't be surprised if you encounter budding starlets sparring with their agents, paparazzi angling for shots, or a starry-eyed soul who wants *your* autograph.

Note that the shops along Hollywood Boulevard typically stay open about a half hour after the rest of the park has closed. (Consult the "Shopping" section in the *Diversions* chapter for specifics on our favorite shops; wares generally include a sampling of movie memorabilia and plenty of Disney character merchandise that's a cut above T-shirts.)

However you get there, it's important to stop at the corner of Hollywood and Sunset boulevards to check the **Tip Board** (one of two trusty boards that list current waiting times for popular attractions—the other board is on New York Street). Until 1 P.M., this is also the place to make priority seating arrangements for full-service restaurants. Lest you ignore breakfast, the Starring Rolls Bakery is constantly auditioning coffee drinkers and croissant and cinnamon roll eaters a few steps away.

Sunset Boulevard

This Studios block is a broad, colorful avenue every bit as glamorous as Hollywood Boulevard. It has the same high-cheekbone style and its own stock of towering palms, evocative facades, and tempting shops. It also has stage presence, in the form of the 1,500-seat Theater of the Stars amphitheater,

•CONTINUED FROM PREVIOUS PAGE

DON'T OVERLOOK
Voyage of The Little Mermaid*; Indiana Jones Epic Stunt Spectacular*/**;
Disney-MGM Studios Backlot Tour; Disney's Doug Live!**; Fantasmic!*;
Disney's Hunchback of Notre Dame—A Musical Adventure**

DON'T KNOCK YOURSELF OUT
Honey, I Shrunk the Kids Movie Set Adventure; Backstage Pass;
Bear in the Big Blue House—Live on Stage

* Fastpass attraction as of press time. Consult your guidemap for new additions.

** Pay close attention to performance schedules.

Quiet Nooks

- Starring Rolls Bakery
- Tune-In Lounge
- Sunset Ranch Market
- Benches on Sunset Boulevard near Theater of the Stars
- Shaded benches around Echo Lake
- Brownstone stoops on New York Street
- Washington Square, at the far end of New York Street

where you can see live performances of *Beauty and the Beast*. Sunset Boulevard begins innocently enough, with a friendly old-fashioned farmers market, and a shop called Once Upon A Time that's housed in a replica of the Carthay Circle Theatre where *Snow White and the Seven Dwarfs* premiered. But none other than the white-knuckle Tower of Terror looms at the end of the road.

Somehow, **Beauty and the Beast—Live on Stage**, a production that was the *raison d'être* behind the Broadway musical, manages to remain oblivious to its eerie neighbor. The show is 20 not-to-be-missed minutes of rich musicality, delightful costuming and choreography, and uplifting entertainment. While a canopy keeps the sun's heat at bay, we still aim for an evening performance during the summer months; note that this show generally opens shortly after the park does.

Then there's **The Twilight Zone Tower of Terror**, a hair-raising experience. Because few of us have a natural yen to drop several stories (more than once, we might add) down a dark elevator shaft, this one requires some bravery. It helps to know what to expect.

Basically, "guests" enter the mysteriously abandoned Hollywood Tower Hotel and are invited into a library, where even the cobwebs seem to be circa 1939. Here, Rod Serling appears on a black-and-white television set to brief you (stormy night, Halloween 1939, lightning strikes, guests disappear from hotel elevator) and welcome you to tonight's episode of *The Twilight Zone*: "If you'll just step this way into the boiler room, this is where you'll board our service elevators." You reach a boarding area—last call for chickening out—and file into an elevator (look at the diagram above the doors to avoid, say, the front row). Once you are seated and the safety bars are secured, the doors shut and the elevator ascends. You're soon so entranced with astonishing special effects—apparitions that appear in a corridor that vaporizes into a dark, star-filled sky and a gigantic eye straight from the fifth dimension—that dread becomes (almost) secondary. When the elevator moves over into a second, pitch-black shaft, anything can happen, since Disney's Imagineers deviously transformed this ride from a two-screamer into a five-screamer. The bottom falls out more than once, and not subtly: Multiple plummets are scripted. One thing's for certain: Your cue to strike a great casual pose—a scream resembling a yawn, perhaps—is when you're at the top of the shaft. You want to look good in the group picture, which is taken as a panorama of the park suddenly gives way to a drop. The big plunges are incredibly fast downward pulls with surprisingly smooth landings. It may be a small comfort, perhaps, but the really hairy part is over faster than many vocal cords are able to respond.

A few notes: The jitters tend to stay with you a bit after the 12-minute drama has ended. If you have back or neck problems, a heart condition, or are pregnant, we suggest that you pass on the Tower of Terror. We urge you *not* to try it on a full stomach.

If you're willing (and able) to continue the thrill-fest after your stay in The Hollywood Tower Hotel, get ready to shake, rattle, and roll on the **Rock 'n' Roller Coaster starring Aerosmith**. This ride is sure to show you some moves that would rival the King himself. As the first WDW roller coaster to flip you upside down, this dark, completely indoor, steel construction goes from zero to 60 miles per hour in just under three seconds. The premise: You've just scored backstage passes and VIP transport to a sold-out Aerosmith concert at the Hollywood Bowl. During your nighttime drive through Southern California, you twist and turn to a rockin' sound track—and feel like you've stepped right inside a runaway music video.

Pay attention to the warning signs posted as you enter the ride. If you have back or neck problems, a heart condition, or if you're pregnant, sit this one out.

Animation Courtyard & Mickey Avenue

Adjacent to Sunset Boulevard and Hollywood Boulevard is the section of the park that takes you under the sea with a diminutive mermaid and into working animation and television production studios. Passing under an archway located off Hollywood Plaza, you see Animation Courtyard immediately in front of you, with Mickey Avenue to your left.

A word about timing: The tours here—The Magic of Disney Animation, the Disney-MGM Studios Backlot Tour, and Backstage Pass—are most exciting on weekdays before 5 P.M., because glimpses of Disney's magic makers at work stop when they call it a day.

A Striking Resemblance

- Chinese Theater— Mann's Chinese Theatre in Hollywood

- Once Upon A Time storefront—Carthay Circle Theatre in Hollywood, where Disney's *Snow White* premiered

- Mickey's of Hollywood storefront—Frederick's of Hollywood

- Jim Henson's Muppet*Vision 3-D theater—the theater from *The Muppet Show*

- Hollywood Brown Derby—Brown Derby of Hollywood's heyday

Consider **The Magic of Disney Animation** a non-negotiable must. A guided walking tour through working animation studios, it's a chance to learn the facts of life as they relate to Mickey Mouse and to see Disney's next animated film as a work in progress. Although big changes were made here in recent years, the tour still includes the uproarious commentary of Robin Williams and Walter Cronkite. The expansion of the animation facility brings Disney animation to life before your very eyes. You don't spend the whole 35 minutes peering over shoulders, however. First, you watch a film that transforms Williams into one of the lost boys from *Peter Pan*. Next, you gather round an actual artist, who reveals still more secrets of animation. Then, you see the animation studios, including part of the new facilities, and view snippets from a future movie release. Finally, you are led into a theater and treated to a finale of great moments from Disney classics, from *Snow White and the Seven Dwarfs* to *Tarzan*.

If you think you'd enjoy a behind-the-scenes look at moviemaking of the "lights, camera, action" sort, take two: The backlot tour and Backstage Pass complement each other well. The **Disney-MGM Studios Backlot Tour** is a two-pronged gig that begins with an entertaining six-minute demo of how a realistic sea storm or naval battle might be filmed (two guests are asked to don yellow raincoats and brave the elements). The second segment, a 29-minute tram ride, starts calmly enough, but sit on the right side to stay dry. You visit the wardrobe area; the lights, camera, and props departments; and the backlot neighborhood of facades where you can see *The Golden Girls* house, or at least its exterior. Then, suddenly, there you are in a special-effects zone called Catastrophe Canyon, which specializes in nature's wrath: violent downpours, fiery explosions, flash floods. Just as you're thinking that New York City would seem calming compared to this, there it is, a realistic-looking Manhattan block made mostly of fiberglass and Styrofoam. Lines here tend to be shorter in the late afternoon (ask the attendant for an E.T.A., and if it's more than 30 minutes, check back later). The tour exits through the **American Film Institute Showcase**, a revolving display of costumes, props, and partial sets that features interactive elements related to film lore and legends.

A matter of yards away, **Backstage Pass** beckons with inside stuff on the challenging process of making television shows and movies. Revamped to include the re-creation of a scene from *Home Improvement*, the 25-minute walking tour lets you see blue-screen technology in action. Sets include Tim (the tool man) Taylor's living room, backyard, and even neighbor Wilson's fence. A lucky guest is chosen to go head-to-head with Tim in a nailing contest.

The guest is placed in front of a blue screen so it appears that he or she is standing side by side with Tim on the television monitors. While Tim Taylor never sets foot on the lot, the finished product makes it seem as though he did. The tour also steals through prop- and set-filled rooms and a special-effects shop, as well as along a soundproof catwalk that overlooks soundstages from which you may see live takes of new programs, if sets are "hot." (NBC's *ER* and HBO's *From the Earth to the Moon* have both filmed here.)

If you can get near **Voyage of The Little Mermaid**—and at this 15-minute musical adapted from the movie, that's no easy task—don't hesitate. It's not the story line that's so compelling. It's the upbeat music, the amazing puppetry, the occasion to watch children ogle this real, live mermaid *whose tail is moving*, and the mist-infused feeling that you are underwater. Voyage of The Little Mermaid always seems to start the day with a 30-minute wait;

Snacker's Guide

For a healthy nibble, seek out the Sunset Ranch Market on Sunset Boulevard for carrot sticks and fruit, or try the small fruit stand located between Hollywood Boulevard and Echo Lake. For a savory bite, try the burgers at Rosie's All-American Cafe on Sunset Boulevard or the nearby turkey-leg cart that also offers hot dogs and baked potatoes. If you need a sweet fix, sample the cookies at Starring Rolls Bakery on Sunset Boulevard or the ones at The Writer's Stop on New York Street, ice cream at Dinosaur Gertie's or shakes at Min and Bill's Dockside Diner, both on Echo Lake.

Pop Quiz

your best bet is to try for the first show in the morning. Check the guidemap for showtimes.

If you're eager to return to your *Romper Room* roots, follow the trail of toddlers to **Bear in the Big Blue House—Live on Stage**. Otherwise, skip it and move on to bigger and better things.

Echo Lake Area

Heading back through the archway into Hollywood Plaza, you come upon **The Great Movie Ride**. This drive-through theater of sorts is a classic in its own right and the best ticket we know to a quick video rental decision your next time out. Housed in an artful replica of Mann's Chinese Theatre, this not-to-be-missed 22-minute attraction is bursting with Audio-Animatronic figures that bring motion-picture legends and moments from almost every genre to life. It's "Chim Chim Cher-ee" meets "Here's looking at you, kid," cigarette-puffing Clint Eastwood meets broom-brandishing Wicked Witch of the West, *Alien* meets *Singin' in the Rain*, and then some—be prepared for surprises. The ride has meticulous detailing and astounding realism. Notice, for example, how Julie Andrews' throat vibrates as she sings. The Great Movie Ride draws large crowds all day long. However, with queues that wind past some *Wizard of Oz* props and a screening of famous movie scenes, it is also one of the most entertaining waits in Walt Disney World. (**Note:** It takes about 25 minutes to reach the ride vehicles when the line extends to the theater entrance.)

Heading through Hollywood Plaza toward Echo Lake, the next attraction you encounter is **Disney's Doug Live!** For those who have never seen Doug canned, and wouldn't know him from Homer Simpson, this original musical stage show is based on *Disney's Doug*, an ABC Saturday morning cartoon. Don't be fooled by the kid quotient here: The show is thoroughly enjoyable, at times, squealingly adorable. After experiencing Disney's Doug Live! you just might roll out of bed early next Saturday to tune in. You needn't watch your back en route to the adjacent ABC Sound Studio, home of **Sounds Dangerous starring Drew Carey**. But you'd better arrive all ears.

The twenty-twentiest vision in the world won't see you through the dark, frantic moments of this astonishingly realistic surround-sound audio adventure. Expect 12 of the most mind-boggling minutes you have ever spent in a pair of headphones. Easy-listening this is not.

Here's the deal. Disney has cast you and every other pair of wired ears in the theater as members of an elite audience (no stretch there!). You're attending a sneak preview of a live-action TV show that stars Drew Carey as an undercover detective. Thanks to a camera discreetly tucked into Carey's tie tack you see everything his tie tack wishes it could see. And, of course, no one whispers, crashes, or so much as whimpers during the determined detective's madcap pursuit of diamond smugglers without word—or major vibrations—getting back to your headphones.

When a bad move by a panic-stricken Carey (open mouth, insert camera) zaps the television picture, you have no choice but to follow the action in the dark. Those clean ears you toted into the theater strain and contort with every twist in the furious plot. Fully enveloped in the audacious realism of 3-D audio, you attempt to sit calmly while your ears carry you into a swarm of 5,000 restless bees. Listen carefully and you'll doubtless marvel at the palpable snip, snip, snip of the barber's scissors. Your head will spin with the wildly screeching tires of Carey's speeding car. And as attuned as you become, you'll likely still be unprepared for the finale (think close encounters with a circus elephant).

If you are an action-movie fan, it's worth risking life and limb to catch the **Indiana Jones Epic Stunt Spectacular**. Arrive a good 45 minutes before showtime to snare a seat toward the front of the 2,000-seat amphitheater. The half-hour performance steals its thunder from *Raiders of the Lost Ark* and begins with the selection of a few fearless "extras" (they're put to use during a scene involving a sword fight in Cairo). Nimble stuntpeople perform one death-defying caper after another, leaping between buildings, dodging snipers and boulders, and eluding fiery explosions. You feel the heat of the flames, you fear for the Harrison Ford look-alike. Tricks of the trade are revealed and you're *still* impressed. The Indiana Jones Epic Stunt Spectacular nearly always plays to capacity audiences, so your best bet for getting a great seat is the first or last show of the day. Keep in mind that seating begins 30 minutes prior to each show.

Did you know...

Although Disney Feature Animation Florida has contributed to hits such as *Beauty and the Beast*, *Aladdin*, and *The Lion King* since 1989, 1998's *Mulan* was actually the first feature film produced primarily in the Florida studios. Thousands of guests watched the film's creation through the glass-walled corridor at The Magic of Disney Animation. During your visit, you might meet an animator who brings new Disney characters to life.

Just Add Tap Shoes

One of the coolest things at the Studios is a certain lamppost (yes, lamppost) on New York Street by the Backlot Theater. It's not just any street fixture, mind you; this one has a (fiberglass) umbrella sticking out from it and a few well-placed sprinkler heads. Simply grab hold of the umbrella's handle and you'll have all the precipitation you need to pretend you're Gene Kelly in *Singin' in the Rain*.

As exciting as the Indiana Jones Epic Stunt Spectacular is, the attraction just around the corner packs even more punch. At **Star Tours**, you don't sit in an amphitheater; you strap yourself into a flight simulator. You don't live vicariously through professional stuntpeople; you experience the extraordinary sensation of barreling through space at the speed of light for yourself. The premise: Enterprising droids R2D2 and C-3PO are working for an intergalactic travel agency whose fleet of spacecraft makes regular trips to the Moon of Endor. As luck would have it, you draw a rookie pilot who gives new meaning to reckless abandon. Soon you're spiraling through deep space, dodging lasers and giant ice crystals. Be prepared for an intense five-minute ride that encompasses a lot of bucking, tilting, and other disorienting movements. Star Tours is an incredible experience—one of those don't-miss-unless-you-have-a-very-good-reason attractions. (Among the very good reasons: just ate, heart condition, pregnancy, susceptible to motion sickness.) The lines are generally shortest in the morning, with waits of about 30 minutes the rest of the day.

New York Street

Moving along, you arrive at the Studios' back corner. This is a glimpse of Manhattan as it used to look, with a few alterations having to do with the Empire State Building's dimensions and the size of the puppet population.

You're here for *one* thing: the fabulously entertaining, special effects-laden presentation of **Jim Henson's Muppet*Vision 3-D**. Miss it and you've deprived your sense of humor. So head straight for the Muppet theater and fill up on a 25-minute stream of amusing Muppet antics that push the creative envelope of 3-D movies with such effects as a cannon blast through the screen, some bubble magic, and a floating banana cream pie. (Yes, the curmudgeons from *The Muppet Show* are in attendance, in their familiar balcony spot, cynical as ever.)

Okay, we lied. There's *another* reason you're here. As you leave the Muppets, veer right to the Backlot Theater. Here, beneath the blissful shade of a canopy, you'll slip away to 15th-century Paris for **Disney's The Hunchback of Notre Dame—A Musical Adventure**, a 30-minute reprise of the animated feature. In this rendition, Gypsies imaginatively reenact the tale of the world's most famous bell ringer, Quasimodo, and his selfless acts in the name of love. The special effects are first rate. Shows start in the late morning.

From the Backlot Theater, walk straight toward New York Street, where you can take in the skyline or sit down on a stoop. A sign in the window of our favorite brownstone cautions NO SOLICITING, but it says nothing about stoop trespassing. So we take a seat, do some people-watching and simply gaze at the

Empire State Building. Disney used a technique called forced perspective to make the four-story version here appear to have 104 floors. If passersby ask for directions, it's good to know that the **Honey, I Shrunk the Kids Movie Set Adventure** playground is behind one of the facades here. And if they want to know where to find the Toy Story Pizza Planet Arcade (and its resident ATM), tell them it's across from the Muppet theater.

Entertainment

Disney's Tinseltown sticks close to its Hollywood heritage in its roster of live entertainment. Because the marquee is ever changing, it's essential to consult a guidemap. You might run into budding starlets and gossip columnists along Hollywood Boulevard, or there may be a visiting celebrity about.

Each afternoon, a stream of performers inspired by characters from the animated film *Mulan* celebrates the ancient Chinese folktale and brings a regal beauty to the Studios' parade route, most notably with an elegant horse-drawn carriage and a 150-foot Chinese dragon.

Last, but hardly least: Fantasmic!—a 26-minute pyrotechnic dazzler— cranes necks nightly in a lagoon-endowed amphitheater behind Tower of Terror. Shown just after dusk, this expression of Mickey's dreams (and nightmares) is filled with dancing fountains, characters galore, and special effects synchronized to classic Disney tunes. Note that the best seats are actually toward the back of the theater.

DISNEY'S ANIMAL KINGDOM

So strong is this park's sense of purpose that it's as if the animals of the world put their antlers and antennae together and created it themselves— to celebrate their aardvark-to-zebra diversity, remind us of their prehistoric heritage, and rally support for wildlife conservation efforts. Not that Disney's creative hand isn't greatly evident in this park. In fact, when Animal Kingdom first opened to homo sapiens, it didn't merely expand the dimensions of a Walt Disney World vacation. It ushered the theme-park genre into wholly uncharted territory.

How so? This park is something of a wildlife preserve, an interactive natural-history museum, and a conservation-minded retreat rolled into one. The natural world dominates the imaginary. And not just on the surface. Endangered-species breeding programs coexist with blockbuster attractions. Sophisticated Audio-Animatronic dinosaurs share the marquee with more than 1,700 animals (some 250 species), whose habitat needs dictate much of the landscape. Dinosaur fossils are abundant; plastic straws and Styrofoam cups, conspicuously absent. (One glimpse at the park and it's no surprise that Animal Kingdom is accredited by the American Zoo and Aquarium Association, an organization that supports conservation, education, science, and recreation.)

Animal Kingdom's biggest attraction, Kilimanjaro Safaris, delivers the high adventure of the African classic, with a bonus: the chance to race across the savanna, chasing ivory poachers. Enter Disney's Africa and you can essentially put a check mark next to that travel fantasy. The transporting effect of elephants and other signature African creatures is not to be denied. And you haven't gotten acquainted with lions and rhinos until you've been mere yards away, with no visible separation between you and them. While the safari is, perhaps, the best example of the inventive realism and evocative entertainment style that define the park's most adult attractions, it's hardly the last word.

The thematic center of Animal Kingdom is—bongo drumroll, please—The Tree of Life, a 14-story monument to creatures large and small, with more than 325 carvings. Call it the animal version of "I claim this land in the name of . . ."

GUIDING PRINCIPLES: The pages that follow are designed to provide a thorough initiation to Animal Kingdom. The fact is, even folks who could find their way from Space Mountain to Pirates of the Caribbean with bags over their heads have had to start from square one in this WDW frontier. Structured as a guided walking tour through the five themed "lands" that make up the park, this section offers a geographic orientation to Animal Kingdom while also taking stock of attractions as they relate to adults.

For at-a-glance recommendations, the Touring Priorities list in the margin on page 136 ranks the park's best adult bets. To learn the most efficient touring strategies, consult the Hot Tips in the margins of this section and the flexible tour plan provided in the *Planning Ahead* chapter. For details on how to get to Animal Kingdom via WDW transportation or by car, turn to the "Getting Around" section of the *Planning Ahead* chapter. For descriptions of shops worth perusing in this particular corner of the World, see the "Shopping" section of the *Diversions* chapter. And, finally, to find out the park's best bets for dining, refer to the evaluative "Restaurant Guide" in the *Dining & Entertainment* chapter.

GETTING ORIENTED: Although greenery reigns in Animal Kingdom, relegating concrete, and indeed most architecture, to garnish status, successful penetration of this particular jungle requires no compasses, scythes, or snakebite kits. (Do work on your Tarzan call, however.) The park is set up as a series of themed lands decidedly unlike any you've encountered in the Magic Kingdom. To see the forest through the trees, look up: Like the icons of its Worldly siblings, Animal Kingdom's Tree of Life serves as an instant beacon for the momentarily disoriented. This massive spectacle also anchors the park's most central land, Safari Village.

The layout of Animal Kingdom might be compared to the silhouette of a simple daisy. Acting as the stem is the lush expanse of The Oasis. Safari Village (the land that serves as the park's hub), encircled by a river, is the flower's center. And extending from the center like petals are bridges leading sharply southeast to the primeval area known as DinoLand U.S.A.; northeast to Asia, the park's newest land; northwest to Africa, the park's largest land; and southwest to Camp Minnie-Mickey, a character vacationland.

It's true that Disney's Animal Kingdom is more than double the size of Epcot, but thanks to the considerable roaming room designated for animal residents only, it takes no more legwork to circumnavigate this park than to explore Epcot. As anyone who's been to Epcot can attest, this is still a good amount of walking—so follow our efficient touring plan and take advantage of the park's many pleasant resting spots. Seniors who choose to tour the smaller parks on foot may choose to rent a wheelchair at Animal Kingdom—or better yet, given the steep inclines throughout the park, a self-driven Electric Convenience Vehicle (ECV).

■ This park's layout can be confusing, especially for first-time visitors. Pick up a guidemap as soon as you enter the park. Use it to help plan your day, allowing enough time to travel from one area to the next for a show with a set start time.

■ Since this park already opens at the crack of dawn, there are no early-entry days for Disney resort guests.

■ Weekends tend to be the most crowded days at Disney's Animal Kingdom.

A Walking Tour

Our tour begins much like any other intrepid adventure, assuming that intrepid adventurers have inexplicably omitted mention of the turnstiles that must be traversed en route from urbane Central Florida to the Great Unknown. No matter. You're about to be enveloped by **The Oasis**, a canopy of nature that serves as Animal Kingdom's inviting foyer. Two paths lead north to Safari Village and the looming Tree of Life. Before you proceed farther into the fragrant tangle of tropical trees and flowers, where you're bound to be distracted by waterfall-laden streams and glimpses of macaws, iguanas, and giant anteaters, *stop!* Tell yourself it's all a mirage and pause only to pick up a guidemap (if you don't already have one) near the front gate or at Guest Relations. You don't have to cool your jets for any other practicalities, unless you're picking up some wheels for the day, using the ATM, renting a locker, or visiting package pickup.

As in the rest of the park, Disney has endowed The Oasis with borders infinitely more discreet than turnstiles, bringing you that much closer to experiencing that rare animals-are-drawn-to-me realm inhabited by Audubon and Snow White. It's tempting to linger, but this is better done later in the day, when there's no rush to beat the masses to the most exciting rides, Dinosaur, Kali River Rapids, and Kilimanjaro Safaris (the left path offers the fewest distractions, but we suggest choosing the path to the right—a main artery to the major attractions).

Emerging from the northern reaches of The Oasis, you arrive at a bridge to the island of Safari Village and receive your cue to gasp—a panoramic view of Animal Kingdom's central land, the moat-like river, the soaring Tree of Life, and the glorious balance of the park before you. Whether you gasp or launch into a tale about the time you stood at just such an overlook and outsmarted a lion, you should proceed across the bridge toward the tree.

Safari Village

Exotic in a neither-here-nor-there-but-certainly-not-North-America sense, Safari Village is awash in the sort of vivid color paintbrushes dream about imparting. Meticulously carved and painted building facades and smatterings of African and Caribbean folk art add to the eye-catching allure of environs intended to replicate a village in the Tropics. Notable as the land that serves as the gateway to all other Animal Kingdom lands, it's also the park's core dining and shopping zone (for humans, at least; the animals try to steer clear of fast food).

N ←

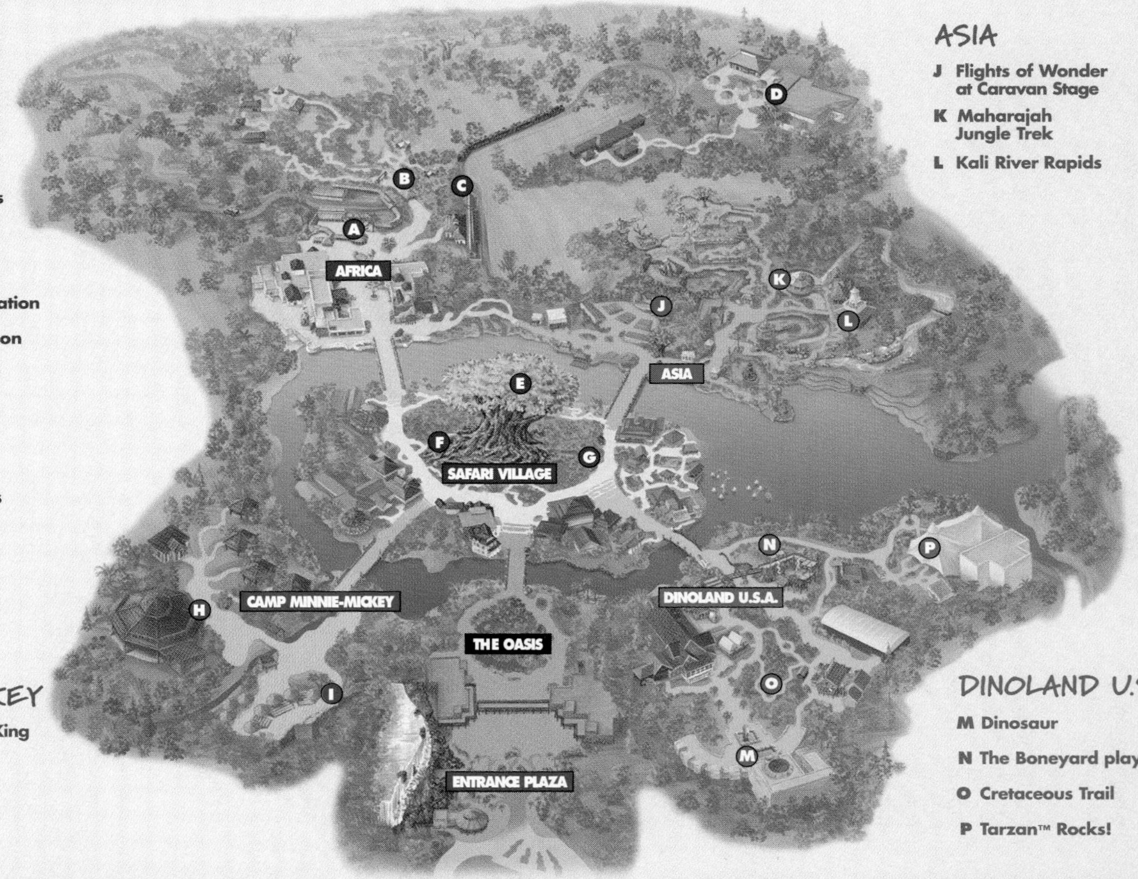

ASIA

J Flights of Wonder at Caravan Stage
K Maharajah Jungle Trek
L Kali River Rapids

DINOLAND U.S.A.

M Dinosaur
N The Boneyard playground
O Cretaceous Trail
P Tarzan™ Rocks!

ASIA

SAFARI VILLAGE

DINOLAND U.S.A.

CAMP MINNIE–MICKEY

THE OASIS

AFRICA

ENTRANCE PLAZA

AFRICA

A Kilimanjaro Safaris
B Pangani Forest Exploration Trail
C Wildlife Express to Conservation Station
D Conservation Station

SAFARI VILLAGE

E The Tree of Life
F Safari Village Trails
G It's Tough to be a Bug!

CAMP MINNIE–MICKEY

H Festival of the Lion King
I Pocahontas and Her Forest Friends

Touring Priorities

* Fastpass attraction as of press time. Consult your guidemap for new additions.

** Pay close attention to performance schedules.

Take a minute to glance at the **Tip Board**, listing showtimes and current waiting times for popular attractions. This board is on the right as you enter Safari Village. Checking the board to align your schedule with certain showtimes helps structure your day.

The biggest draw here—quite obviously, **The Tree of Life**—is as awe-inspiring on close inspection as it is from afar. The man-made, banyan-like tree looms 145 feet over the Animal Kingdom as its central icon. Even dung beetles have their place on this arboreal masterpiece, whose 50-foot-wide trunk and wind-blown limbs contain nose-to-nose carvings of every animal Disney artists could fit. Certainly, Mickey's lineage is represented. The carvings are an elaborate tribute to the richness and diversity of animal life on Earth. To get a better look at them, do your best imitation of a dachshund that thinks it's a giraffe. Also, be especially nice to anyone carrying binoculars—there's a lot to be seen. Don't neglect to check out the cockatoos, flamingos, deer, and other wildlife living among the tree's roots along the **Safari Village Trails**.

Before you leave The Tree of Life, consider the possible advantages of starting small. If you can bear eight minutes of animated insects creeping and crawling into your personal space, see **It's Tough to be a Bug!**, a 3-D special-effects film shown—where else?—inside the tree. It's a decidedly off-Broadway show, starring Flik (from the film *A Bug's Life*) and a cast of a million billion bugs whose previous credits include *Beauty and the Bees* and *My Fair Ladybug*. You become honorary bugs in an effort to understand their world, but things go humorously awry when several of Flik's buddies don't appreciate a visit from *you*. After a demonstration of their talents, you may suddenly cease to be fazed by any creature with fewer than six legs. **Note:** Anyone leery of spiders, roaches, and the like is advised to skip the performance, or risk being seriously bugged.

DinoLand U.S.A.

As you pass underneath the immense brachiosaurus skeleton and into what appears to be a kitschy park created around a remote paleontological dig site, picture this: a huge crocodile, having suavely inherited the planet, filing under a human skeleton at the entrance to HumanLand U.S.A. theme park. Kind of a nifty perspective, eh? Anyway, this wryly wrought land is the park's most imaginative, filled with wacky details that make it feel like a little-known curiosity off Route 66 (songs like "It's the End of the World as We Know It" and "Bad to the Bone" fill the sound track). Attractions feature intimate rendezvous with winners (suave crocodiles) as well as sore losers of the Cretaceous period's Survival of the Meteorproof. The biggie, sure to elicit lots of white lies ("I didn't even flinch") and skepticism ("Yeah, right"): **Dinosaur**, an exciting time-travel journey fraught with errant asteroids and frightening run-ins with Disney's largest and most realistic Audio-Animatronic figures yet.

A 3½-minute thrill attraction that has earned raves, Dinosaur is found inside the Dino Institute, a staid museum-like building that reveals nothing of the fast, jarring, and heart-pounding ride ahead. Of course, there's a larger mission that has nothing to do with any personal desire for an adrenaline rush and everything to do with selfless intentions to save an iguanodon. (Don't worry, we'll explain.) Basically, you have it on good authority that if you shoot 65 million years back in time, pronto, there's a chance you can bring back an iguanodon for paleontologists to study. The catch is that you have to do this seconds before the meteor blast thought to have sealed the dinosaurs' fate and ended the Cretaceous period. So you strap yourself into the vehicle, and think about what you will say to the 16-foot-tall creatures when you get there. Need a lift? You *are* vegetarians, right?

And so it is that you find yourself in this perilous race against time, ducking meteors and attempting to blink away encroaching nonvegetarian dinosaurs as your vehicle rages out of control. Just when you think you've spied some friendly faces in the crowd, you notice the nostril-flaring carnotaurus hot on your tail. What happens next, alas, is for us to know and for you to find out. Dinosaur is not to be missed (unless, of course, you have dinophobia, are pregnant, suffer from back or neck problems, or have a heart condition).

The nearby **Cretaceous Trail** offers a much tamer path to this bygone era. Along this short pathway, you'll discover an American crocodile and a red-legged seriema (a type of bird); these animals' ancestors were dinosaurs' compatriots. **Note:** This area may have undergone substantial changes by the time you visit.

Because it's rare that you get a chance to compare shoe sizes with a dinosaur, traipse over an arch made of dinosaur bones (OldenGate Bridge), and unearth

---

The Better to See Them With

Have a pair of binoculars? The 14-story Tree of Life is reason to tote them along—unless you like craning your neck. There are more than 325 animals carved into the tree, and you'll want to be able to see the ones at the top.

Quiet Nooks

Who says you can't find peace in a jungle? Consider these relatively relaxing spots and seek out others.

- The Oasis in the afternoon

- Safari Village Trails (especially near the back of the Tree of Life)

- Pangani Forest Exploration Trail

- Tables along the river at Flame Tree Barbecue in Safari Village (except at lunchtime)

- Cretaceous Trail

- Conservation Station

- Anywhere but Camp Minnie-Mickey

the fossils of an American mammoth. **The Boneyard** playground is worth a passing glance, even if it's mainly meant for kids. Just cross your arms as if you were supervising the dig, and listen up as they uncover clues to how the mammoth died.

There's the potential for one last stop in these parts: a detour to the Theater in the Wild to take in **Tarzan Rocks!** In-line skaters and singers rock out as a live band plays tunes from Disney's animated feature.

Asia

A footbridge that might not look out of place in the Himalayas, were it not filled with theme park guests, leads from Safari Village to this exotic chip off Earth's largest continent. Your gateway to Asia is the village of Anandapur, an enchanting blur of Asian architectural styles and cultures that sits on the fringes of a made-in-Florida rain forest. The musical welcome is provided by tiny brass bells that dangle from the eaves of pagodas, dancing in the wind.

At first, Anandapur (Sanskrit for "place of delight") comes off as a bustling intersection. But deep in this land, civilization seems to have graciously bowed to nature. Speckling the landscape are temples overtaken by gibbons, ruins frequented by Asian tigers, a pavilion leased to fruit bats, and the like.

The age-old man versus nature conflict surfaces as a bitter battle between loggers and ecotourists over the rain forest's fate. This being Animal Kingdom rather than Lumberjack Kingdom, you are necessarily cast as an adventure-minded ecotourist. Simply act as if you're here on vacation (now *there's* a stretch) to take a rafting expedition, trail Komodo dragons and other local fauna, and do some theater-in-the-round bird-watching. It's a nonspeaking part, but feel free to ad-lib.

If you're up for some adventure (and a quick shower) get over to the local river-running outfit, **Kali River Rapids**. You're in the right queue if you crash a gecko party and see shadows of circular rafts screaming by under a bridge. Once your own community-sized raft shoves off from the boathouse, it parts the waters beneath a fog-shrouded steeple of greenery that might have been made by an elite class of beavers. Don't allow yourself to be lulled into security, no matter how sweetly the birds chirp. Any minute you'll be trading this calm for a smoldering obstacle course lined with freshly shish-kebobbed forest. Yes, just ahead lies a precarious game of limbo under an abandoned logging truck and a burning tree, not to mention fast-moving rapids that have a penchant for displaying the hats of passersby. The sum total is a jostling five-minute ride that is best left to non-pregnant people sans heart conditions and neck or back problems.

Hydrophobes, note: This one's apt to get you completely drenched. If it's a hot day and you'd like to cool off, it's possible you will cherish the flood of water that is likely to cover you from head to toe. However, a chilly morning ride could make a poncho (sold in line and at stores and carts around the park) a wise investment. Also note that cameras, film, and other non-waterproof valuables should not be taken on Kali River Rapids. While there is a storage space in the middle of the raft for loose items, we suggest entrusting them to a nice, dry locker or non-riding member of your party.

Continue your Far East itinerary with the **Maharajah Jungle Trek**, a tour through the nearest Southeast Asian rain forest in the most primitive of tour vehicles (your own two feet). Led by an unobtrusive, insightful guide (yourself), you do what great explorers in the wilds can't: parade unharmed past roving tigers and Komodo dragons. Don't be afraid to linger. Even Olympians of these species can't breach Disney's security systems. Chicken out on passing through the darkened (fruit) bat chamber, and you may never see a *Pteropus vampirus*—the closest thing to a Chihuahua with a six-foot wingspan—eating pineapple chunks. But you'll still spot Malaysian tapir, birds, and acrobatic gibbons galore.

Speaking of chickens, here's another feather for your explorer's cap. The Caravan Stage, which struts out performances of **Flights of Wonder** several times daily, can accommodate 1,000 people and all manner of flappers. These airborne forces, from falcons to parrots, could entertain an aviary. Check a guidemap for times.

Africa

If imitation is the sincerest form of flattery, then Africa has got to be blushing. In creating this largest section of the park, itself bigger than the Magic Kingdom, Disney seems to have stopped just shy of moving mountains (Kilimanjaro is conspicuously missing). The artfully reconstructed African savanna and woodland aren't merely stunning to behold. They're designed to satisfy the habitat specifications of each meerkat, zebra, and elephant. Countless trips to the continent, exhaustive planning, and some slick adaptations have enabled Disney to mesh the intimacy of a zoo with the aura of a safari.

Snacker's Guide

For a healthy treat, try the juice blends at the outdoor Safari Bar next to Rainforest Cafe or fruit from a stand in Africa. If you need a sweet break, brave the crowds for the fresh-baked cookies or ice cream in Camp Minnie-Mickey, or the pastries at Kusafiri Coffee Shop & Bakery, in Africa. For a cool pick-me-up, try chocolate-covered frozen bananas or Simba's Paw Print ice cream bars from a vendor, or the ice cream or frozen yogurt from Tamu Tamu Refreshments, in Africa. For a savory snack, consider the broiled burgers from the stand between Africa and Asia, or the smoked turkey legs in Safari Village.

Did you know...

■ The carvings on The Tree of Life represent only about 325 of the 1.4 million existing species.

■ Every plastic bench in Animal Kingdom is made of recycled material—1,350 milk jugs, to be exact.

■ The Disney Wildlife Conservation Fund helps nonprofit organizations protect endangered and threatened animals. You can donate by adding a dollar to your shop purchase.

■ Most of the animals here were born in other zoological parks. Many are registered in special breeding programs called SSPs (Species Survival Plans).

■ WDW has eliminated most of its insecticide use, replacing chemicals with millions of predatory insects—many of which are bred at The Land in Epcot.

Disney's Africa is truly a land of opportunities, among them: treading just yards from cavorting gorillas; observing rhinos, gazelles, and hippos en masse; exchanging glances with a passing giraffe; getting up to speed on wildlife protection and conservation efforts; and chasing renegade ivory poachers.

Of course, you don't cross the bridge from Safari Village and find yourself suddenly surrounded by gorillas and elephants. You acclimate to the continent in the atmospheric village of Harambe, patterned after modern coastal communities in East Africa. Harambe is important as the best spot for food, drink, and shopping during your stay in Africa. Particularly tempting is the Tusker House Restaurant, conveniently flanked by an alfresco watering hole serving African music and Safari Amber beer. Harambe is also the gateway to the land's several exceptional attractions.

Kilimanjaro Safaris, Disney's enticing variation on the classic African travel adventure is one to beat a path to. The 20-minute guided trip through a simulated savanna escorts you within boasting distance of many of the world's most beloved animals—so close you'll begin to wonder which of the 32 people in your open-air gawkmobile (as we've loosely dubbed the roofed, rugged transportation of choice) has irrepressible animal magnetism. As the vehicle bumps along the dust-caked road, you'll observe animals on the move; watch for elephants, gazelles, rhinos, baboons, and lions. Such animals as giraffes and zebras may draw quite near. Your guide will fill you in on less familiar species; for a preview, steal quick glances at the species identification cheat sheet on the seat-back in front of you. These animals have room to roam and thus better things to do than stare back at you—graze, frolic, yawn, pick fights, tend their young, head for the water hole, and socialize, for starters. Of course, as on a real safari, you might not see certain animals on a given trip; they could be sleeping, hiding, or otherwise engaged. For this reason, you may consider riding more than once during your visit.

As we see it, this not-to-be-missed safari has five advantages over the real thing, proximity aside. (1) This African landscape was designed to provide good vantage points of animals' stomping grounds. (2) The rocky road is for effect only; the prime photo junctures are smooth. (3) Creature comforts (i.e., favorite vegetation for four-footed snackers) are strategically located to provide up-close encounters with the animals. (4) Just because giraffes and

other harmless species can come near enough to read the words on your T-shirt (doubtful, given the literacy rate), that doesn't necessarily mean the cheetahs or lions can. Virtually undetectable topographical separations ensure that predatory types maintain a safe distance from people. So you needn't sweat it when a fierce-looking cat licks its chops while staring precisely in your direction. (5) Adventure is built into the experience. In addition to being a virtual who's who of animal crackers, Kilimanjaro Safaris is an unpredictable ride in which close calls are as endemic as close encounters.

Throughout the trip, you hear reports from a bush pilot flying overhead. Among your adventures is a brief stop within close range of the open mouths of genuine snap-happy crocodiles. Shortly thereafter, the vehicle creeps over a rickety bridge, it begins to bow under, nearly spooning you and your safariing friends

Entertainment

A small lineup of amusements supplement the inherently entertaining antics of the animals. Entertaining distractions include African musicians, wacky student paleontologists, and keepers who wander the park with interesting animals. Consult a guidemap for entertainment schedules.

Animal Kingdom Unplugged

If Conservation Station doesn't sate your curiosity, this three-hour behind-the-scenes tour should do the trick. Backstage Safari, basically Animal Care 101, takes you through such animal facilities as the elephant barn and the nursery. The tour is offered on Monday, Wednesday, and Friday, and costs $60 plus park admission. Call 407-WDW-TOUR (939-8687) for reservations.

into a ravine. Suddenly, your guide breaks from the planned route and you embark on a furious chase for ivory poachers in the area. The vehicle careens as it speeds through water-filled canyons. You learn the poachers' fate at journey's end.

A good follow-up to the safari is a walking tour that invites lingering and offers a closer look at gorillas and other animals. Also accessible from Harambe, **Pangani Forest Exploration Trail** segues from the enchanting environs of a free-flight aviary and an aquarium filled with exotic fish to a research lab in which you view a colony of naked mole rats. Beyond that, you'll come upon a stream dammed with glass—the site of a synchronized swimming demonstration by hippos. Okay, so maybe it's not synchronized. But the buoyant beasts don't have to wear nose plugs to be amusing in their underwater glory. Even so, we know what you're thinking: "Are we there yet? Where are the gorillas?" Rest assured, the chest thumpers are close at hand.

There's more to see before you reach the gorilla sanctuary, however, namely, a scenic overlook of the savanna and an ensemble of Timon's meerkat cousins. Chances are, one will be posted on the rocks as a lookout. Although you might think he's searching for his buddy Pumbaa, the warthog, these animals don't demonstrate such fine chemistry in the real world as they do in the movies.

After you peer into their habitat at close range through floor-to-ceiling glass, walk over a suspension bridge to the gorilla valley, and begin turning your head U.S. Open-style to take in the antics of the family brood and the bachelor brood now flanking you (provided, of course, that they're in the mood to see and be seen). What does it feel like to walk alongside these expressive creatures with little between you and their *Planet of the Apes* physiques? Privileged.

Back in Harambe, you'll find the depot for the **Wildlife Express to Conservation Station**, a narrated 5½-minute train trip that chugs quietly behind the scenes of Africa, providing a reverse perspective of Kilimanjaro Safaris along with insights into the park's inner workings. For those looking to take a load off their feet, it offers a leisurely lift (and the only mode of transportation) to and from **Conservation Station**, the attraction that serves as Animal Kingdom's ideological cornerstone. As the park's center for wildlife preservation efforts and veterinary care, Conservation Station acts as a sweeper of sorts, crystallizing the environmental themes presented in the other areas of the park and encouraging active support of wildlife programs while the safari's still fresh.

If EcoWeb, with its Internet link to international conservation organizations, is the most practical of Conservation Station's hands-on exhibits, the Animal Cams are the ones David Letterman would doubtless make a beeline for; in the latter, you zoom, tilt, and pan one of many cameras set up to surreptitiously monitor activity on the savanna and in animals' "backstage" areas. (And you thought they didn't study their lines.) Another highlight is Song of the Rainforest, a binaural booth that lets you vicariously experience the drama of the Amazon with nothing more than a simple headset. The interactive video displays of Rafiki's Planet Watch (endangered animal alert) and Eco Heroes (meet the conservationists) are potential points of interest. Animal Health & Care, a look at the park's working veterinary facilities, can be fascinating, depending on what's happening the day you visit. Overcome by an urgent need to make some tails wag? Follow the tykes to Affection Section, where you can scratch some tame fur balls behind the ears.

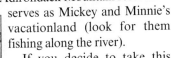

Camp Minnie-Mickey

If you want to commune with animals more accustomed to standing still for pictures, the trail heading left (southwest) of Safari Village goes to Camp Minnie-Mickey, a character-size version of an Adirondack Mountain resort that serves as Mickey and Minnie's vacationland (look for them fishing along the river).

If you decide to take this detour, do it outside the park's prime migration periods (opening and closing) and note that you may encounter a lot more than you bargained for—namely, alfresco frolicking and singing by the characters in two stage shows. The one to head for (well before showtime) is **Festival of the Lion King**, an entertaining 30-minute spectacle of dance, song, and acrobatics by a troupe of talented tribal performers. In **Pocahontas and Her Forest Friends**, a 12-minute performance presented in Grandmother Willow's Grove, live critters scamper across the stage as Pocahontas searches for a protector of the forest. Check a guidemap or the Tip Board for specific showtimes.

143

The sky's the limit for recreational activities beyond the theme parks.

Diversions: Sports, Shopping & Other Pursuits

I t's a cool April morning and you are posing for a picture with an eight-pound largemouth bass. You've caught so many fish over the past two hours, you're wondering if, given more time, you couldn't hook them all. You'd signed on for this guided catch-and-release fishing trip around Seven Seas Lagoon expecting a relaxing morning on the water and a few polite nibbles, but here you are, no more than a few hundred yards from Disney's posh Grand Floridian resort, catching bass that require muscle. And this is not an isolated occurrence. Though fishing may not be the first sport that comes to mind when you think of the Royal Mousedom (that would be golf), in angling circles Walt Disney World is fondly known as the theme park metropolis with world-class bass fishing. In lay terms that means big fish (and a lot of them) showing a great time to even the most inexperienced angler who drops them a line.

. . .

It is nearing 10 P.M. on a January night, and a group of sophisticated shoppers are fawning over such things as shortbread baked in the image of Mickey Mouse's shorts. One of them wants Mickey-shaped pasta, while another has a $100 Mickeyfied tea kettle under one arm. A third is off playing credit card bingo with Disney-characterized Christmas ornaments and office accoutrements. If the shops at the Downtown Disney Marketplace don't close their doors soon, these purchases are not going to fit through them. We've made a startling discovery about the shopping scene at Walt Disney World: It can throw unsuspecting adults—even shopping phobes—into a frenzy. The bottom line: Shops here are loaded with nicely evolved character goods and lots more merchandise (labels such as Waterford and Liz Claiborne, for example) that's simply way beyond kid stuff.

...

It is a steamy afternoon in July and you are treating yourself like an indulgent movie star at the Grand Floridian Spa & Health Club. You've already been buffed to baby softness with Dead Sea salts and essential oils, and experienced the thrill ride of tension relief—namely, a good hot soak in a 70-jet hydrotherapy massage tub. As you contemplate whether you're perhaps a bit too relaxed to stay awake for your aromatherapy facial, you look at your feet, now perfect examples of the rejuvenating powers of a paraffin treatment and pedicure. Even if you and your (currently golfing) beloved skipped your 3 P.M. couples massage, you suspect that you might feel a bit self-conscious gliding through your hotel tonight—a renewed being among weary theme park goers.

Here's the point: The World beyond the major theme parks offers a slew of terrific diversions that, interspersed between park visits, help establish perfect symmetry in a well-rounded Walt Disney World vacation. Once you get over the shock of finding such activities here in the first place, you're *still* pinching yourself because the quality of the experiences is so good. You'll find that even more world-class adventures for adults (thoroughly described on the following pages) exist within the playground that is Walt Disney World.

We're just hinting at the possibilities when we mention golf courses, widely considered among the country's best; state-of-the-art tennis facilities, health clubs, and the spectators' dream known as Disney's Wide World of Sports complex—all perfect examples of Disney's ability to dazzle in the most unexpected arenas. On the shopping front, tantalizing stores (including a collection of character-defying options at Downtown Disney) are popping up propertywide. Add the last word in water parks, including a sky-scraping water slide and a humongous wave pool, and the list is still incomplete. For a full inventory of distractions (the categories: sports, shopping, and other pursuits) so compelling you might wonder why anyone bothers with those theme parks, read on.

SPORTS

O kay, sports fans, it's time for our play-by-play guide to Walt Disney World. First and foremost, you can play some of the finest golf courses in the country. There are 99 holes here (available in increments of 9 or 18), and you can take your pick from five designer-name par 72s that individually and collectively have earned hosannas from *Golf Magazine* and *Golf Digest*. And as we can personally attest, you need not possess a smidgen of ability in order to enjoy yourself. Whatever your skill or mood, there's a course in Walt Disney World's diverse lineup to suit; each venue is a unique challenge, and opportunities abound to test your mettle on fairways that have humbled the pros.

You can also play some serious (or casual) tennis on the most advanced surface that exists, right here at Disney's Racquet Club or The Villas at the Disney Institute. You can angle for largemouth bass weighing eight pounds or more (waterways here are teeming with trophy-scale bass). Prefer to catch a wave? There's waterskiing. Want to get above it all? Try parasailing. Feel like a round of one of the most juvenile sports you can think of (hint: not T-ball or kickball)? Take your pick of several artfully designed miniature golf courses. In these parts, you can not only rent boats and bikes galore but you can actually buzz around on a Water Mouse speedboat or on a tandem bike and never get a second glance. The Walt Disney World Speedway stands by with racer's ed. Plentiful pools invite you to swim yourself into a waterlogged prune.

In other words, you are not lacking for sporting opportunities at Walt Disney World. All of these playful options plus a few more, including health clubs, jogging trails, and spectator sports (what can we say? it's a big World out there), are fully detailed in the sections that follow. Of course, you may also choose to play couch potato, although, after you know your options, it will no doubt require some willpower.

In the Rough

"There's a lot of wildlife around the Palm course's property," says a former Disney pro. "People have seen deer, otters, turkeys, bobcats, and even panthers. One day, someone said he saw a couple of bald eagles."

Golf Rates

The following greens fees were in effect at press time for the WDW golf courses. Prices do not include tax, and they are subject to change. Prices fluxuate between Peak (1/1–4/25) and Nonpeak (4/26–12/31) seasons. WDW resort guests get $5 off the Day Visitor Rate.

DAY VISITOR RATES

■ Osprey Ridge: from $60* to $160.

■ Eagle Pines: from $50* to $145.

■ Magnolia: from $45* to $135.

■ Palm and Lake Buena Vista: from $45* to $125.

Summer discounts (May 22 through October 2) lower rates for all WDW courses to about $50 as of 10 A.M.

* Twilight rates begin at 3 P.M. during much of the year, starting an hour earlier in certain seasons. Rates range from $45 to $60 depending on tee time and course chosen.

Golf

Disney's 99-hole "Magic Linksdom"—second only to the Mouse in drawing power—is renowned for the challenge, variety, and fairness of its courses. Walt Disney World has become a familiar name on *Golf Magazine*'s biennial list of the best golf resorts in the country. *Golf Digest* has tabbed four of the World's five par-72 courses as outstanding ("plan your next vacation around it") or very good ("worth getting off the interstate to play"). And noted golf writer Glen Waggoner is hardly alone in giving Mickey Mouse's backyard the nod as America's greatest golfing haven. In Waggoner's words, "Some other places have an individual course that is superior to any in Walt Disney World's lineup, but no other resort in the entire country has five courses this good." Solidifying this reputation is the National Car Rental Golf Classic (October 14–22) at WDW, a PGA tour event with over a quarter century of prestige behind it.

Depending upon the tee box chosen, the immaculately kept Disney courses provide challenging or relaxed play; while the layouts are quite distinct in their design, they are all constructed to be especially forgiving for the mid-handicap player. Of the original three Joe Lee-designed courses, the Palm and the Magnolia get the most attention, but the Lake Buena Vista is a popular layout that more than holds its own. Tucked into a corner of the Magnolia is Oak Trail, a par-36 walking course especially suited to beginners. Rounding out the mix are the two challenging venues added in 1992: the Tom Fazio-designed Osprey Ridge and the Pete Dye-designed Eagle Pines.

KNOW BEFORE YOU GO: WDW's peak golfing season extends from January through April. During this period it is especially important to secure reservations well in advance for play in the morning and early afternoon (though starting times after 2 P.M. are usually available at the last minute). Tee times are particularly difficult to get during the third and fourth weeks of January, when some 30,000 truly serious golfers descend on the area for the PGA of America's Merchandise Show, and during the National Car Rental Golf Classic (October 14–22). The Citrus Bowl (January 1) and Daytona 500 (February 17–18) have also proven capable of filling the courses quickly. During such busy periods, the advance reservations and guaranteed tee times afforded by golf packages can be absolutely indispensable. Call 407-WDW-GOLF (939-4653) for package details.

Rates: Greens fees for the 18-hole courses vary according to when you visit (peak versus nonpeak seasons), which course you play (Osprey Ridge and Eagle Pines are more expensive), and your guest status (WDW resort guests get a break). A listing of rates is provided in the margin on page 148. Basically, though, you can count on paying $45 to $160 per round (depending upon your tee time), including the required cart. Throughout the year, golfers can save some money by teeing off in the late afternoon, when twilight rates afford savings of more than 50 percent. The most dramatic savings can be had from May 22 through October 2, when rates for all courses drop to about $50 after 10 A.M. At Oak Trail, a 9-hole walking course, play ranges from about $32 (half price on your second round), depending on the time of day. Annual Golf Memberships ($53), available to Florida residents only, can provide substantial savings (depending on the season) for play after 10 A.M., and also include complimentary use of a cart and a 20 percent discount on golf lessons given by the PGA teaching staff.

Mickey and Mini Golf

Leave it to Disney to create 18-hole miniature golf courses that eschew the typical tackiness for clever designs, both fanciful and devious. The first round is $9.25; it's half price for the second round. Hours are usually 10 A.M. to 11 P.M. Call 407-560-8760 for information on any of these locations.

■ **Disney's Fairways,** one of the two courses at the Fantasia Gardens Miniature Golf complex near the BoardWalk, is ruled by daunting doglegs, sand traps, water traps, par 3s, and par 4s. Astute players may notice shrunken signature holes from famous links. (Play time: about 1½ hours.)

■ At **Fantasia Gardens,** the second course near the BoardWalk, whimsical tees offer odes to *Fantasia*. En route, balls hit chimes and xylophone stairs, and spur water spouts and fife playing. (Play time: about an hour.)

■ **Disney's Winter Summerland,** vacation spot to Santa and Christmas elves, offers the best of both seasons. Near Blizzard Beach, surfboards and sand castles speckle the summer-themed course, while igloos and ice sculptures give the winter-themed course the freeze. (Play time: about an hour per course.)

Tee Time

Want to increase your chances of getting on one of the courses? Heed the following:

- Try to play on Monday or Tuesday.

- Tee off in late afternoon.

- Come in the summer (when special rates are available).

Reservations: Anyone buying a golf package may reserve tee times up to 90 days ahead. Golfers who book lodging at any on-property resort may also secure tee times up to 90 days in advance. For everyone else, the window of opportunity is 30 days out. The practical effect of these rules is that it's difficult for guests staying outside WDW to obtain prime tee times during busy weeks. Note that four golfers are assigned to each starting time, so parties may be matched up. To book tee times, call 407-WDW-GOLF (939-4653). Reservations must be secured with a credit card. Cancelations must be made 48 hours in advance or you'll be charged the full amount.

Transportation: Complimentary taxi service to the Palm, Magnolia, Osprey Ridge, Eagle Pines, and Lake Buena Vista courses is available for all WDW resort guests. Call Guest Services; the taxis work on a voucher system.

Dress: Proper golf attire is required on all courses. Shirts must have collars, and if shorts are worn, they must be Bermuda length.

Equipment rental: Good-quality gear, including Footjoy shoes ($6) and range balls ($6 a bucket), are available for rent at all WDW pro shops. Golf-club rentals run $35 to $45 per set for men, $25 to $35 for women, depending on the season, plus a refundable $500 credit card deposit; photo ID required.

INSTRUCTION: Players looking to improve their game have several options: one-on-one instruction, swing analysis sessions, and playing lessons. At the Walt Disney World Golf Studio, based at the Palm and Magnolia, PGA professionals offer 45-minute sessions that concentrate on improving players' swings through video analysis; cost is $79.50 including tax. Playing lessons, in which a PGA pro provides on-course instruction, delve into strategy, club selection, and short game skills, as well as the psychological side of golf, are $159. Private lessons are available for $63.60 per half hour. Reservations are required for all lessons; call 407-WDW-GOLF (939-4653) up to one year ahead.

The Bonnet Creek Golf Club, based at Eagle Pines and Osprey Ridge, boasts a state-of-the-art machine that allows golfers to compare different clubs and balls, and evaluate their swings. Call 888-223-7842 to reserve a free 45-minute session.

TOURNAMENTS: The National Car Rental Golf Classic, which draws top PGA Tour players every fall, is among the most celebrated events on Disney's sports calendar. The tournament has been a major magnet for golf fans since 1971 when, two months after Walt Disney World opened its gates, Jack Nicklaus won the inaugural event. Because the Classic is one of the last regular PGA Tour stops of the year (it's usually held in October; this year, 14–22), exciting competition is a given; pros are looking to vault themselves into the Tour Championship or secure their spots on the top 125 money list.

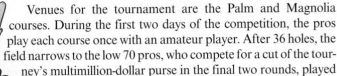

Venues for the tournament are the Palm and Magnolia courses. During the first two days of the competition, the pros play each course once with an amateur player. After 36 holes, the field narrows to the low 70 pros, who compete for a cut of the tourney's multimillion-dollar purse in the final two rounds, played on the Magnolia. Tickets are available on-site each day of the tournament, with one-day admission ranging from $15 for the first two rounds to $20 for the third round and $25 for the final round. A badge good for all of the rounds costs $50. Practice rounds (held several days before the tournament) are open to spectators at no cost. For more information, call 407-824-2250.

Those who are willing to pay big dues may play the Classic alongside the pros. Card-carrying members of the Classic Club play side by side with a different competing pro each day for the first two rounds of the tournament. Some memberships include lodging, reduced greens fees on Disney courses for a year, and admission to the theme parks for a week. For additional details, call 407-824-2250.

The Courses

PALM: This prickly yet picturesque course (located just west of the Polynesian resort, with the Magnolia to its immediate north) is marked by tight wooded fairways, a wealth of water hazards, and elevated greens and tees, which bear Joe Lee's unmistakable signature and make for challenging club selections. The par-72 Palm plays shorter and tighter than its mate, the Magnolia, and measures 5,311 yards from the front tees, 6,461 from the middle, and 6,957 from the back. The palm-dotted venue hosts the National Car Rental Golf Classic, along with a fellow Lee design, the Magnolia course. Of the holes garnering the most locker-room curses (numbers 6, 10, and 18), the sixth, a 412-yard par 4, is the most notorious. There's a lake on the left, woods and swamp on the right, and more water between you and the two-tier green. The course—whose greens were rebuilt in 1993 from the drainage basin up—opened in 1971 with the Magnolia and the Magic Kingdom itself. Facilities shared by the Palm and the Magnolia include two driving ranges, two putting greens, and a pro shop. The Walt Disney World Golf Studio is also based here. Course record: 61 (Mark Lye, 1984).

Slope Scope

The slope ratings for the five Disney courses from the back tees are: Osprey Ridge, 135; Magnolia, 133; Palm, 133; Eagle Pines, 131; Lake Buena Vista, 128. By way of comparison, an average slope rating is around 115. The famously challenging links at Pebble Beach check in at 139; the formidable TPC Stadium course at Ponte Vedra, at 135.

18

The Ten Most Humbling Holes

Cumulative toughest-playing Classic holes since 1983:

1. Palm No. 6
2. Palm No. 18
3. Palm No. 10
4. Lake Buena Vista No. 18
5. Magnolia No. 18
6. Palm No. 4
7. Magnolia No. 17
8. Magnolia No. 5
9. Lake Buena Vista No. 11
10. Magnolia No. 15

MAGNOLIA: Like the Palm, the Magnolia opened with the Magic Kingdom in 1971. It received a major face-lift in 1992. Course designer Joe Lee realigned teeing areas, recontoured greens, and replaced the original playing surface with a "faster" grass, among other things. The Magnolia features abundant water and sand, but what really sets it apart—aside from the 1,500 magnolia trees in its permanent gallery and a mouse-eared bunker beside the sixth green—is exceptional length, vast greens, and a flaw-exposing layout requiring precision and careful course management. Meandering over 175 acres of wetlands and gently rolling terrain, the par-72 course measures 5,232 yards from the front tees, 6,642 from the middle set, and 7,190 from the back markers. Among the signature holes is number 17, a long par-4 dogleg left that dares long hitters to bite off the edge of a lake, then avoid more water to the right of the green. It is the Magnolia that has final say in the outcome of the National Car Rental Golf Classic, and it takes full advantage with a final hole that rates among the tournament's testiest. Facilities shared by the Magnolia and the Palm are two driving ranges, two putting greens, and a pro shop. The WDW Golf Studio is based here. Course record: 61 (Payne Stewart, 1990).

OAK TRAIL: This nine-hole par-36 walking course ensconced in a 45-acre corner of the Magnolia is worth noting as an unintimidating venue for beginners, yet it's no cream puff for better players. The 2,913-yard layout unleashes plenty of challenges—including two fine par 5s—and boasts well-maintained greens.

OSPREY RIDGE: Tom Fazio has taken his signature mounding along fairways and around greens to monumental heights here—most dramatically with a namesake ridge that meanders through the property and elevates some greens as high as 25 feet above the basic grade. The designer counts Osprey Ridge among his best efforts, and the sentiment is echoed in the course's considerable popularity among experienced golfers. The long par-72 layout winds through a beautifully remote and thickly forested part of the property near Fort Wilderness; it has a deceptively gentle start, then raises the stakes en route to its three great finishing holes. Along the way, players will confront the signature par-3 third hole, with its elevated tee, and the fierce fourteenth, a long par 4 with a carry over water. Osprey Ridge plays to 5,402 yards from the front tees, 6,680 from the middle, and 7,101 from the back. Facilities shared by Osprey Ridge and Eagle Pines include a driving range, a putting green, a pro shop, a restaurant, and a lounge. Course record: 65 (Daniel Young, 1992).

EAGLE PINES: The subtle contours of this low-lying link provide a decided contrast to the dramatic landscaping of its companion course, Osprey Ridge, which also plays from the Bonnet Creek Golf Club. Designed by Pete Dye on a (successful) mission to create a unique challenge for players of all levels, Eagle Pines features target fairways, expansive waste areas, and roughs lined with pine needles. True to its rustic environs (it's located on the outskirts of Fort Wilderness), the course is sufficiently nestled in foliage and marshlands to summon comparisons to a nature preserve. Although water comes into play on 16 holes, the overall impression is one of great variety, from short par 4s to far sterner challenges—this is one course that lives up to the cliché of making you use every club in the bag. The course measures 4,838 yards from the front tees, 6,309 from the middle, and 6,772 yards from the back markers. Facilities shared by Eagle Pines and Osprey Ridge include a driving range, a putting green, a pro shop, a restaurant, and a lounge. Course record: 60 (Bart Bryant, 1993).

LAKE BUENA VISTA: This Joe Lee design is a Rodney Dangerfield of sorts. One of the shortest of the five 18-hole courses, it features a good amount of water, and its fairways, hemmed in by stands of pine and oak, are Disney golf's tightest. Lake Buena Vista honors its reputation as a friendly course for less experienced golfers. But it is also well equipped to challenge more-skilled players. As golf writer Glen Waggoner puts it, Lake Buena Vista may be the weakest link in the Disney chain, but it's still head and shoulders above the number two venue at most other golf resorts in the United States. The course's toughest holes—the 11th and the 18th—were at one time counted among the ten most humbling tests in the history of the National Car Rental Golf Classic. But perhaps no one has greater respect for the course than Calvin Peete, who, during the 1982 Classic, blitzed the Palm in a record-breaking 66 strokes, only to give it all back—and more—on little ol' Lake Buena Vista. The course plays to 5,194 yards from the front tees, 6,268 from the middle, and 6,819 from the rearmost markers. Facilities at Lake Buena Vista include a driving range and a practice green. The course is immediately adjacent to the Disney Institute. Course record: 61 (Bob Tway, 1989).

Course for Celebration

Disney's town of Celebration, Florida, is home to the first collaboration of famed father-and-son designers Robert Trent Jones, Sr., and Robert Trent Jones, Jr. Fees for the par-72 course range from $32 to $120, depending on the time of day and season; call 407-566-4653.

Want to Up the Ante?

Tennis

Even if you can't quite picture Mickey with a mid-size racquet in his hand, Walt Disney World can still serve up plenty of tennis action for players of any caliber. There is a total of 25 courts scattered around the World, including four located at the Dolphin hotel, and shared with the Swan. You'll find a pair of hard courts at the Yacht and Beach Club, two at BoardWalk, two more at Fort Wilderness (watch out for swinging toddlers), and a nice, quiet trio (the courts, not the players) at Old Key West.

The Grand Floridian's duo boasts clay surfaces while The Villas at the Disney Institute feature four hydrogrid clay courts. Courts lighted for night play are available at many resorts; this is a big deal, given the daytime heat during much of the year. For quality court time, the most important three words that serious tennis buffs need to remember when planning a visit are: Disney's Racquet Club.

Disney's Racquet Club

Disney's Racquet Club should please even the pickiest players. The six courts, lighted for night play, are state-of-the-art hydrogrid clay, with a subterranean irrigation system that keeps them evenly watered without sprinklers. The pro shop carries (character-endowed) tennis wear and high-quality equipment, from Wilson's Hammer series racquets to Mickey Mouse socks.

KNOW BEFORE YOU GO: Disney's Racquet Club is located just beyond the Contemporary resort's north wing. Courts are busiest during June and July, when tennis leagues may take over from 10 A.M. to 4 P.M. Two courts are open to guests at these times, but they are first-come, first-served (so to speak). February, March, and April also tend to be busy, especially around holidays and spring break. January, October, and November should be considered prime time to play. The courts and pro shop are generally open from 7 A.M. to 7 P.M., but hours vary seasonally.

Rates: Court rentals are $15 per hour. Racquets can be rented for $5 if you haven't brought your own from home. Ball-machine rental is $12.50 per half hour. Locker room facilities are available at no charge.

Reservations: Courts may be reserved up to 90 days in advance. Call 407-WDW-PLAY (939-7529). Need a partner? Call 407-824-3578 and ask for the player match-up sheets.

Dress: It's hot down here, so we recommend cool, loose-fitting tennis whites. As for showing up in footwear other than flat-bottom tennis shoes, note that cross-trainers and running shoes tear up clay courts. The pro shop staff will politely, but firmly, recommend you purchase the proper shoes on the spot.

INSTRUCTION: The tennis program at Walt Disney World is under the direction of Peter Burwash International. Disney's Racquet Club offers instruction from pros for all levels of play. Private lessons cover everything from strokes to strategy and cost about $60 per hour (including racquet rental). Group lessons for three to five people run $80 per hour, while hitting lessons go for $40 per hour. Fast-paced drill sessions ($20 per hour) and nonstop tennis (also $20 per hour), as well as themed daily clinics ($25 per 1½ hours), are available. Call 407-WDW-PLAY (939-7529) for lesson reservations.

TOURNAMENTS: Private tennis tournaments may be arranged. For information and pricing, call 407-827-4433.

Fishing

Drop a line, it's promptly answered. That's typical fishing at Walt Disney World. Bay Lake, which adjoins man-made Seven Seas Lagoon, was stocked with 70,000 largemouth bass in the mid-1960s. A restrictive fishing policy allowed the fish to swell in both numbers and size. Even today angling is permitted on Bay Lake and Seven Seas Lagoon strictly in the context of guided expeditions, so the fish have gotten only so wise to plastic worm tricks. Bass pro Bob Decker, a longtime WDW fishing guide who has pursued his sport in lakes and tournaments all over Florida, has given Bay Lake his hard-earned vote for the best bass fishing in Florida. On these waters you're not just likely to catch fish; you're apt to catch largemouth bass weighing eight pounds or more. And

Tennis Tips

■ Court fees are $15 per hour at Disney's Racquet Club, Grand Floridian, and Dolphin. Use of courts at The Villas at the Disney Institute is included in a $15 one-day health club pass. All other courts are free.

■ The courts at the Dolphin are illuminated all night long.

■ Want to play hard but don't have a partner? Note that drill sessions at Disney's Racquet Club cost only $5 more than court rental.

■ New tennis balls cost about $6 per can on-property. Take some from home.

The World's Most Striking Feature

it's not uncommon for a group to catch 15 to 20 fish over a couple of hours, or for a first-timer to reel in half a dozen good-size bass.

While the guided fishing trips that comb the picturesque waters of Bay Lake and Seven Seas Lagoon generally net the biggest catches, there's more to the WDW fishing scene. Additional guided expeditions lead anglers to a few of Disney's more scenic waterways. And those who prefer to go it alone have some tempting options in the canals of Fort Wilderness and the stocked fishing area—dubbed the Ol' Fishin' Hole—at Dixie Landings.

The official policy is catch-and-release, and no license is required for fishing on Walt Disney World waterways. Disney's guides know their territory well, keep track of where the fish are biting, and serve in whatever capacity guests prefer—from straight chauffeurs to casting coaches and even all-out facilitators. Reservations for all fishing excursions must be made at least 24 hours in advance and may be made up to 90 days ahead by calling 407-WDW-PLAY (939-7529).

Guided Fishing Trips

BAY LAKE & SEVEN SEAS LAGOON: Guided expeditions offering first-rate largemouth bass fishing depart from the Fort Wilderness marina at 7 A.M., 10 A.M., 1:30 P.M., and 4:30 P.M. (hours vary seasonally) for two-hour trips on Bay Lake and Seven Seas Lagoon. Trips are made on pontoon-style boats and can accommodate up to five people. The fee per boatload is $150.94 for two hours (about $60 more for an extra hour) and includes guide, gear, and beverages. Guides will pick up guests at the Contemporary, Fort Wilderness, Grand Floridian, Polynesian, and Wilderness Lodge marinas. Call 407-WDW-PLAY (939-7529).

LAKE BUENA VISTA: Guided two-hour excursions plying Lake Buena Vista and adjacent waterways depart at 6:30 A.M. and 9 A.M. from the Downtown Disney Marketplace marina. On 6:30 A.M. trips, anglers have the lake and the largemouth bass therein all to themselves (later, rental boats may infringe on prime fishing territory). The cost for up to five people, including guide, gear, and beverages, is $150.94. Individuals pay $56.60 per person. Guides will also pick up guests at Dixie Landings, Port Orleans, and Old Key West. Call 407-WDW-PLAY (939-7529).

SASSAGOULA RIVER: The daily two-hour fishing trip that escorts anglers on the bass-infused Sassagoula River and Lake Buena Vista is sold by the seat rather than by the boat. Guides pick up at Dixie Landings. The trip accommodates up to four people; includes guide, gear, and refreshments; and costs $56.60 per person. Parties of one or two will come out ahead, while larger groups will pay less per person if they opt for one of the other excursions. Trips begin between 6:30 A.M. and 9 A.M., depending on the season. Call 407-WDW-PLAY (939-7529).

CRESCENT LAKE: Daily fishing excursions depart at 7 A.M. from the BoardWalk dock and 7 A.M. and 11 A.M. from the Yacht and Beach Club marina. Cost is $150.94 for two hours (about $60 more for an extra hour) for up to five people, including guide, gear, and refreshments. Call 407-WDW-PLAY (939-7529).

Fishing on Your Own

Individuals who prefer to fish solo may do so on the myriad canals of Fort Wilderness, BoardWalk, and off the dock at the Downtown Disney Marketplace—catch-and-release only. Poles may be rented for about $4 per hour at the Marketplace, BoardWalk, and at the Fort Wilderness Bike Barn (the latter also rents rods and reels for $6 per hour or $9 per day; bait costs $3.50). While it's possible to toss in a line right from the shores of Fort Wilderness, canoes allow anglers to slip into some peaceful, and often fruitful, channels. Canoes may be rented from the Fort Wilderness Bike Barn. Call 407-824-2742.

Dixie Landings has a pond called the Ol' Fishin' Hole that's stocked with catfish, bass, and bluegill. Catch-and-release only, the quiet spot features a small dock among tall reeds where, from 8 A.M. to 4 P.M. every day (hours may vary seasonally), fishing is returned to its cane-pole-and-worm roots. Pole rental is $4 per hour, including worms. Call 407-934-6000, ext. 6278.

Fishing Tips

Although the fishing is good here year-round, it's most pleasant from November through May, when temperatures are cooler. As for strategy, one local recommends going with plastic worms, the red shad-like ones, in particular. To stack your odds, he suggests shiners (about $12 for a dozen; ask for them when you make reservations). Also, top-water baits work well in spring and fall.

Despite pleasant terrain that looks like it's been spread with a rolling pin, Walt Disney World can be a rough place to pursue the world's most mobile form of exercise. From late spring through early fall, comfortable running conditions are fleeting, with early birds getting the best shot at an enjoyable run. In the cooler seasons, joggers have greater freedom to explore the many compelling choices here.

Inquire about maps of the jogging trails and footpaths accessible from most WDW resorts at the hotel's Guest Services desk. Courses range from one mile to just over three. Dixie Landings, Old Key West, and Fort Wilderness offer some of the most extensive and scenic venues.

Boating

Guests looking to cruise, paddle, or even create a small wake on the pristine lakes and waterways of Walt Disney World have nothing short of the largest fleet of pleasure boats in the country at their disposal. Resort marinas stand by with sailboats, pontoon boats, canopy boats, canoes, pedal boats, and mini-speedboats, all of which are available for rent on a first-come, first-served basis.

On the World's most expansive boating forum, the 650-acre body of water comprising Bay Lake and the adjoining Seven Seas Lagoon, watercraft from the Contemporary, Wilderness Lodge, and Fort Wilderness marinas converge with boats lighting out from the Polynesian and Grand Floridian. Other areas are more contained. Craft rented at the Caribbean Beach cruise around 45-acre Barefoot Bay. As boats on brief loan from the Downtown Disney Marketplace roam 35-acre Lake Buena Vista, small flotillas of rental craft drift in from the upriver marinas of Old Key West, Port Orleans, and Dixie Landings. Meanwhile, watercraft from the Yacht and Beach Club and the Swan and Dolphin make ripples on 25-acre Crescent Lake, while pedal boaters ply the World's newest cruising zone—the 15-acre Lago Dorado at Coronado Springs.

All the marinas are open from 10 A.M. until early evening (hours vary seasonally). No privately owned boats are permitted on WDW waterways. Renters must present a WDW resort ID card, a valid driver's license, or a passport. Some boat rentals carry other restrictions (described below).

CANOEING: Paddling among the narrow channels of Fort Wilderness during the peaceful morning hours, canoers pass through forest and meadows, encountering solitary anglers and quacking contingents along the way. Fishing and canoeing are an irresistible combination for many, with fishing gear available for rent right alongside the canoes (which run $6 per half hour or $12 per hour) at the Fort Wilderness Bike Barn. Canoes may also be rented at Caribbean Beach, Port Orleans, Dixie Landings, and The Villas at the Disney Institute. Use of these watercraft is restricted to WDW canals.

CRUISING: For groups interested in taking a leisurely sunning, sightseeing, or party excursion on the water, motorized canopy boats and pontoon boats are the only way to go. Sixteen-foot canopy boats accommodating up to eight

adults (about $21 per half hour) and 21-foot pontoon boats holding ten adults (about $29 per half hour) are available for rent at most marinas. Guests must be 19 years old to rent a pontoon boat and 16 years old to rent a canopy boat. For information on special occasion and fireworks cruises, see page 179.

PEDAL BOATING: For those who prefer pedal-pushing to paddling, pedal boats (accommodating two pedaling passengers and two free-loaders) are available for $6 per half hour or $12 per hour at most marinas. Rentals are restricted to Disney resort guests at the Caribbean Beach, Port Orleans, Dixie Landings, Swan and Dolphin, Coronado Springs, and Yacht and Beach Club marinas, The Villas at the Disney Institute, and Fort Wilderness. The Swan and Dolphin, and Old Key West also rent Hydro Bikes (singles, $8 per half hour; doubles, about $16 per half hour), which resemble upright bicycles affixed to pontoons. Guests of Animal Kingdom Lodge and the All-Star resorts can rent boats at any of the above-mentioned locations.

SAILING: Bay Lake and Seven Seas Lagoon offer pretty reliable winds and unparalleled running room. Sailing conditions are generally best in March and April. Sailboats may be rented at the Grand Floridian, Polynesian, Contemporary, Wilderness Lodge, and Caribbean Beach marinas. Rental fees range from $12

Stock Car Racing 101

The drone of stock cars burning up a one-mile oval sets most anyone's mind to racing. So it is that a pumped-up driver's ed. has been introduced at the Walt Disney World Speedway, near the Magic Kingdom parking lot. The Richard Petty Driving Experience even welcomes backseat drivers.

Prefer to keep your sweaty palms off the steering wheel? Try the Riding Experience, about $90 for three laps in a slick stock car; no reservations necessary. Want your foot on that gas pedal? Reserve ahead for the three-hour Rookie Experience (about $370), including instruction and eight high-speed laps; the 18-Lap King's Experience (about $740); or the Experience of a Lifetime (about $1,270), delivering three rounds of Petty practice. To put yourself in the driver's seat, call 800-237-3889.

Which Way to the Beach?

WDW resort guests need not set out for the coast to find pretty strands to sunbathe on and get sand between their toes. Between the resorts fronting Bay Lake (the Contemporary, Wilderness Lodge, and Fort Wilderness) and those alongside Seven Seas Lagoon (the Grand Floridian and Polynesian), there are over five miles of white-sand beaches. And that doesn't include the powdery white stretches at the Caribbean Beach, Yacht and Beach Club, Swan and Dolphin, and Coronado Springs resorts. The beach fronting the Polynesian's Tahiti guest building is among the more secluded shores. All beaches are reserved exclusively for guests staying at those properties. Note that swimming is not permitted.

to $20 per half hour. Among the options are SunFish (two passengers max), Monohulls (good beginner boats holding up to six), and catamarans for two or three people (experience required).

SPEEDBOATING: Among the most enjoyable ways to cool off at WDW is the legion of mini-speedboats called Water Mouse boats (which replaced Water Sprites). The boats' small hulls ride a choppy surface as if they were galloping steeds, maxing out at 22 miles per hour. (An additional boon: Drivers must be 12 to pilot Water Mouse boats.) Fort Wilderness Marina offers one of the more uncrowded arenas at WDW. While the boats ostensibly seat two, adult boaters will reach greater speeds going solo (and creating tiny wakes for one another). Water Mouse boats are restricted to lakes only and are available for about $19 per half hour at the Grand Floridian, Polynesian, Contemporary, Wilderness Lodge, Fort Wilderness, Yacht and Beach Club, and Caribbean Beach marinas. At Dixie Landings, Port Orleans, and Coronado Springs, Water Mouse boats rent for $20 per half hour.

WATERSKIING AND WAKEBOARDING: Enthusiasts interested in hitching a ride around Bay Lake and Seven Seas Lagoon will pay about $100 per hour for a boat and instructor. Cost is by the boatload, and up to five people can be accommodated at a time. Trips depart from the Contemporary marina. Reservations must be made at least 24 hours in advance and can be made up to 90 days ahead. Call 407-WDW-PLAY (939-7529).

Swimming

A s if it weren't enough to have an inside track to three water parks (see "Other Pursuits" in the latter part of this chapter), WDW resorts are themselves bursting at the seams with watery playgrounds. With no fewer than 60 pools spread throughout Disney's hotel grounds, guests at each resort can be assured of easy access to at least one pool. However, it is important to note that due to a policy initiated to prevent overcrowding, WDW hotel pools are open only to guests staying at that resort; pool-hopping is permitted strictly between sister resorts (the Yacht and Beach Club; Port Orleans and Dixie Landings; All-Star Movies, All-Star Music, and All-Star Sports; and the Swan and Dolphin).

As a general rule, the hotels with multiple pools afford the most pleasant swimming for adults. This is because one pool is tailored (mostly via a delightfully rendered theme) to attract the splashy crowd, thereby freeing up the other(s) for swimmers in search of calmer waters. The Yacht and Beach Club offer the best of both

worlds: two secluded pools with whirlpools, and an extraordinary mini water park, called Stormalong Bay, that sprawls over three acres and features current pools, jets, and a sand-bottomed wading lagoon. The Swan and Dolphin also do things right: A grotto pool filled with waterfalls and alcoves is punctuated by whirlpools and complemented by two rectangular pools.

Among resorts with one swimming hole, the Grand Floridian's pool is vast, unthemed, and open 24 hours; the Animal Kingdom Lodge's, poised for animal viewing; and Port Orleans', fun but generally overrun with children (although you can also swim next door at Dixie Landings). Featuring two pools apiece are the Contemporary, Polynesian, Wilderness Lodge, Fort Wilderness, All-Star Movies, All-Star Music, and All-Star Sports resorts. (**Note:** The All-Star resorts are exceptions to the two-pools-means-at-least-one-quiet-pool rule.) BoardWalk boasts three pools, Coronado Springs and Old Key West have four pools apiece, Dixie Landings and The Villas at the Disney Institute each have six, and the Caribbean Beach resort has seven. Each of the resorts on Hotel Plaza Boulevard checks in with one pool. Lap swimmers will be happiest with the spacious rectangular pool at the Swan and Dolphin.

Biking Around the World

While Fort Wilderness is certainly prime territory for leisurely cycling, the World is filled with picturesque roads that wind within some of its most sprawling and scenic resorts.

Bikes are available for rental (about $6 an hour or $15 per day, with some variation among locations) in precisely the spots where guests will want to ride: Fort Wilderness, Wilderness Lodge, Old Key West, Port Orleans, Dixie Landings, Caribbean Beach, BoardWalk, The Villas at the Disney Institute, and Coronado Springs.

Disney's Wide World of Sports Complex Tips

- For a complete event calendar, call 407-363-6600 or check *www.disneyworldsports.com*.

- WDW resort guests may take buses from Blizzard Beach (10 A.M. to 6 P.M.) or from Downtown Disney (6 P.M. to 11 P.M.). Note that transfers can take quite a bit of time.

- Tailgating in the parking lot is not permitted. (Parking is free.)

- Take an umbrella to outdoor contests (the area's prone to afternoon showers), and know that games may be canceled due to inclement weather.

- Want to be a part of the action? Volunteer to work at a Wide World of Sports event. Call 407-363-6600.

Disney's Wide World of Sports Complex

Should your definition of paradise include slam dunks, screeching fastballs, and the intoxicating aroma of steamed weenies, welcome to nirvana. Disney's Wide World of Sports complex, which sprawls over 200 acres, is one agile place. Capable of hosting a dozen events at once, the immense facility has an archery-to-wrestling lineup that makes channel surfing in a sports bar seem positively passive. As the spring-training ground for Major League Baseball's Atlanta Braves, the home of Minor League Baseball's Orlando Rays, the Amateur Athletic Union (AAU), and a veritable turntable of tournaments, it's the biggest thing to hit the Florida sports scene since the Orlando Magic.

Despite its enormity, the complex somehow comes off as almost quaint. Its old-time Floridian architecture harks back to a simpler era. It recaptures the essence of a neighborhood ballpark, beckoning friends and families to spend a lazy afternoon together.

The complex, near the junction of I-4 and U.S. 192, has an armory of box seats and bleachers to accommodate all manner of spectators. There's a 9,500-seat baseball stadium; a 5,000-seat field house that hosts basketball, wrestling, and volleyball; a track-and-field complex; 11 clay tennis courts; and four multipurpose fields for football, soccer, lacrosse, and more. Not content to remain a spectator? Another area is devoted to the NFL Experience (included with general admission), where you can test your *own* football skills.

The $9 general admission ticket allows you the freedom to take in a number of nonpremium events—that is, competitions that are worth watching, but not quite major league. Tickets for all premium events, such as Atlanta Braves games and Orlando Rays Minor League Baseball, are available through TicketMaster (407-839-3900; *www.ticketmaster.com*) and include license to roam the complex. Premium tickets can also be purchased at the complex's ticket office on the day of the event, if still available. Click on *www.disneyworldsports.com* for information on the entire sports lineup.

If an afternoon of cheering (pom-poms optional) and rooting for the next-best-thing-to-the-home-team leaves you with a linebacker-style appetite, head straight for the Official All Star Cafe. The burgers are good, the atmosphere's festive, and as far as restaurants go, it's the only game in town. Vendors offer a variety of stadium snacks for those dining in their seats or on the run.

Health Clubs

Not all fitness centers located within the WDW resorts are reserved strictly for guests staying under the same roof. Olympiad Health Club at the Contemporary (407-824-3410), Grand Floridian Spa & Health Club (407-824-2332), Muscles & Bustles at BoardWalk (407-939-2370), La Vida at Coronado Springs (407-939-3030), R.E.S.T. at Old Key West (407-827-7700), Ship Shape at the Yacht and Beach (407-934-3256), Sturdy Branches Health Club at The Villas at Wilderness Lodge (407-938-4222), the Disney Institute Spa and Fitness Center (407-827-4455), and Zahanati Health Club at Animal Kingdom Lodge are accessible to all WDW resort guests; Body By Jake at the Dolphin (407-934-4264) is open to all.

The bare-bones facility at the Swan (free for all Swan and Dolphin guests) is fine for on-the-road maintenance. Better equipped—more cardiovascular machines and saunas—are the Contemporary Fitness Center, Muscles & Bustles at BoardWalk, La Vida at Coronado Springs, Sturdy Branches at The Villas at Wilderness Lodge, and Ship Shape at the Yacht and Beach, which has a whirlpool, steam room, and sauna; cost is $12 per day, $30 for length of stay, or $40 for length of stay per family of up to five to use any of the four clubs. R.E.S.T. at Old Key West is free for WDW resort guests.

The best of the lot distinguish themselves by offering exceptionally pleasant environs and the likes of personal trainers and Cybex machines. Body By Jake at the Dolphin ($10 per day; free for Swan and Dolphin guests) offers aerobics and Polaris equipment, and the Grand Floridian Spa & Health Club ($12 per day, $30 for length of stay) comes with frills; for details, see this chapter's "Spas" section. The well-appointed Fitness Center at The Villas at the Disney Institute ($15 per day, $35 for length of stay, or $50 for length of stay per family of four) could be a Cybex warehouse if not for its airy setting. Zahanati Health Club at Animal Kingdom Lodge boasts a steam room plus spa services including massages, manicures, and pedicures.

Getting Above It All

If the notion of flying like a kite above Bay Lake with a panorama of the Magic Kingdom appeals to you, factor in a contoured chair that allows you to sit in a reclined position and you have an idea of the parasailing experience as it exists at Walt Disney World.

The flight lasts seven to ten minutes, and the landing is quite soft, thanks to the parachute and the two-person crew's skillful handling (as one reels in the cord, the other slows the boat just so).

Parasailing excursions are offered at the Contemporary marina, with none other than four-time World Overall Champion Sammy Duvall and his world-class instructors. The cost is about $75 for single riders and $115 for tandem riders. Make the requisite reservations up to 90 days in advance by calling 407-939-0755. Guests must check in 20 minutes before departure.

Did you know...

Enough Mouse ear hats are sold each year to cover the head of every person in Pittsburgh.

SHOPPING

There's more to the shopping scene at Walt Disney World than Mouse ears, Mickey Mouse watches, and sweatshirts ad infinitum. Indeed, Disney character merchandise has reached a level of taste and sophistication that will amaze even the most demanding souvenir hunter. The options range from dark chocolate molded in the image of a certain mouse's face to exclusive pieces of Disneyana created by world-class design houses, including Waterford, Goebel, and Lladró. For adults looking to find a grown-up forget-me-not, the pickings have never been better. There are T-shirts, sweatshirts, and denim shirts playfully adorned with tasteful character appliqués. Silk ties, hair accessories, and dress socks feature surprisingly subtle Mickey Mouse designs. And product lines earmarked for executives and gourmands have deftly infused the World's most recognizable silhouette into the likes of black leather portfolios, fine writing implements, and sugar bowls and creamers.

Although much of the commerce here revolves around Disneyana, most shops offer character merchandise within the context of a broader theme (jewelry or books, for instance). Others, such as a certain shop in the Magic Kingdom, eschew the stuff altogether, offering such unlikely items as beer steins and crystal,

instead. Yes, that's right, crystal. In the Magic Kingdom. A bit bizarre, granted. But the fact that such a possibility exists on this prime piece of "Please, Daddy, please!" real estate serves as a nice elbow-in-the-ribs allusion to what fills shelves and racks in more adult corners of the World.

When we say that Epcot's World Showcase is no United Nations of Kmarts, no international convention of Disney paraphernalia, we mean (1) merchandise eloquently represents a who's who of world nations; (2) we'd trust the folks who stock some of the shops here to choose a gift for our mothers; and (3) the place is a dangerous buying spree waiting to happen. Then there's the Downtown Disney Marketplace, an attractive enclave of boutiques and restaurants on the shores of Lake Buena Vista that (from 9:30 A.M. to 11 P.M. daily, until midnight in some busy seasons) offers the best one-stop shopping in the World. And it's not just because it boasts the biggest hoard of Disney merchandise on the planet: The whirlwind shopping potential of the Marketplace extends to animation cels, books, Christmas trimmings, designer clothing, environmentally themed goods, fine jewelry, and gourmet gifts (and that's just from *A* to *G*). The sort of place that inspires shoppers to drag companions by the arm to see this great thing or that, the Marketplace is loaded.

Because it wouldn't be right to send you out into the World without an itemized shopping list, we've pulled together a diverse selection of the best shops in the World. While particular items may not be in the store when you are, comparable goods should be available.

In Downtown Disney Marketplace
Standouts

THE ART OF DISNEY: If you skip this showroom brimming with limited-edition art pieces, collectibles, and animation cels, you've missed out on some of the most spectacular ogling to be had at Walt Disney World (Disney characters masterfully rendered by the likes of Lladró and Waterford). A Disney artist is on hand daily to draw personalized sketches of favorite characters, as well as answer questions about the animation process and past Disney animated films.

DISNEY'S DAYS OF CHRISTMAS: It even smells like Christmas here in the World's largest excuse to say "Ho, ho, ho." Rather than tick off the many delightful trimmings—both traditional and Disney-style—proffered at this trove of decorative items, ornaments, and collectibles, we'll cut to the chase: Just add eggnog.

DISNEY AT HOME: One look around this shop might inspire you to reaccessorize the house with subtle Mickey-revering dishware, blankets, clocks, shower curtains, and (dare we suggest) furniture. Or (more likely) to find a good home for a signature piece of embossed pottery or a wrought-iron candle holder.

Downtown Disney, Defined

In addition to the World's best shopping, the Downtown Disney Marketplace offers restaurants, lounges, a marina, special events, and interactive fountains. Walkways link the Marketplace to its spirited neighbors: Pleasure Island and Downtown Disney West Side. The three locales (and the stockpile of clubs, shops, and restaurants therein) are collectively known as Downtown Disney—a district zoned exclusively for entertainment. Buses and boats service the area. Marketplace shops are described in this section (starting above), while Pleasure Island and West Side shops are summed up in the margin on the next page. See our "Restaurant Guide" and "Nightlife Guide" in the *Dining & Entertainment* chapter for further details on the restaurants and clubs located here.

Beyond the Marketplace

Rather than invent new ways to immortalize the Mouse, the shops at Pleasure Island and Downtown Disney West Side specialize in offbeat goods with adult appeal.

At Pleasure Island, Reel Finds yields stars' collectibles; Suspended Animation showcases cels and such; and Island Depot delivers novelty T-shirts.

On the West Side, Starabilias peddles Hollywood memorabilia; Hoypoloi stocks Zen gardens and artsy glass sculptures; and Magnetron houses umpteen magnets. More obviously, the Guitar Gallery is the vintage guitar source; Virgin Megastore is CD central; and Sosa Family Cigars offers premium smokes.

GOURMET PANTRY: This Marketplace institution stocks a full line of Gourmet Mickey cookware, including the latest in Mouse-inspired dishes. It is also positively crammed with delectables; while many sweets and savories are meant for instant gratification, others (Mickey-shaped pasta and Mickey Shorts Bread) make good souvenirs.

TEAM MICKEY'S ATHLETIC CLUB: This expansive shop specializes in sport-specific Disney character apparel and gear that run the gamut from Goofy golf club covers to Minnie tennis whites.

2R'S READING AND RITING: In this book nook, you'll find best-sellers, children's books, and Disney tomes; gifts for the office, such as Mickey Cross pens and Disney's Executive Collection desk accessories, which take Mickey to sophisticated heights; and a ready supply of both artful and adorable stationery, journals, and greeting cards. Plus cappuccino.

WORLD OF DISNEY: The most comprehensive collection of Disney character merchandise available anywhere and a shopper's concierge desk equipped to locate any item in stock make this emporium an unbeatable venue for one-stop souvenir sprees. As you make your way through the maze of displays, ranging from limited-edition watches to stuffed animals, from intimate apparel to office accessories, and from frames to photo albums, notice how each room is themed, replete with colorful murals and whimsical character sculptures. One area, presided over by Disney villains, is overflowing with tempting stuff: watches, jewelry, and some great decorative accessories for the home. The most eye-catching room's travel theme is evident in the totes, packs, and hats sold there, not to mention the character-piloted contraptions hung from the high ceilings. Avid cooks will savor the goods in the "Enchanted Dining Room." While conspicuous characters are the rule storewide, there is also a lot of great Mickey Mouse innuendo to be found.

Good Bets

EUROSPAIN: Presented by Arribas Brothers, this shop offers crystal keepsakes (engraved on-site), porcelain figurines, glass slippers, and more.

GENERATION BENEFITS: Mickey makes himself very scarce at this upscale spot—a reliable resource for men's and women's sportswear and accessories, branded by the likes of Tommy Hilfiger and Liz Claiborne.

RESORTWEAR UNLIMITED: With classic sportswear separates from such labels as Liz Claiborne and Ralph Lauren, and a small stash of accessories (sandals, handbags, and jewelry), this shop is equipped to plug most any hole in a woman's travel wardrobe. It also has a Lancôme cosmetics counter.

SUMMER SANDS: A beach fix minus the high tide, with Walt Disney World's largest selection of swimwear, cover-ups, and hats.

In the Parks
Magic Kingdom Standouts

BRIAR PATCH (Frontierland): The specialty of the house is merchandise that sweetly portrays Winnie the Pooh and cohorts.

CRYSTAL ARTS (Main Street): This shop offers cut-glass bowls and vases and clear-glass mugs and steins similar to those found at Eurospain in the Downtown Disney Marketplace. Items can be engraved on-site, and guests have the opportunity to observe an engraver or glassblower at work.

Shopping Tips

■ Not enough time in the day? The Downtown Disney Marketplace keeps long hours—9:30 A.M. to 11 P.M. daily, occasionally leaving its doors open until midnight.

■ Short on cash? Stop by the ATM on the West Side (near Forty Thirst Street), in the Marketplace (in Guest Services, near Toys Fantastic), or at Pleasure Island (near Rock N Roll Beach Club).

■ Valet parking is available at Downtown Disney (near Fulton's Crab House and by Cirque du Soleil) from 5:30 P.M. to 2 A.M. Cost is $6; the service is complimentary to guests with disabilities.

■ Shopped until you're ready to drop? Head to the umbrella-dotted Sunset Cove near the marina and relax with a margarita; hours are seasonal.

■ Guest Services (near Toys Fantastic) will wrap your gift for about $2 to $8 and ship it anywhere in the world.

Pin Trading

In the mood for some Olympic-Village-style pin trading? You're in luck. A veritable bartering brouhaha has erupted at Walt Disney World. Here's how it works:

Simply purchase—or pack—some starter pins (available throughout WDW). Put the pins in a highly-visible place (say, on your hat). Then keep your eyes peeled for pin-bearing park-goers or Disney cast members.

If your pin-trading etiquette is not up to snuff, ask a cast member for advice. Remember: If you're displaying a pin, it's assumed you are willing to trade it—so don't wear family heirlooms or other pins you are unable to part with. And when it comes to swapping with cast members, it's strictly Disney pin for Disney pin.

DISNEY & CO. (Main Street): Victorian wallpaper, elaborate woodwork, and old-fashioned ceiling fans are a fitting backdrop for the intimate apparel at this lovely shop on Center Street, just off Main.

DISNEY CLOTHIERS (Main Street): Souvenir clothing earns big style points here, as various Disney characters appear on silk scarves, ties, and leather goods, and are appliquéd on collared shirts, denim shirts, sweaters, jackets, and nightshirts. Selection is small but choice.

EMPORIUM (Main Street): The Magic Kingdom's largest gift shop offers an array of WDW logo and character merchandise (including lots of stuffed animals, T-shirts, sweatshirts, and hats) whose variety is eclipsed only by that found at the Marketplace. Be sure to get a glimpse of the display windows out front.

THE KING'S GALLERY (Cinderella Castle): You'll pay a king's ransom to walk off with some of the treasures at this richly appointed shop with suits of armor and Spanish-made swords. But don't overlook the Cinderella keepsakes.

MAIN STREET ATHLETIC CLUB (Main Street): A nifty stash of sports-related character apparel. If you want to score some great gear sporting classic characters in action, don't pass.

MAIN STREET CONFECTIONERY (Main Street): The sweet-toothed fall in line for peanut brittle, fudge, and marshmallow crispie treats made on the premises. For Pooh's Hunny Pots (chocolate filled with gooey caramel), chocolate-covered Mickey-shaped pretzels, and creatively candy-coated marshmallows, this is the source.

MAIN STREET GALLERY (Main Street): One of five WDW showrooms featuring limited-edition art pieces, collectibles, and animation cels (an extraordinary eyeful that should not be missed). Displays are different at each gallery.

MAIN STREET MARKET HOUSE (Main Street): Brass lanterns and oak floors provide the background for a selection of old-fashioned snacks and dishware.

UPTOWN JEWELERS (Main Street): If you're shopping for a character watch, 14K gold or sterling silver jewelry, or souvenir charms, this elegant catchall is the place. There is also a selection of ceramic character figurines.

THE YANKEE TRADER (Liberty Square): A front porch with a rocking chair sets the tone for this cozy niche chock-full of Disney country kitchenware.

YE OLDE CHRISTMAS SHOPPE (Liberty Square): Although smaller than Disney's Days of Christmas at the Downtown Disney Marketplace, this locale is a fine resource for traditional and character holiday decorations.

Epcot Standouts

THE AMERICAN ADVENTURE (World Showcase): Heritage Manor Gifts waxes patriotic with Americana in the expected colors. Highlights include decorative throws, history books, and colonial memorabilia.

THE ART OF DISNEY (Future World): The Art of Disney serves as the park's repository for Disney animation cels and limited-edition art pieces and collectibles. It is one of five such showrooms at Walt Disney World.

CANADA (World Showcase): An array of Canadian handicrafts and Indian artifacts puts the Northwest Mercantile on the essential-shopping circuit. But don't neglect the refined pottery and pewter candlesticks at La Boutique des Provinces.

CHINA (World Showcase): Yong Feng Shangdian is so huge, it's almost a province; the montage of paper fans, Chinese prints, silk robes, antiques, vases, and tea sets is truly something to behold.

FRANCE (World Showcase): Boutiques offering things beautiful and French. Our favorites are Plume et Palette (artwork upstairs, collectibles downstairs);

The Mouse Delivers

■ Prowling the property but can't find the object of your obsession? Ask a park employee, and if that must-have Donald Duck screen saver or Tinker Bell tea set exists, he or she should be able to find out where it's sold.

■ Have a sudden, not-to-be-denied yearning for a certain music box, watch, or tie that you saw in a shop during your visit? Call WDW Mail Order at 407-363-6200.

■ Still have unfulfilled Disney cravings? Call 800-237-5751 for The Disney Catalog, call 818-265-4660 to find The Disney Store nearest you, or browse through The Disney Store's offerings online at *www.disneystore.com*.

■ Theme park shoppers may arrange to have purchases sent to a location near the gates for later pickup. WDW resort guests may have purchases delivered to their hotel at no charge.

Talk About an Eclectic Mix...

The unique array of merchandise found in shops at the Studios is best quantified by example. At last check, you could fill the following unlikely shopping list:

- An end table once owned by Cecil B. DeMille

- China that belonged to Elvis and Priscilla

- Limited-edition Disney animation cel

- Frank Sinatra's electric piano

- Dumbo tea set

- Pooh dinnerware

- *I Love Lucy* silk tie

- *Austin Powers* movie lot crew I.D. badge

- Mickey golf shirt

- Brandon Lee's black jacket from *The Crow*

La Maison du France (wine, cookbooks, and hand-painted dishes); and La Signature (Guerlain cosmetics and fragrances).

GERMANY (World Showcase): Shops here are simply irresistible. Die Weihnachts Ecke (bursting with cuckoo clocks, nutcrackers, and wood carvings) is joined by Volkskunst (beer steins in all sizes); Der Teddybär (a delightful toy shop); Weinkeller (with bottlings from the vintage German vintner H. Schmitt Söhne); Kunstarbeit in Kristall (steins, crystal, and Christmas goodies); and Glas und Porzellan (a boutique with Goebel's M. I. Hummel figurines, where an artist demonstrates the process by which the rosy-cheeked creations are painted and finished).

GREEN THUMB EMPORIUM (The Land, Future World): Do not be misled. While this great shop is flush with seeds, kits, and garden-themed knick-knacks, gardening prowess is not sold here. Repeat: No green thumbs change hands.

ITALY (World Showcase): When in this multishop pavilion, we gravitate toward La Bottega Italiana for cannoli and vino, Delizie Italiane for fine chocolates, and Il Bel Cristallo for Armani figurines, silk scarves, and leather purses.

JAPAN (World Showcase): In the vast emporium known as the Mitsukoshi Department Store, kimono-clad dolls (priced from $20 to $500) merit special attention, as do kimonos, origami kits, and bonsai.

MOUSE GEAR (Innoventions, Future World): Epcot's best address for character merchandise also stocks a selection of souvenirs relating to surrounding pavilions. (This shop was formerly known as Centorium.)

MEXICO (World Showcase): While the vibrant piñatas presented in the central plaza are great for effect, the ceramics and other handicrafts at adjacent Artesanías Mexicanas tend to be marked by a more enduring appeal.

MOROCCO (World Showcase): At least half the fun of shopping in this pavilion's maze of Berber bangles, basketry, and clothing is never knowing just what awaits around the bend (we found a lovely little bottle filled with rosewater, known as *cortas*). Carpet-making demonstrations are held from park opening until about 6 P.M.

NORWAY (World Showcase): The Puffin's Roost is undoubtedly Central Florida's best source for trolls and gorgeous, often hand-knit, Norwegian ski sweaters (bargains when compared to the cost of flights to Oslo). Miniature wood carvings and handcrafted jewelry add to the interesting purchase panorama.

UNITED KINGDOM (World Showcase): Some of Epcot's finest shops lie within this pavilion's borders. There's The Toy Soldier (where Winnie the Pooh and Teletubbies star); The Crown & Crest (a British free-for-all complete with intricately designed chess sets and pub glasses); Pringle of Scotland (a bounty of cashmeres and sports apparel); The Queen's Table (with fragrances and collectibles from Lilliput Lane, David Winter, and Wedgwood); and The Magic of Wales (handcrafted gifts). And, of course, there's a prime spot for tea lovers—The Tea Caddy.

Disney-MGM Studios Standouts

ANIMATION GALLERY: One of five WDW venues showcasing limited-edition art pieces, collectibles, and animation cels from a variety of Disney movies. The difference here: the chance to watch an artist creating and to buy the resulting artwork right on the spot.

KEYSTONE CLOTHIERS: Characters turn up on smartly styled men's casual wear, luggage, and shoes, not to mention accessories of the silk character tie and boxer short sort.

MOUSE ABOUT TOWN: A well-heeled wardrobe of subtly mouse-infused jackets, sweatshirts, and sports apparel in the sort of deep, dark colors a man-about-town would also appreciate. Golf-related accessories and apparel abound.

ONCE UPON A TIME: . . . there was a little shop that offered one of the classiest souvenir collections the World over—musical snow globes featuring artfully rendered Disney characters and lovely character-infused housewares.

SID CAHUENGA'S ONE-OF-A-KIND: Celebrity encounters abound in this den of movie and television memorabilia. There are scads of autographed photos,

---

Walt Disney World Jingles

Yo ho, yo ho . . . You can relive the sounds of Walt Disney World with a customized CD of music and dialogue from park shows and attractions. Simply stop in at a custom-CD kiosk—at Main Street Exposition Hall in the Magic Kingdom, the Imagination! pavilion at Epcot, across from the Caravan Stage, in Animal Kingdom's Asia, or Studio M, in the Downtown Disney Marketplace—and pick ten favorites for $19.98.

Conservation Initiative

As anyone who has ever given a gorilla a dollar could tell you, animals aren't great money managers. Which is why initiatives like the Disney Wildlife Conservation Fund come in handy.

This fund was established to support conservation efforts worldwide. You can help by tacking on a dollar for the Wildlife Conservation Fund when you make a purchase at any Animal Kingdom shop. If you're interested, pick up a brochure from a shop display for a list of nonprofit organizations assisted to date.

Expect a gentle solicitation at the cash register. Don't expect a gorilla looking for a handout.

original movie posters, and if you time it right, belated premiere invitations to Disney animated films. There's also ample opportunity to snap up hand-me-downs direct from the stars, so when someone compliments your handbag, you can say, "Yeah, Mae West liked it, too." Closet contents turn over too frequently to allow for specifics, but past fashion statements have come courtesy of Clark Gable, Cher, and Elizabeth Taylor.

SUNSET CLUB COUTURE: This purveyor of jewelry and limited-edition timepieces has the sort of incomparable selection that makes collectors' eyes widen. Consider gold pocket watches with conspicuous ears, marcasite pieces with stylized Mickey designs, and custom-made watches with tremendous face value (namely, your choice of characters, drawn and then sealed onto the watch's face).

THE WRITER'S STOP: This cozy commissary of cappuccino, cookies, and Hollywood-themed page-turners regularly hosts book signings.

Animal Kingdom Standouts

WONDERS OF THE WILD (Safari Village): Nature-themed apparel and descriptive gifts can be found here. Selections vary from everything you need to start your own backyard habitat to tinkling chimes, aromatic candles, soothing fountains, as well as many other unique treasures.

ISLAND MERCANTILE (Safari Village): The park's largest shopping oasis in a nutshell: stuffed animals on safari. Certainly, this is the last word in safari hat style, as interpreted by every Disney character that ever saw the embroidered front of a sweatshirt.

MOMBASA MARKETPLACE/ZIWANI TRADERS (Africa): Take one of the striking Kenyan-made walking sticks for an in-store test stroll, and you may well receive raves on your carving skills while perusing the soapstone elephants, hand-painted boxes, raku animal figurines, straw hats, and such.

OTHER PURSUITS

Y ou're at Walt Disney World, but you're not in the mood for a theme park, don't feel much like swatting a little yellow ball or sitting by the pool, and have already shopped (and dropped). You're up for something, but lack inspiration. What do you do? Don't despair. Disney's got this one covered.

If you'd like to select from the aquatic side of the adventure menu, Disney has channeled its usual creative flair, and no less than 4.3 million gallons of H_2O, into three parks that are to water what Elvis was to music. There's River Country, an old-fashioned swimming cove with several water slides and a

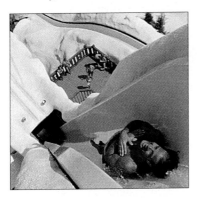

Huckleberry Finn sense of fun; Typhoon Lagoon, where tsunamis are a house specialty; and Blizzard Beach, with all the trappings of a winter ski resort, including a ski jump-style centerpiece.

Perhaps you'd prefer something more nature-oriented. For a blur of greenery and recreation, nothing beats Fort Wilderness, Disney's most unassuming attraction. Its 700 acres of woodland are rife with picturesque trails and canals, and lots of ways—including biking, canoeing, fishing, and horseback riding—to enjoy them.

Maybe you're a pie-in-the-sky romantic without a game plan. You can't bear to simply toast the setting sun from your hotel balcony. You want to celebrate— or simulate—a special occasion. Suffice it to say that Disney yachts and pontoon boats spend many sunsets and fireworks displays ferrying those in the know. The tough part is deciding between wine and champagne, yacht and pontoon, Epcot's IllumiNations and the Magic Kingdom's Fantasy in the Sky fireworks.

Another alluring choice from the dessert portion of the menu finds you in a white robe and slippers between a massage and a facial. It's a tough job, dallying at the World's resort spas while others trod through the parks, but someone's gotta keep the massage therapists in peak condition. Peruse the expansive offerings, and you'll discover the challenge of choosing indulgences. As the tempting array of massages, body treatments, aromatherapy baths, and facials clearly shows, there is great sport in the pursuit of serenity.

Disney Institute undergrads take note: at press time, courses were scheduled for suspension. Class dismissed.

Did you know...

Pontoon boats may be chartered for a party cruise at any time of day. The cost for a one-hour excursion—including snacks, soda, and champagne or cake—is $175 for up to five guests, $230 for as many as ten. Call 407-WDW-PLAY (939-7529) for details.

River Country Tips

- Don't arrive expecting to find a water park of Typhoon Lagoon or Blizzard Beach sophistication or proportions. River Country (just one-seventh the size of Typhoon Lagoon) is much more quaint and contained.

- Know that the park may close because of inclement weather or capacity constraints.

Water Parks
River Country

Disney's original watery playground holds its own with the sort of old-fashioned swimming area Tom Sawyer would have tried to keep a lid on: a walled-off area of Bay Lake furnished with rope swings and a ship's boom that swimmers may also enter via two fast-moving water flumes. A raft ride deposits passengers into this freshwater cove a bit more gently. River Country's other swimming area has charms of its own. A 330,000-gallon pool ensconced in man-made boulders, it is fitted out with two steep chutes that stop seven feet above the water's surface; unlike the swimming cove, it's heated during cooler months. River Country honors its rustic Fort Wilderness surroundings with a short nature trail along the lake's edge that offers a peaceful retreat among egrets and a telescopic perspective of Bay Lake. Note that during the summer, the All-American Water Party brings Fourth of July festivities to River Country: water-balloon tosses, music, and fireworks, plus character greetings.

KNOW BEFORE YOU GO: River Country is located in the northwestern corner of Fort Wilderness on a shore of Bay Lake roughly opposite the Contemporary. The park is usually closed for refurbishment for about two months each year (typically around September and October; call 407-939-4636 for exact dates). During the summer, crowds may push capacity as early as 11 A.M. When the magic number comes up, no one is admitted until crowds subside later in the day, generally around 3 P.M.

How to get there: Buses from the TTC and the Wilderness Lodge, and boat launches from the Magic Kingdom and the Contemporary, deliver passengers within walking distance. Buses transport all other guests from the Fort Wilderness parking lot to the park entrance.

Where to eat: Guests may bring their own lunch (no alcohol or glass containers). Pop's Place (sandwiches, fried chicken, snacks) is the main spot to nosh. Shaded picnic areas stand by.

Vital statistics: Hours vary, but are generally 10 A.M. to 5 P.M., with extended hours in effect during the summer (call 407-939-4636 for current times). Adult admission is $16.91, including tax. River Country admission is also included with an Ultimate Park Hopper Pass and is an option on the Park Hopper Plus Pass. Dressing rooms are available, and lockers and towels may be rented.

Typhoon Lagoon

T he centerpiece of this 56-acre state-of-the-art water park—ostensibly a small resort town transformed by nature's wrath—is a surf lagoon larger than two football fields that incites happy pandemonium with every five-foot wave it unleashes. But there are also three speed slides (which drop 51 feet at 30 miles per hour), three quick and curvy body slides, and a trio of white-water raft rides (one of which accommodates foursomes) that send tubers rollicking through caverns and waterfalls. It's all encircled by a lazy, floatable river in which swimmers—or more accurately, inner-tube innards—leisurely beat the heat.

KNOW BEFORE YOU GO: Typhoon Lagoon is located near Downtown Disney. Pools are heated during winter, and the park is typically closed for refurbishment for about two months each year (usually around November and December; call 407-939-4636 for exact dates). During warmer months, the masses arrive early, often filling the parking lot before noon. When peak capacity is reached, no one is admitted until crowds subside, often around 3 P.M. (Typhoon Lagoon is usually the second water park to reach capacity. Blizzard Beach is the first.).

How to get there: Direct buses from the TTC and all WDW resorts except the Grand Floridian, Contemporary, Polynesian, Wilderness Lodge, and Fort Wilderness (which require transfers at the TTC).

Where to eat: Guests may bring food and drinks into the park (no alcohol or glass containers permitted). Of the two main snack stands, Leaning Palms offers a larger selection than Typhoon Tilly's. Shady picnic areas are close at hand.

Typhoon Lagoon Tips

■ Tidal conditions in the lagoon change every hour, alternating (with warning) between gentle waves and surf city. Call 407-WDW-SURF (939-7873) for current conditions or to inquire about early-morning surfing lessons.

■ For time checks, look to the shrimp boat marooned atop Typhoon Lagoon's makeshift mountain; it sounds its horn and shoots a 50-foot flume of water into the air every 30 minutes.

■ Bad weather or capacity crowds can prompt the park to close.

■ Women will find that one-piece suits fare better on the speed slides here.

Blizzard Beach Tips

■ The chairlift that transports guests to the summit of Mount Gushmore affords a wonderful view, as does an observatory located at the summit itself.

■ Women will find that one-piece suits fare better on the speed slides here.

■ Inclement weather or maxed-out crowds can cause the park to close.

■ The concrete pathways can get hot, making water shoes a coveted commodity.

Vital statistics: Hours vary, but are generally 10 A.M. to 5 P.M., with extended hours in effect during summer months (call 407-939-4636 for current times). Adult admission is $29.63, including tax. Entry to Typhoon Lagoon is included in an Ultimate Park Hopper Pass and is an option on a Park Hopper Plus Pass. Dressing rooms are available, and lockers and towels may be rented. Singapore Sal's stocks beach basics.

Blizzard Beach

Disney legend has it that this 60-acre water park—Walt Disney World's newest and largest—is the melted remains of a failed Disney ski resort. Call it a not-so-little white lie. The bottom line on this place built around a "snow-covered" man-made peak called Mount Gushmore: It has some amazing runs. Chief among them is a ski jump-turned-speed slide that sends riders feet-first down the watery equivalent of a double-black-diamond run (a 120-foot drop at a 66-degree angle, in which speeds reach 60 miles per hour). A second speed slide plunges from 90 feet. Less intimidating highlights include an extra-long white-water-raft ride accommodating five people per raft, side-by-side "racing" slides, and flumes that slalom. For cool yet calm, there's a lazy floatable creek that encircles the park (though it does at one point run through a cave dripping with ice-cold water) and a free-form pool with gently bobbing waves.

When you've finished slipping and sliding down Mount Gushmore, gear up to do the unthinkable: Climb it. This may seem like an odd place for rock-climbing, but the 25-minute Mount Gushmore Expedition Climbing Experience, under the supervision of a rock-climbing expert, lets you scale 15 to 35 feet. Equipment is provided and excursions can be arranged at the Ski Patrol Area. Ask a Disney employee for details.

KNOW BEFORE YOU GO: Blizzard Beach is located near the Disney-MGM Studios, adjacent to Disney's Winter Summerland miniature golf course. All pools are heated during the winter; the park is typically closed for refurbishment for at least one month each year (usually January and part of February; call 407-939-4636 for exact dates). During the warmer months, the masses descend upon Blizzard Beach early in the day, and the parking lot frequently closes before noon. When peak capacity is reached, no one is admitted until crowds ease up, usually around 3 P.M. The park may also close due to inclement weather.

How to get there: Buses are available from all WDW resorts and parks.

Where to eat: Guests may bring their own food and drinks (no alcohol or glass containers permitted). Of the four snack stands, Lottawatta Lodge is the largest and most centrally located. Picnic areas are nearby.

Vital statistics: Hours vary, but are generally 10 A.M. to 5 P.M., with extended hours in effect throughout the summer months (call 407-939-4636 for current times). Adult admission is $29.63, including tax. A Blizzard Beach/Disney's Winter Summerland pass, including Blizzard Beach admission and a round of mini golf, costs $37.05. Entry to Blizzard Beach is included with an Ultimate Park Hopper Pass and is an option on a Park Hopper Plus Pass. Dressing rooms are available, and lockers and towels may be rented. The Beach Haus stocks fun-in-the-sun essentials.

Natural Distraction
Fort Wilderness

Simply put, no place on Walt Disney World property is better equipped to satisfy yens related to the great outdoors than this campground and recreation area, set on 700 forested, canal-crossed acres on the shore of the World's largest lake. (For information about Fort Wilderness accommodations, see *Checking In*. For details about dining, see *Dining & Entertainment*.) Between its wonderfully canoe-worthy canals and its guided fishing excursions, Fort Wilderness gives anglers unparalleled access to Bay Lake's largemouth bass. Since the lake was stocked with over 70,000 bass in the sixties, this waterway is teeming with fish that are ready to tangle with your line.

A marina invites guests to strap on water skis and rent all manner of boats for explorations of the lake. (See "Sports" earlier in this chapter for more details on fishing and boating excursions.) Escorted trail rides and a three-quarter-mile hiking path deliver nature lovers into peaceful areas where it's not uncommon to see deer, armadillos, and birds. (Yes, you're still in Walt Disney World!) Myriad pathways provide inspiring venues for joggers and cyclists (bikes are available for rent), and tennis, volleyball, and basketball courts are scattered about the property. While the two swimming pools and the white-sand beach are open only to campground

Fort Wilderness Tips

■ You can survey the natural beauty of Fort Wilderness via bicycle rentals from the Bike Barn for $5 per hour or $12 per day.

■ Because getting to and from this area can take a lot of time (inquire at WDW resort Guest Services as to the most efficient route), it's worthwhile to combine a visit to Fort Wilderness with an excursion to River Country.

guests, the River Country water park (described on page 174) is close at hand. In the evenings, hayrides, Mickey's Backyard Barbecue, and the World's most-popular dinner show, the Hoop-Dee-Doo Musical Revue (see *Dining & Entertainment* for details), keep things humming.

KNOW BEFORE YOU GO: Fort Wilderness is located east of the Contemporary on a large plot of land stretching south from Bay Lake to Vista Boulevard. It's open year-round.

How to get there: Preferably by car, for efficiency's sake. Guests at WDW-owned properties and those with River Country tickets may take boat launches from the Magic Kingdom, Wilderness Lodge, or the Contemporary resort. Buses from the TTC transport guests with a WDW resort ID or a multi-day admission pass.

Getting around: Only vehicles bound for campsites are permitted beyond the guest parking lot. Fort Wilderness is serviced by an internal bus system that links all recreation areas and campsites (buses circulate at 20-minute intervals from 7 A.M. to 2 A.M.). Guests who prefer greater independence may rent bikes or electric carts from the Bike Barn.

Where to eat: The Settlement Trading Post and the Meadow Trading Post stock staples and prepare made-to-order sandwiches; there's also Trail's End Buffet for all-day dining.

Vital statistics: Admission to Fort Wilderness is free for Walt Disney World resort guests. The Bike Barn in the Meadow Recreation Area is the place to pick up trail maps and to rent bikes ($5 per hour, $12 per day), canoes ($6 per half hour, $12 per hour), rods and reels ($6 per hour, $9 per day), fishing poles ($2 per hour, $4 per day), and electric carts (about $40 for 24 hours; reservations necessary; call 407-824-2742). Hayrides depart twice nightly at 7 P.M. and 9:30 P.M. from Pioneer Hall and last about an hour ($6; call 407-939-7529 to confirm times). Guided 45-minute trail rides depart four times daily from the Tri-Circle-D Livery near the visitor lot; reservations suggested ($23; call 407-939-7529 up to 90 days ahead).

Romantic Excursions and Fireworks Cruises

Breathless

Moored at the Yacht and Beach Club marina, the *Breathless* is a sleek 24-foot Chris-Craft reproduction of a 1930s mahogany runabout. The motor boat, named after the Dick Tracy character, is equipped with bench seats and accommodates up to seven people (the fewer, the better). Refreshments can be served on the boat, which day and night escorts private parties around 25-acre Crescent Lake and adjoining waterways at speeds up to 50 miles per hour. From 2:30 P.M. to 5:30 P.M. daily, 10- and 30-minute excursions plying Crescent Lake and adjoining canals are available. But the *Breathless'* most romantic outings are its dusk IllumiNations cruises, which zip past BoardWalk, the Swan and Dolphin, and the Disney-MGM Studios en route to providing prime views of the show (from beneath the bridge at the World Showcase France pavilion).

KNOW BEFORE YOU GO: All cruises on the *Breathless* depart from the Yacht and Beach Club marina. On request, guests may be picked up from the dock at BoardWalk. No sunset cruises are available on the *Breathless.*

    Rates: Cost is per boatload (up to seven passengers); driver is provided. Ten-minute and 30-minute excursions go for about $25 and $75, respectively. The one-hour IllumiNations cruise runs $160.

    Reservations: Advance reservations, which can be made as far ahead as 90 days, are strongly recommended for the *Breathless*; reservations must be made at least 24 hours ahead. Call 407-WDW-PLAY (939-7529).

Grand 1

This striking 44-foot Sea Ray is the sort of craft that escorts VIPs on private tours of the Seven Seas Lagoon and Bay Lake before nightfall, pausing in just the right spot as the Fantasy in the Sky fireworks explode above Cinderella Castle. But don't be misled: The *Grand 1* defines VIPs quite broadly, to encompass any group of up to 12 passengers lucky enough to snare a reservation. Although providing tantalizing vistas of the Magic Kingdom fireworks are the *Grand 1's* specialty; the elegant craft can be booked for most any hour, most any day. You may content yourself with feasting merely on the fireworks and the stars, or you may have your excursion catered, courtesy of chefs at the Grand Floridian. Thus, the possibilities extend from a private cruise for two, complete with dinner and champagne, to a cocktail party for 12, with as much shrimp, chips and salsa, chicken wings, beer, and wine as the boat can hold.

KNOW BEFORE YOU GO: All cruises on the *Grand 1* depart from the Grand Floridian marina. On request, guests may be picked up from the Polynesian, Contemporary, Wilderness Lodge and Villas, or Fort Wilderness dock.

Spa Tips

■ Reserve treatments well in advance; confirm your appointment before you arrive.

■ Request a female or male spa therapist if you have a preference. The spa will honor your wishes, if at all possible.

■ Drink plenty of water to counter the dehy-drating effects of these indulgences.

■ Jewelry and spa treatments don't mix. Plan ahead and leave yours in a safe at your hotel.

■ If it's a body treatment, leave underwear in the locker. The provided robes are sized for modesty, and therapists are trained to discreetly cover your most private parts during treatments.

■ Bathing suits are optional for the separate men's and women's saunas and whirlpools.

Rates: You'll pay $275 per hour to rent the *Grand 1.* Cost is per boatload (up to 12 passengers); a driver and deckhand are included, refreshments are not.

Reservations: Reservations for excursions on the *Grand 1* should be made as far in advance as possible, preferably at the time you book your accommodations; they must be made 24 hours ahead. Call 407-824-2439 to book the *Grand 1.* For more information about having your affair catered, call 407-934-3946.

Pontoon Boats

No one will ever confuse a pontoon boat with a yacht, but when it comes to fireworks cruises, no one's looking at the boat anyway. What matters: comfort, capacity, a great vantage point, and timing. And so it is that Disney's pontoon boats, which accommodate up to ten people on private one-hour cruises, provide some of the best seats around for the Fantasy in the Sky fireworks and IllumiNations. Fantasy in the Sky cruises ply the Seven Seas Lagoon and Bay Lake, making quiet ripples on the water just outside the Magic Kingdom; those who want to dine out on the water may commission finger food or a whole seafaring buffet from, for example, the Wilderness Lodge's restaurant menus. As a hint to the possibilities, consider a buffet of Pacific salmon, two-ounce tastings of selected Oregon wines, and berry cobbler all around. Illumi-Nations excursions prowl the waters of Crescent Lake, where Epcot's Spaceship Earth beams like a second moon on the horizon. On these cruises, chefs from the Yacht and Beach Club, or Board-Walk send splurgers off with made-to-order buffets.

KNOW BEFORE YOU GO: Pontoon fireworks cruises last about an hour, and begin 30 minutes before the fireworks are scheduled to start. Fantasy in the Sky excursions depart from the Grand Floridian, Polynesian, Contemporary, Wilderness Lodge, and Fort Wilderness marinas. IllumiNations cruises depart from the BoardWalk and Yacht and Beach Club marinas.

Rates: Cost for one-hour Fantasy in the Sky or IllumiNations pontoon cruises is $120 per boatload (up to ten passengers); driver is provided, food is extra.

Reservations: Pontoon boats must be reserved at least 24 hours ahead; advance reservations, accepted up to 90 days ahead, are strongly recommended. Call 407-WDW-PLAY (939-7529). For catering information, contact Guest Services at the resort from which you wish to depart.

Spas

Grand Floridian Spa

Although more pocket-size than palatial, this elegant peach- and aqua-hued retreat has ample space to coddle 17 people at once—provided that there's a twosome being pummeled to contentment in the couple's treatment room. His and hers lounges, saunas, steam rooms, and whirlpools make worthy hangouts of the locker rooms. Signature services include baths steeped in native Floridian flowers and a deluxe facial complete with two masks and hand and foot massages. A cooling wrap incorporating lavender oil and calendula soothes the sunburned. Ultimate Relaxation pairs a traditional massage with a soak in a hydrotherapy tub that's equipped with 70 jets.

WORTH NOTING: The treatment menu includes aromatherapy; reflexology; shiatsu; Swedish, sports, and hydrotherapy massages; as well as a relaxing massage designed especially for expectant mothers. Massages last 25 to 80 minutes. Manicures, pedicures, and soothing hand and foot treatments are administered in the comfort of chairs that massage the lower back; feet are soaked in whirlpool baths. The spa offers a variety of body wraps (lavender and calendula, marine algae, clay, paraffin) and exfoliating scrubs 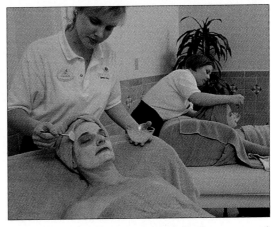 (herbal, sea salt); an array of facials, including one especially for men; and several therapeutic and aromatherapy baths. Couples may receive side-by-side aromatherapy massages or a hands-on massage lesson in the couple's treatment room.

KNOW BEFORE YOU GO: The Grand Floridian Spa is located right next to the health club at its namesake hotel, near the Magic Kingdom. Hours are from

Did you know...

You're not only welcome, you are wholly encouraged to show up at least 30 minutes before your scheduled spa service to lounge in the sauna, steam room, and whirlpool. Similarly, all three spas are linked to first-rate health clubs, which you are free to use before or (yeah, right) after your treatment.

Spa 101

As a rule, aromatherapy massages are the lightest (and most aromatic); reflexology (all in the feet) and shiatsu involve precise pressure points rather than the (light or deep) kneading motions of Swedish massage; hydrotherapy massage (delivered by jets or a water-jet wand as you float in a tub) is as deep as it gets.

6 A.M. to 9 P.M. (varies seasonally). Reservations may be made up to one month in advance. Call 407-824-2332.

How to get there: Monorail and boat transport is available to WDW resort guests from the Magic Kingdom. Similarly, guests may take the monorail from Epcot and the TTC, and buses from Downtown Disney, the Studios, and Animal Kingdom.

Rates: Expect to pay about $50 for a 25-minute massage and about $100 for a facial. Prices include an 18 percent gratuity.

Packages: Both half-day and full-day options are available. They range from the basic Spa Sampler (about $180; facial, manicure, and pedicure) to The Ultimate Day ($430; seven treatments, plus lunch).

The Spa at the Disney Institute

This sweat-free zone within Sweat Central (a.k.a. the Disney Institute Fitness Center) is a realm of unaffected calm, from its potted-plant accents to its teal towels and terra-cotta-colored tiles. The ten treatment rooms couldn't feel farther removed from the clanks of weight machines and the mechanical whirr of treadmills. Signature services include the tingling Warm Seafoam Mud Wrap and Seaweed Hydro-Massage, a penetrating immersion in saltwater and seaweed. The locker rooms are each equipped with a steam room, sauna, and whirlpool. Ordering a spa cuisine lunch is an option in the spa's coed lounge.

WORTH NOTING: The treatment menu includes aromatherapy, reflexology, sports, and Swedish massages, as well as hydrotherapy massages that combine an aromatherapy bath in a 48-jet tub with a traditional massage. Massages last about 25 to 80 minutes. The extensive lineup of body wraps and scrubs includes several that incorporate marine substances (seaweed, saltwater, sea salt, and sea mud). In addition to a large variety of specialty manicures and pedicures, the spa offers a diverse array of facials, from seaweed to aromatherapy.

KNOW BEFORE YOU GO: Located on the northern shore of Lake Buena Vista, near Downtown Disney, the spa is tucked within the Disney Institute Fitness Center at The Villas at the Disney Institute. Hours are from 8 A.M. to 8 P.M. (varies seasonally). Reservations are taken up to six months ahead. Call 407-827-4455.

How to get there: Buses transport WDW resort guests from the Magic Kingdom, Epcot, the Disney-MGM Studios, Animal Kingdom, and Downtown Disney. There are paved foot paths to the spa from the Downtown Disney Marketplace and West Side.

Rates: Expect to pay about $50 for a 25-minute massage and about $85 for a facial (including an 18 percent gratuity).

Packages: Choices range from the half-day Men's Programme ($150; sports massage, men's facial, and manicure) to the Full Day of Restoration ($265; four treatments, plus lunch).

The Spa at Wyndham Palace

Opposite Downtown Disney in more than location, this peaceful piece of the Wyndham Palace Resort offers a pampering repertoire that's about as deep and diverse as they come. Snazzy pedicure chairs with built-in whirlpool foot baths and back-massage capability overshadow the locker room saunas and steam rooms. Other clever touches include lushly landscaped outdoor whirlpools and use of one-way glass to provide views from the 14 treatment rooms. An herbal bath borrowed from Germany and Shirodhara (a calming hair and scalp treatment with Asian origins) are among the more esoteric specialties. The cool-mud Theme Park Leg Relief Wrap shows the spa's lighter side. Speaking of light, spa cuisine can be delivered poolside.

WORTH NOTING: The lineup of treatments includes aromatherapy, sports, shiatsu, Swedish, deep-tissue, reflexology, and hydrotherapy massages lasting from 25 to 80 minutes. An adjoining full-service salon offers the usual (highlights to bikini wax) services; normal pedicures and manicures are eclipsed by the likes of the 80-minute Sports Pedicure, complete with whirlpool foot bath, heated mud pack, aromatherapy massage, paraffin dip, and reflexology. The spa offers a variety of specialty baths (mineral, herbal, mud, seaweed) and a number of facials, including one designed to relieve sun-stressed skin. Its menu of body scrubs and wraps incorporate cool and warm mud, sea salt, and Asia's ancient Ayurvedic therapies.

KNOW BEFORE YOU GO: The Wyndham Palace Resort & Spa is located on Buena Vista Drive, right across the road from the Downtown Disney Marketplace. Hours are from 6 A.M. to 9 P.M. (varies seasonally). Call 800-981-1472.

How to get there: The resort is a short walk from Downtown Disney, which can be reached from the Magic Kingdom, Epcot, the Disney-MGM Studios, and Animal Kingdom via bus.

Rates: A 25-minute massage runs about $50 and facials cost about $85 (including an 18 percent gratuity).

Packages: The scripted half-day and full-day options range from the Royal Sampler (about $160; body scrub, hydrotherapy massage, neck and shoulder massage) to the Man's Day Away ($325; personal training session, four treatments, plus lunch). Customized packages are also available.

From casual to posh, Disney dining offers a delicious world of possibilities.

Dining & Entertainment

I t's late in the book and we're sure you must be dying of hunger by now, so we'll begin by quickly running through the food specials. But first, you'll be happy to hear that the outfit you are wearing at this moment, plus shoes, will be just fine for most any WDW restaurant (assuming that you didn't get all gussied up to read this chapter and that you're not in your pajamas or reading on the job). And second, atmosphere—the sort that mere ambience wouldn't recognize—is a specialty of the house (you won't simply dine on seafood here, you'll do it cheek to cheek with a bustling coral reef or within the effervescent context of a New England clambake). Sampler platters include such unfamiliar cuisines as Norwegian and Moroccan. And if you're looking for some sophisticated eats, you're in luck. In response to patrons' demands for fresher, more imaginative, fare, Disney has given its chefs greater freedom. With WDW's chefs doing their own grocery shopping (more accurately, blanketing the country to find the most flavorful ingredients) and having more fun, not to mention flexibility, in the kitchen, the World's menus have closed their historic culinary gap by targeting discriminating taste buds. As an example of the quality of dining that can now be found all over Walt Disney World, consider Artist Point restaurant, which features the likes of just-hooked king salmon, creatively prepared and served with hard-to-find pinot noirs from the Pacific Northwest. But we're getting carried away and you're hungry and need to make a decision. Our "Restaurant Guide" will help; it cuts to the chase and describes the best dining opportunities for adults in the World.

Of course, you also need to be thinking about what you want to do later, so let us quickly outline the basics. For your nighttime entertainment, you won't simply find a tremendous variety of clubs; you'll find them shoulder to shoulder in a section of Downtown Disney—called Pleasure Island—that takes the hassle out of club-hopping. The place gets going early and doesn't turn into a pumpkin until 2 A.M.; dress is weekend casual.

Next door to Pleasure Island, you'll find some good excuses to stay out late in Downtown Disney West Side. This waterfront area's ultra-hip pair of hot spots provides opportunities to groove to live blues and dance to a Latin beat (complemented, if you wish, by Mississippi Delta or Cuban cuisine). Out of oomph? You may simply sit and feast on a first-run movie in the vast 24-screen theater here or an original big-top production by none other than Cirque du Soleil (an unforgettable experience).

Take a stroll along the BoardWalk and you'll stumble upon nostalgic snacks such as caramel apples and saltwater taffy, plus a brewpub with great grub, a grand old-fashioned swing hall, a lively sports bar with more TVs than Sony, and a casual sing-along spot with dueling ivory ticklers. Look around the other resorts and you'll discover hotel lounges that defy their ho-hum roots and make nightcaps an event—by evoking a locale such as Polynesia, New Orleans, or the Old West, and by specializing; there's an outstanding wine bar, a beer lover's paradise, and several enterprising lounges that offer choice microbrews.

Please, take your time, and when you're ready to think about after-dinner entertainment, know that this chapter's "Nightlife Guide" provides the complete scoop on Pleasure Island, the West Side, and BoardWalk, as well as compelling spots in the theme parks and resorts.

Bon appétit!

RESTAURANT GUIDE

The dining scene at Walt Disney World has evolved into a vast array of possibilities that span the price, cuisine, and atmosphere spectra. It stretches from the theme parks to the resorts and beyond, also encompassing Downtown Disney (the Marketplace, Pleasure Island, and the West Side). Memorable dining experiences abound for adults who prefer meals to fast-food fixes. Peruse the World menu and you'll find such diverse combos as meat loaf with a side of "Father Knows Best," tiramisu served with an aria, and a sumptuous seven-course splurge complete with harpist and Royal Doulton china.

Collectively, WDW's many eateries can satisfy most any craving. The key is to think with your stomach as you plot your days and nights at the World. Recognize Epcot's World Showcase as a gastronomic stronghold, and plan to arrive with appetite and priority seating time. Although edibles in the other theme parks tend toward fast food, Disney has taken the genre well beyond burgers, particularly in Animal Kingdom, and there's no shortage of tasty sit-downs. Note that Downtown Disney has some mouthwatering distractions—including Fulton's Crab House, Portobello Yacht Club, Planet Hollywood, and Wolfgang Puck Cafe—that you might want to figure into your meal plan. Be sure to look beyond the restaurants at your own hotel to consider mealtime pilgrimages to others, as the resorts contain some of the World's most pleasant dining rooms and most enticing menus. And don't neglect to discover the far-reaching dining frontier at the BoardWalk.

To make priority seating arrangements for WDW restaurants, dial 407-WDW-DINE (934-3463.)

We're happy to report that Walt Disney World has more tempting cuisine for the sophisticated palate than ever before, as behind-the-scenes improvements—from fresher, more flavorful ingredients to stronger wine lists—have quietly pushed the epicurean envelope. Also, healthier, more interesting grazing options in the theme parks (see our snacking suggestions in the margins of the *Theme Parks* chapter) can provide inexpensive treats that help subsidize the sit-down meals.

To ease the task of deciding among the World's innumerable eateries, we've whittled the list down to a diverse selection of full-service restaurants and more casual noshing spots that we recommend as the best adult bets. The intention is not to diminish the value of establishments not included, but to underscore the greater appeal certain restaurants hold for adults.

Fare Thee Well

This restaurant guide is not a comprehensive listing of the World's eateries, but a selective roundup of the best adult dining and snacking venues. Those restaurants designated as "Standouts" are dining rooms and fast-food places whose exceptional flair, distinctive fare, and/or terrific setting have earned our highest recommendation. "Good Bets" are additional locales that offer consistently rewarding dining experiences.

Priority Seating, Explained

A system known as priority seating takes the place of reservations for all WDW restaurants, with the exception of the dinner shows. You receive a seating time but must check in at the restaurant to become eligible for the next available table. (Our advice: Arrive 15 to 20 minutes early.)

Here's how the system works: (1) Those with priority seating will be seated at or near their assigned time, and (2) walk-ins will have a shot at any open tables. To make arrangements, call 407-WDW-DINE (939-3463) up to four months in advance. Hours are weekdays from 7 A.M. to 10 P.M. and weekends until 8 P.M. Because procedures are subject to change, it's best to confirm policies with 407-WDW-DINE.

Our dining recommendations, which touch down all over the World and provide options for all taste buds and budgets, are presented within three distinct contexts—in the theme parks, in the resorts, and elsewhere within WDW boundaries. Within each of these locales, we have roped off for extra consideration those restaurants that offer some of the most consistently rewarding dining experiences. Under the heading "Standouts," you'll find stellar places to grab a great bite on the quick, moderately priced restaurants with exceptional flair, and extra-special havens worth every hard-earned dollar for their distinctive food and setting. Under the designation "Good Bets," we've corralled additional locales, also highly regarded, that we've come to know as fine places to have a meal. Because Walt Disney World's theme parks are unique terrain calling for both firm arrangements and flexible eating plans, we have included recommendations for fast-food as well as full-service options.

Individual entries offer characterizations of each restaurant and provide such essential information as location, price, and the kind of meals served there (represented by B, L, and D for breakfast, lunch, and dinner, with S symbolizing availability of snacks). As an indication of what you can expect to spend for a meal, we have classified restaurants as very expensive (dinners $46 and up), expensive (dinners $21 to $45), moderate (dinners $10 to $20), or inexpensive (dinners under $10). The prices represent a meal (one entrée, one beverage, and either one appetizer, one side order, or one dessert) for one person not including tax or tip. As a rule, tabs for lunch are a bit lower, while those for breakfast are considerably less.

We also denote in each entry the necessity of reservations or priority seating (the system that has replaced reservations at WDW restaurants). In the adjacent margins, we explain priority seating and outline protocol for booking tables in and around the World. For the rundown on dinner shows, strategies for eating your way around the World, and the scoop on where to find an afternoon tea, dining rooms with terrific views, late-night bites, great wines by the glass, and more, check the margins. A final word of advice: You might *not* want to read this section on an empty stomach.

In the Theme Parks
Table Service

Standouts

AKERSHUS (Norway, Epcot's World Showcase): The ambience of a medieval Norwegian fortress—marked by dramatic cathedral ceilings, stone archways, and iron chandeliers—is not to be denied. Nor is the delicious novelty of the Norwegian smorgasbord served here. Known as *koldtbord* (or "cold table"), the buffet includes hot and cold selections. There's plenty for the unadventurous palate, from creamy potato salad to savory Norwegian meatballs, but don't stop there. This is your chance to sample well-prepared signature dishes that don't often leave Scandinavia; there's smoked mackerel, herring prepared every which way, mashed rutabagas (don't wince; they're good), and a whole lot more. It all washes down quite nicely with a tall draft of Ringnes beer. Wine selection is limited. Priority seating suggested. Moderate to expensive. L, D.

BISTRO DE PARIS (France, Epcot's World Showcase): An intimate bistro that puts on romantic airs rather than the usual bustle. If you think the elegant decor, with its evocative interplay of brass sconces, milk-glass chandeliers, mirrors, and leaded glass, is convincingly French, wait until you swallow your first morsel. The menu is executed with a rich authenticity that will astonish any unsuspecting gourmand. This is hearty dining, so you might want to take a stroll around the promenade to walk off your escargots, rack of lamb, and chocolate soufflé. The impressive wine list is *très* French. Priority seating suggested. Expensive to very expensive. D.

How to Book a Table

■ **IN THE THEME PARKS:** Priority seating is suggested for nearly all table-service restaurants in the theme parks; simply call 407-WDW-DINE (939-3463). For same-day arrangements in the Magic Kingdom, report to City Hall; in Epcot, head to Innoventions Plaza; in the Disney-MGM Studios, go to the corner of Hollywood and Sunset; in Animal Kingdom, ask at Guest Relations in The Oasis (go to Rainforest Cafe for a table at the restaurant itself). Same-day plans can also be made at all park restaurants or by dialing *88 from a pay phone within a theme park.

■ **IN WDW RESORTS:** Priority seating for Disney resort restaurants may be made by calling 407-WDW-DINE or by dialing *55 on any house phone. For reservations at any of the full-service eateries at the Swan, call 407-934-1609; for the Dolphin, call 407-934-4889.

■ **ELSEWHERE AT WDW:** Any necessary reservations or priority seating arrangements at Downtown Disney and the resorts on Hotel Plaza Boulevard may be made using the number provided in the restaurant entry.

Smoker's Alert

With the exception of specifically designated areas, all public parts of the theme parks and WDW-owned resorts are now strictly nonsmoking. Tobacco products are no longer sold in the parks. However, smokers may still find refuge in some Swan, Dolphin, Board-Walk, and Downtown Disney eateries.

CRYSTAL PALACE (Main Street, Magic Kingdom): A landmark of sorts, this restaurant—our favorite in the Magic Kingdom—could be a Victorian garden if not for the existence of walls and a ceiling. The airy atmosphere provides a pleasant escape from the crowds on Main Street and the all-you-can-eat buffet is easily the most bountiful spread of any meal in the park. It's driven by fresh produce, including a salad bar (with peel-and-eat shrimp) and pasta selections for lunch, and adds carved meats, fish, and creative sides for dinner. Friends from the Hundred Acre Wood wander about during all meals. It's the ever-changing inventive fare that makes Crystal Palace perhaps the best spot for adults to dine in the company of characters. Priority seating suggested. Moderate to expensive. B, L, D.

50'S PRIME TIME CAFE (Disney-MGM Studios): In a word: *cool*. This good-humored retreat to the era of *I Love Lucy* is an amusing amalgam of comfort food, kitschy 1950s-style kitchen nooks, and attentive servers of the "No talking with your mouth full" ilk. Expect Mom or her favored offspring to meddle in your affairs here ("Did you wash your hands? All right, then; what color was the soap?"). And recognize that the best fun is had by doing some regressing of your own. One Prime Time regular we know—a troublemaker appropriately in his mid-fifties—has gotten major entertainment mileage from such lines as "Mom, she

says I'm a tattletale!" and "Mom, can I sleep over at Suzy's house? Her parents aren't home and she's afraid to be alone." As for the fare, it's tasty home cooking as it used to be (heavy on the meat and potatoes), served forth in generous-to-the-point-of-grandmotherly portions. Most guests find that it honors their memory of fried chicken, meat loaf, s'mores, and root beer floats. A full bar is available. Priority seating suggested. Moderate to expensive. L, D.

GARDEN GRILL (The Land, Future World): When your assigned priority seating time comes due at this lazy Susan-turned-dining area (it rotates slowly above the rain forest, desert, and prairie scenes visited by the Living with the Land boat ride below), you are politely informed by a "farmhand" that you have some chores to do. Bessie has been milked, apparently, but the table hasn't been set. And so it is that you are seated, only to have to stand and harvest your place setting from the center of the table. As the meal and the setting progress, you steal through a squawking rain forest, observe a strong wind kicking up desert sand, watch buffalo graze on a prairie, and visit a farmhouse (request a table on the lower tier for the best view). Mickey and pals make rounds at each meal. The full country breakfast is served family-style, as are lunch and dinner, which feature vegetables grown in The Land's greenhouses, fried fish, rotisserie chicken, and grilled flank steak. Save room for the warm apple crisp. When all's said and done, you're glad you did your chores. Priority seating suggested. Moderate to expensive. B, L, D.

HOLLYWOOD BROWN DERBY (Disney-MGM Studios): The Studios' most gracious dining is found at this faithful revival of the original cause célèbre, which opened on Hollywood and Vine back in 1926. Dressed to the nines in chandeliers and celebrity caricatures, the restaurant stokes the appetite with its finely chopped signature Cobb salad and fabulous grapefruit cake. The California wine list is excellent. Priority seating is suggested. Expensive. L, D.
   Note: Guests who make dining arrangements at their Disney resort or at any of the parks can take advantage of the Fantasmic! Dining Opportunity. Special seating for the evening's performance of Fantasmic! is included with the meal at no additional cost. (The Fantasmic! Dining Opportunity cannot be booked through WDW-DINE, but can be reserved in person up to seven days ahead.)

LES CHEFS DE FRANCE (France, Epcot's World Showcase): "Bright lights, big dining room" describes this airy restaurant. With three of France's best chefs—Paul Bocuse, Roger Vergé, and pastry guru Gaston Lenôtre—keeping tabs on

---

Special Dietary Requests

Walt Disney World restaurants can accommodate special dietary requirements (vegetarian, low-sodium, lactose-free, and kosher meals, for example) if requests are made at least 24 hours in advance. Make your personal needs known when you make your priority seating arrangements by calling 407-WDW-DINE (939-3463).

Secrets to Success

Hungry and in no mood to wait in line? To avoid the inevitable crunch, plan to eat an early (or late) meal. Restaurants that offer table service are usually less crowded at lunch than at dinner, so you might want to make lunch the main meal of the day. But if it's a dinner spot you relish, choose a restaurant where priority seating is available (see page 189 for details on making these arrangements). Also, be on the watch for discounted early-bird specials, which arise on occasion from 4:30 P.M. until 6 P.M.

this nouvelle French kitchen, the broth is far from spoiled. We love the mere thought of their Lyons-style onion soup and the luscious ways in which they fill a puff pastry. Wine pairings are suggested from the modest list. Priority seating strongly suggested. Expensive. L, D.

L'ORIGINALE ALFREDO DI ROMA RISTORANTE (Italy, Epcot's World Showcase): Adorned with massive murals that evoke the Italian countryside, this restaurant inspires a "when in Rome" frame of mind from the outset. You suddenly hear an Italian grandmother's voice in your head, urging you to "eat, eat." But do you go with the specialty of the house, fettuccine Alfredo? Perhaps the veal parmigiana? Or maybe lasagna is more to your liking? It's hard to go wrong at Alfredo's, as fresh pasta is made right on the premises and fine Italian wines are in ready supply; of course, you could blow it and neglect to save room for dessert. This restaurant is a favorite, also, for its atmosphere, which is at once romantic and festive. Between arias, roving Italian singers have been known to choreograph a napkin-twirling tarantella. Priority seating suggested. Expensive. L, D.

Good Bets

BIERGARTEN (Germany, Epcot's World Showcase): Prepare for the best of the wurst. A buffet of traditional German cuisine (don't miss the red cabbage, spaetzle, or sauerbraten) is the main attraction in this charming makeshift courtyard. Adding to the fun are long communal tables, 33-ounce steins of Beck's beer, and a selection of German wines and liqueurs. Follow it up with homemade apple strudel. Priority seating strongly suggested. Moderate to expensive. L, D.

CINDERELLA'S ROYAL TABLE (Cinderella Castle, Magic Kingdom): The grand medieval setting provides a suitable backdrop for the equally grand American fare. Roast prime rib ("king" or "queen" cut, as you wish), herbed-chicken, and spice-crusted salmon are just a few of the castle specialties. We're never sure if it's the stained glass windows, the majestic blue goblets, or the *milady* and *milord* salutations from our waiter that make us feel like queen and king for a day (or at least a meal). But long live the royal treatment. Priority seating strongly suggested for all meals, especially the daily character breakfast. Expensive. B, L, D.

CORAL REEF (The Living Seas, Future World): It's all about sneaking bites of fresh fish under the watchful eyes of sea turtles, dolphins, and gargantuan groupers. Every table in the dining room has a panoramic view of the living coral reef; some are right up against the glass. Menu items run the gamut from traditional seafood dishes such as broiled salmon to more outrageous entrées like grilled alligator sausage (yes, *really*). Tender filet mignon and pan-seared chicken breast are also on the menu for those members of your group who are satisfied simply *watching* the fish. Priority seating suggested. Expensive. L, D.

HOLLYWOOD & VINE (Disney-MGM Studios): An Art Deco-style restaurant with Tinseltown flourishes, this entertaining character-hosted buffet offers a grand breakfast spread complete with eggs, french toast, and frittatas. Highlights from the luncheon buffet include grilled flank steak, pasta in a pesto sauce, and a self-serve ice cream bar. Beer and wine are served at an additional cost. Expensive. B, L.

LE CELLIER STEAKHOUSE (Canada, Epcot's World Showcase): We love retreating to this peaceful wine cellar-like spot, a favorite place for a hearty yet reasonably priced meal. An updated menu features such savory additions as stuffed filet, T-bone, and New York strip steaks. Grilled vegetarian napoleon and Canadian cheddar cheese soup round out the options. Then there's potential for maple-Butterfinger crème brûlée. Microbrews from Quebec and Canadian lagers are served. Priority seating suggested. Moderate. L, D.

MAMA MELROSE'S RISTORANTE ITALIANO (Disney-MGM Studios): A pleasantly removed bastion of movie star photographs and thin-crust pizzas. The menu highlights Italian favorites, such as linguini with clams, and meats cooked over an oak-burning oven. The wine list includes selections from California and Italy. Priority seating suggested. Moderate to expensive. L, D.

Note: Guests who make dining arrangements at their Disney resort or at any of the parks can take advantage of the Fantasmic! Dining Opportunity. Special seating for the evening's performance of Fantasmic! is included with the meal at no additional cost. (The Fantasmic! Dining Opportunity cannot be booked through WDW-DINE, but can be reserved in person up to seven days ahead.)

Cheap Eats

Our suggestions for spur-of-the-moment fast food:

- **ABC Commissary** (Disney-MGM Studios)
- **Columbia Harbour House** (Liberty Square, Magic Kingdom)
- **Pecos Bill Cafe** (Frontierland, Magic Kingdom)
- **Sunshine Season Food Fair** (The Land, Epcot's Future World)
- **Tusker House** (Africa, Animal Kingdom)
- **Wolfgang Puck Express** (Downtown Disney West Side)

Grape Expectations

Grown-ups who are surprised by the fine dining (and snacking) all over the World will be absolutely delighted by the selection of wines to accompany their food. From the pavilions of World Showcase to the lounges and restaurants of the WDW resorts, here are our favorite ways to sample the fruit of the vine.

■ La Maison du Vin (France, Epcot's World Showcase): Tastings and sales from the country synonymous with wine. A chance to sample top-quality vintages before you buy a whole bottle.

■ Weinkeller (Germany, Epcot's World Showcase): Daily tastings from the shop's 54 varieties. Don't miss the rich, flowery dessert wines, gloriously sweet (and not inexpensive).

•CONTINUED ON NEXT PAGE

MARRAKESH (Morocco, Epcot's World Showcase): It's not every day that you can slip into an exquisitely tiled Moroccan palace and expect to be entertained by belly dancers and musicians as you polish off a sampler plate of distinctive Moroccan cuisine, such as couscous or kebobs. The volume of the music here can be a drawback. Priority seating suggested. Expensive. D.

THE PLAZA (Main Street, Magic Kingdom): Frozen desserts outnumber the fine burgers and sandwiches on the menu in this charming spot. Consider this ratio a gigantic hint to rope off some stomach space for one of the enormous sundaes or floats. Priority seating suggested. Moderate. L, D, S.

RAINFOREST CAFE (Animal Kingdom and Downtown Disney Marketplace): The inside of this place is as lush (and loud) as a jungle, thick with tropical vegetation and fish-filled aquariums. Dishes answer to names like Mgambo (pasta with shrimp), Plant Sandwich (veggies), and Mojo Bones (barbecued ribs). Appetizers and desserts can easily be shared, but you might not want to. Priority seating strongly suggested (available 30 days ahead for breakfast; four months prior for lunch and dinner). Moderate to expensive. B, L, D, S.

ROSE & CROWN PUB AND DINING ROOM (United Kingdom, Epcot's World Showcase): The menu ventures only a tad beyond fish-and-chips, but outdoor tables offer a front-row view of the fireworks over the lagoon, and the pub's downright neighborly. Priority seating suggested. Expensive. L, D, S.

SAN ANGEL INN (Mexico, Epcot's World Showcase): The lights are low, the mood is romantic, and there is a smoking volcano poised almost tableside. If that's not enchantment enough, there's a mystical pyramid and a moonlit river. The menu? You may need to bring the table candle closer to read it, but you'll find Mexican fare from margaritas to chicken mole. Priority seating suggested. Expensive. L, D.

SCI-FI DINE-IN THEATER (Disney-MGM Studios): The huge salads, sandwiches, and desserts here are more creative than at your average drive-in, but the food still takes a backseat to the campy setting. As the parking attendant leads you to your car (the tables resemble 1950s-era convertibles), she reminds you of some drive-in

etiquette ("The speed limit is 5 miles per hour," "Dim your lights and watch for on-coming traffic"). Science fiction and horror trailers play on a large screen. Wine and beer are available. Priority seating suggested. Moderate to expensive. L, D.

TEPPANYAKI DINING ROOMS (Japan, Epcot's World Showcase): It's not exactly an authentic dose of Japanese cuisine (Tempura Kiku next door gives a closer approximation with its sushi, sashimi, and tempura), but it offers a great time and a terrific meal. Guests sit around a large teppan grill and watch as a nimble, white-hatted chef deftly demonstrates just how quickly enough chicken, beef, seafood, and vegetables to feed eight people can be chopped, seasoned, and stir-fried (knives fly at speeds that could dust a food processor). Entrées are sizzling and flavorful. Because smaller parties are seated together, Teppanyaki becomes a social affair, and it's a fine place for outgoing singles. Priority seating suggested. Expensive. L, D.

Fast Food

Standouts

BACKLOT EXPRESS (Disney-MGM Studios): Shady and inconspicuous (it's tucked away by the Indiana Jones Epic Stunt Spectacular theater), this is a sprawling spot with both indoor and outdoor seating and unusual potential for quiet. Paint-speckled floors and assorted auto debris give you an idea of the

•*CONTINUED FROM PREVIOUS PAGE*

■ Artist Point (Wilderness Lodge): Want to know why pinot noir and grilled salmon are a match made in heaven? Here's where to find out.

■ California Grill (Contemporary): The list has great depth and breadth, with all of the restaurant's many California wines available by the glass; the possibilities change daily to complement new dishes.

■ Cítricos (Grand Floridian): An ample selection of international wines marries nicely with cuisine from the south of France—especially with the $22 three-course pairings.

■ Martha's Vineyard (Beach Club): Samples from this lounge's savvy list of vintages are a delicious way to explore wine regions from across the country.

■ Victoria & Albert's (Grand Floridian): The World's most upscale dining room boasts a grand wine list. For $35 or $40, you can get four glasses of wine chosen to complement individual courses on the prix fixe menu.

S.O.S. for the Sweet Tooth

The following theme park spots are sure to satisfy:

Boulangerie Pâtisserie (France, Epcot's World Showcase)

Fountain View Espresso and Bakery (Future World, Epcot)

Kringla Bakeri og Kafe (Norway, Epcot's World Showcase)

Kusafiri Coffee Shop & Bakery (Africa, Animal Kingdom)

Main Street Bake Shop (Main Street, Magic Kingdom)

Main Street Confectionery (Main Street, Magic Kingdom)

Sleepy Hollow (Liberty Square, Magic Kingdom)

Starring Rolls Bakery (Disney-MGM Studios)

Süssigkeiten (Germany, Epcot's World Showcase)

decor. Chicken Caesar salads, grilled chicken sandwiches, chili, and brownies are among the more tempting fare. Beer is available. Inexpensive. L, D, S.

BOULANGERIE PATISSERIE (France, Epcot's World Showcase): The chocolate croissants, blueberry tarts, apple turnovers, and such are timeless. Follow your nose, and don't neglect to notice the sweet temptation aptly known as the Marvelous. Kronenbourg beer and French wines are also offered. Inexpensive. S.

CANTINA DE SAN ANGEL (Mexico, Epcot's World Showcase): Forget for a moment the *churros*, the frozen margaritas, and the Dos Equis drafts: this place has south-of-the-border charm. When the weather cooperates, the outdoor lagoonside seating makes the experience even better. Inexpensive. L, D, S.

COLUMBIA HARBOUR HOUSE (Liberty Square, Magic Kingdom): This spot distinguishes itself from the rest of the fast-food crowd by emphasizing things from the sea—among them, clam chowder, fried fish, and harpoons (which are strictly for decor). The apple pie is not to be missed. Bypass the tables in the main room for one of the quiet nooks upstairs. Inexpensive. L, D, S.

FOUNTAIN VIEW ESPRESSO AND BAKERY (Innoventions Plaza, Future World): This ode to pastries and specialty coffees is a veritable oasis any time of day. Wine and beer are also available. Inexpensive. B, S.

KRINGLA BAKERI OG KAFE (Norway, Epcot's World Showcase): Simply a super place for a sweet fix or a light lunch. Among the tasty morsels here are open-face sandwiches (roast beef, turkey, and salmon), sweet pretzels called *kringles*, and *vaflers* (heart-shaped waffles freshly made as you wait and topped with powdered sugar and preserves). Ringnes beer is on tap. The outdoor seating area is shaded by a grass-thatched roof. Inexpensive. L, D, S.

MAIN STREET BAKE SHOP (Main Street, Magic Kingdom): This dainty spot is renowned for quick breakfasts (from bagels to warm cinnamon rolls) and enormous fresh-from-the-oven cookies (we love the chocolate chip). The ice cream cookie sandwiches make good use of flavors from the Plaza Ice Cream Parlor next door. Inexpensive. B, S.

SOMMERFEST (Germany, Epcot's World Showcase): Here, quick sustenance takes such classic forms as bratwurst, soft pretzels, Black Forest cake, German chocolates, Beck's beer, and German wine. The nicely shaded outdoor seating area sports a festive mural. Inexpensive. L, D, S.

STARRING ROLLS BAKERY (Disney-MGM Studios): Have croissant and cappuccino, will travel. This is the place in the Studios to get the day off to a sweet start or to take an impromptu cookie or coffee break under umbrella-shaded tables. Inexpensive. B, L, S.

SUNSHINE SEASON FOOD FAIR (The Land, Future World): This bumper crop of food stands, located directly beneath the hot-air balloons on the pavilion's lower level, is the best place in Epcot to strap on the ol' feed bag and graze. It's a finicky eater indeed who can't find temptation among this court's count-less offerings. For dining on the lighter side, select from fresh salads, soups, and handsomely garnished baked potatoes. Heartier fare comes in the form of pastas, sandwiches, and barbecued pork. Baked goods, ice cream, and refresh-ing libations round out the options. The eating's significantly more peaceful here outside prime dining hours. Inexpensive. B, L, D, S.

TUSKER HOUSE (Africa, Animal Kingdom): Wild elephants, or at least gazelles, couldn't keep us away from this, the park's most civilized grazing option. Consider fried or rotisserie chicken, beef stew, turkey sandwiches, and grilled chicken salad in a bread bowl, and you may wish your safari vest came with Tupperware attachments. We dig the carved chairs inside, but somehow the Safari Amber beer tastes better out under the thatched roof. Inexpensive. L, D, S.

Good Bets

COSMIC RAY'S STARLIGHT CAFE (Tomorrowland, Magic Kingdom): A one-size-fits-all establishment that's a choice spot to get fast food in the Magic Kingdom for two reasons: variety and elbow room. Burgers, salads, and rotis-serie chicken all have a place on the menu. Inexpensive. L, D, S.

No Priority Seating?

If you're caught without priority seating arrangements in the theme parks, you can sometimes snag a table at one of these recommended full-service eateries (if you're willing to wait a bit):

- **Hollywood Brown Derby** (Disney-MGM Studios)
- **Le Cellier Steakhouse** (Canada, Epcot's World Showcase)
- **The Plaza** (Main Street, Magic Kingdom)
- **Rainforest Cafe** (Animal Kingdom)

Coffee Couture

For java as main course (or cause), skip the usual cup o' automatic drip and head to one of these fine coffee houses—they know double lattes from skim mocha cappuccinos. Sometimes aroma *is* atmosphere.

■ **Sleepy Hollow** (Liberty Square, Magic Kingdom)

■ **Fountain View Espresso and Bakery** (Future World, Epcot)

■ **Starring Rolls Bakery** (Disney-MGM Studios)

■ **Kusafiri Coffee Shop & Bakery** (Africa, Animal Kingdom)

■ **Forty Thirst Street** (Downtown Disney West Side)

■ **Ghirardelli Soda Fountain and Chocolate Shop** (Downtown Disney Marketplace)

FLAME TREE BARBECUE (Safari Village, Animal Kingdom): Take a good gander and you'll sight fingers being licked about as far as the eye can see at the pleasant riverfront tables bounding this pulled-pork and barbecued-brisket hut. Don't miss the self-serve barbecue-sauce stations. Inexpensive. L, D, S.

LOTUS BLOSSOM CAFE (China, Epcot's World Showcase): The menu's on the short side, but what's here—basic Chinese takeout—is a good call when hunger strikes and you're in the neighborhood. Outdoor tables line the sidewalks. Inexpensive. L, D.

PIZZAFARI (Safari Village, Animal Kingdom): When the name of the craving is a perfectly unaffected individual pizza, consider a spot that still prefers pepperoni to funky nouveau toppings. The menu does stray a bit more than the average pizza place (grilled chicken Caesar salad), but we like to stick to the basics. Spin on your heels for a stationary safari featuring this satisfying den's muraled menagerie. Inexpensive. L, D, S.

PLAZA ICE CREAM PARLOR (Main Street, Magic Kingdom): Simply the park's most bountiful stash of ice cream. Head here when you want a choice of flavors. Inexpensive. S.

PURE AND SIMPLE (Wonders of Life, Future World): The place merits attention by offering healthy pickings like fruit smoothies, fruit-topped multigrain waffles, vegetable pizzas, tuna pitas with reduced-calorie mayonnaise, and papaya juice. Inexpensive. B, L, S.

YAKITORI HOUSE (Japan, Epcot's World Showcase): This pleasant spot (named for the specialty of the house, savory skewered chicken) is one of the most relaxing settings in all of Epcot for a quick and satisfying bite. Sake and Kirin beer are available. Inexpensive. L, D, S.

In the Resorts

Standouts

ARTIST POINT (Wilderness Lodge): The Pacific Northwest theme of this restaurant is beautifully announced in two-story-high landscape murals, while tall red-framed windows look out to Bay Lake. Artist Point's hallmark is its knack for translating fresh seasonal ingredients from the Pacific Northwest into flavorful creations. An excellent example is the wild king salmon marinated in maple whiskey, then roasted with apples and herbs and served on a smoking cedar plank, accompanied by winter squash. The desserts are so heavenly that you should make room no matter how full you think you are. It's just the fork-licking finale you'd expect from a restaurant of this caliber. The wine list features some of the best pinot noirs coming out of Washington and Oregon right now. The cumulative effect is an artist's palette for the sophisticated palate. Priority seating suggested for breakfast (a character affair) and for dinner. Expensive. B, D.

BIG RIVER GRILLE & BREWING WORKS (BoardWalk): A standout for its fresh-brewed ales alone, this unassuming place delivers huge portions of satisfying pub grub. The straightforward please-all menu runs from burgers and steaks to lobster pot pie and yellowfin tuna. The kitchen takes full advantage of the ready availability of great beer for its sauces, and, yes, that Rocket Red Ale Chicken is as good as it sounds. The small partitioned dining area somehow possesses a cozy air in spite of the factory motif. This restaurant tends to be more low-key than the other BoardWalk eateries, and makes for a peaceful retreat during the day. Seating is available outside on the boardwalk. First-come seating. Moderate. L, D, S.

BONFAMILLE'S CAFE (Port Orleans): This restaurant offers an absolutely endearing introduction to Creole cooking in a casual courtyard setting that neatly evokes New Orleans' French Quarter. Bonfamille's was inspired by a tale of a matriarch, Memere, who conjured up this advice for all who dine here: "Loosen up your belt and enjoy what you've put past your tongue," which is all the more relevant after you've experienced the generous portions served here. Try the jambalaya or seafood etouffée with a bottle of Dixie Blackened Voodoo Lager. Priority seating available for dinner. Moderate. B, D.

The Inside Scoop

Hungry enough to eat Everything but the Kitchen Sink? That's what you'll get in this aptly named colossal sundae, served at Beaches & Cream Soda Shop in the Yacht and Beach Club. Expect eight scoops of ice cream smothered in every topping conceivable.

Runnin' On Empty

Chefs at the California Grill use ingredients so fresh that there's hardly a thing in the restaurant's freezer. Except ice cream.

CALIFORNIA GRILL (Contemporary): The fresh seasonal ingredients credo gets an artistic interpretation at this casual feast for the eyes (and stomach) on the Contemporary's 15th floor. Chefs at this acclaimed restaurant keep no culinary secrets as they prepare dishes in the exhibition kitchen. The West Coast theme shines through in such market-fresh dishes as alderwood-smoked salmon with whole roasted onions, and grilled-pork tenderloin with balsamic vinegar-smothered mushrooms and polenta. If there's a bit of a din in the dining room, it's partly because of unsuppressible raves and the waitstaff's collective ability to elaborate on any dish, ingredient, or wine. The star-studded wine list, ranging from traditional chardonnays to new-wave viogniers, is a striking mix of greatest hits and good finds, all available by the glass. Also drawing a crowd: the Grill's divine California-style pizza, fine sushi bar, and a host of vegetarian choices. Home-baked desserts along the lines of butterscotch crème brûlée provide the finishing touches, as do sweeping views of the Magic Kingdom. Priority seating strongly suggested. Expensive. D.

CAPE MAY CAFE (Beach Club): The all-you-can-eat New England-style clambake held nightly in this whimsical, beach-umbrella-decked dining area is among the best values at Walt Disney World. The groaning board includes mussels, fish, clams, oysters, peel-and-eat shrimp, corn-on-the-cob, ribs, red-skin potatoes, chowders, and salads. Lobster is available for an extra charge. If you like, dessert can be milk and chocolate chip cookies. Priority seating suggested for breakfast (served with a side of characters) and for dinner. Moderate to expensive. B, D.

CITRICOS (Grand Floridian): The sun-drenched disposition of this gastronomic breath of fresh air is probably to be expected. From the aromas wafting from the open kitchen, it's clear that the chef has vowed to wow you with cuisine from the south of France herb by fragrant herb. Even if the kitchen were sealed off from view and scent and there were no pastry chefs at work in the dining room, no loaves of bread baking, no private party room or artful wine pairings or potential for a plate of lobster crepes stuffed with parsnips and served with vanilla sauce, we'd still . . . Strike that. There's no changing the essence of Cítricos. Priority seating suggested. Expensive to very expensive. D.

FLYING FISH CAFE (BoardWalk): Expect an earful when you ask about the catch of the day at this compelling eatery bound and determined to serve seafood "so fresh it has an attitude." Fun, sophisticated decor from the designer of the Contemporary's California Grill elevates the appeal. As an example of the (exhibitionist) kitchen's knack for light, creatively prepared dishes, consider barbecue-glazed salmon with sweet-corn pudding and potato-wrapped yellowtail snapper. The menu items vary daily, but steaks and vegetarian choices are usually offered. And whatever you do, make sure you save room for the Chocolate Lava Cake, a concoction so delicious it was voted Best Dessert in Central Florida by at least one restaurant critic. Priority seating suggested. Expensive. D.

NARCOOSSEE'S (Grand Floridian): Within the conspicuous octagonal building that looks out over Seven Seas Lagoon, you'll find a casual restaurant whose open kitchen presents such not-so-casual fare as filet mignon and garlic stuffed Maine lobster. Yet on the recently revised seasonal menu, you may also discover luscious wild salmon, lamb chops with garlic mashed potatoes, and penne pasta with sautéed vegetables. Although this is not your secluded romantic retreat (children are not scarce), the food is excellent, and the international wine selection is quite good—you might enjoy a pre-dinner glass on the veranda. Priority seating suggested. Expensive. D.

OLIVIA'S CAFE (Old Key West): We like the Key Western manner with which Olivia's approaches its theme; certainly, the enthusiastically laid-back setting and menu convey the spirit of the leisure-centric locale. Oh, there are menu selections that work the theme hard—salads with Key lime-honey Dijon dressing, conch chowder, and Key Lime Kooler, a creamy blend of rum and Key lime juice—but there are just as many offered strictly for fun. Cases in point: pan-seared beef tenderloin in lobster bourbon sauce, shrimp fritters with roast-pepper puree, and black-bottom pie. Wine, beer, and specialty drinks are served. On Monday, Wednesday, and Sunday, breakfast comes with characters. Menu changes seasonally. Priority seating suggested. Moderate. B, L, D.

VICTORIA & ALBERT'S (Grand Floridian): Indulgent without being too haute to handle and stunningly luxurious without being pretentious, this grande dame of the Walt Disney World dining scene is in a class all its own. Elegant touches include Royal Doulton china, Sambonet silver, and Schott-Zweisel crystal. The

Cook Nook

You're on vacation from cooking, but you still might relish some time in the kitchen. No stirring, roasting, or chopping is required. Victoria & Albert's Chef's Table in the Grand Floridian lets you chat up the masters in the kitchen as they prepare culinary delights. To book this aromatic roost, call 407-WDW-DINE six months in advance. The Chef's Table costs $115 per person (plus tax). The meal with wine pairings is $160 per person.

Two for Tea

Teatime with all the trimmings—scones, dainty sandwiches, and pastries served on bone china—is 2 P.M. in the Garden View lounge at the Grand Floridian. An extensive selection of teas and tasty accompaniments are offered every day until 6 P.M. (first-come seating).

seven-course prix fixe menu changes daily, always offering an array of fish, poultry, beef, veal, and lamb selections as well as a choice of soups, salads, and desserts. The delectable $85-per-person adventure begins with the arrival of hors d'oeuvres. As an example of what could follow, consider Oriental shrimp dumplings, chicken consommé with pheasant breast, poached Maine lobster with passion fruit butter, mixed field greens with raspberry-pinot noir vinaigrette, and a dark chocolate and strawberry soufflé. Perfect portions keep it all surprisingly manageable. The beautifully appointed room is well designed for intimate dining. The strains of a harp or violin provide a romantic backdrop. The wine list is encyclopedic, and the wine pairings (you'll pay about $35 or $40 more for four selected glasses) provide fitting complements. At the end of the meal, you're presented with a souvenir menu and a red rose. In sum, an extremely expensive, extremely special experience. Did we mention that every host and hostess at the restaurant is named Victoria or Albert? Jackets are required for men. Priority seating necessary. Very expensive. D.

YACHTSMAN STEAKHOUSE (Yacht Club): Our stomachs couldn't possibly be as big as our eyes at this carnivore's paradise, where on at least one occasion a server has kindly saved us from ourselves. The generous portions begin with truly massive rolls and continue with the imperative spicy fried onion skillet and the Yukon Gold mashed potatoes; of course, there's no skimping on the excellent and expertly prepared aged beef entrées (prime rib, filet mignon, and chateaubriand, to name a few), so good luck finding room for a piece of tiramisu or Jack Daniels' cake. While the menu emphasizes steak, it also includes seafood and chicken dishes. This atmospheric restaurant is possessed of country club elegance and is filled with intimate dining nooks perfectly suited for special occasions. Priority seating suggested. Expensive. D.

Good Bets

BEACHES & CREAM SODA SHOP (Yacht and Beach Club): Every inch a classic soda fountain, it's the site for egg creams, malts, milk shakes, and hand-dipped ice cream and frozen yogurt, plus burgers and sandwiches. Continental breakfast is also offered. First-come seating. Inexpensive to moderate. B, L, D, S.

BOATWRIGHT'S DINING HALL (Dixie Landings): Reasonably priced Cajun specialties are the draw at this unique eatery, where the centerpiece is a riverboat under construction, boat-making tools are mounted on the walls, and tables are set with condiment-filled toolboxes. Try the baby-back ribs and Cajun dirty rice. Full bar. Priority seating available. Moderate to expensive. B, D.

CONCOURSE STEAKHOUSE (Contemporary): If filet mignon stuffed with wild mushrooms speaks to you or you'd like to sample some of the best mashed potatoes in the World or you just want a quick, civilized bite one step removed from the Magic Kingdom, here you have it. Individual pizzas and salads are a good bet for lunch. Priority seating suggested. Expensive. B, L, D.

GRAND FLORIDIAN CAFE (Grand Floridian): Tall, wall-length windows incorporate the hotel's central courtyard into this inviting restaurant's potted-palm greenery. It's a pleasant spot morning, afternoon, and evening, and a reasonably priced way to check out the World's poshest resort. The cafe's tasty seasonal dishes have a southern flavor, and the menu includes many light selections. Try the citrus french toast with cinnamon, the crab cakes with Key lime remoulade, or the roast mango chicken. Excellent wine selection. Priority seating available. Expensive. B, L, D.

Walt Disney World Microbrews

- Safari Amber at Animal Kingdom (African lounge and most restaurants)
- Lodge House Brew at Territory lounge (Wilderness Lodge)
- Fulton's Honey Wheat Lager (Fulton's Crab House)
- Flying Fish Brewing Co.'s Extra Pale Ale and Extra Special Bitters at Flying Fish Cafe (BoardWalk)
- Three house ales—Wowzer's Wheat, Tilt Pale Ale, Rocket Red—and two ever-changing specialty brews handcrafted at Big River Grille & Brewing Works (BoardWalk)

We (Almost) Never Close

The following hotel eateries offer limited menus 24 hours a day during busy seasons (hours are subject to change):

Captain Cook's Snack Company
(Polynesian)

Gasparilla Grill & Games
(Grand Floridian)

Food and Fun Center
(Contemporary)

Tubbi's
(Dolphin)

Watercress Pastry Shop
(Wyndham Palace)

B-Line Diner
(Peabody Orlando)

JUAN & ONLY'S (Dolphin; 407-934-1609): It'll cost you a few pesos, but for generous portions of exceptional Southwestern fare, head for this colorful spot. Whether you take a white-corn tortilla chip to the Seven Sins Dip is up to you. There's *cerveza*, margaritas, and both red and blond sangria by the pitcher, and the bar stocks rare tequilas. Reservations suggested. Expensive. D.

KIMONOS (Swan; 407-934-1609): This is the place for good sushi (prepared as you watch) and tempura in a peaceful lounge styled with bamboo and kimono accents. A respectable wine selection is complemented by sake, Japanese beers, and specialty cocktails. The calm is occasionally interrupted by karaoke. Smoking is permitted. Reservations accepted. Moderate to expensive. D, S.

'OHANA (Polynesian): The beauty of this family-style dining experience—a South Pacific feast prepared in the restaurant's prominent open-fire cooking pit—is that the hickory-grilled skewers of turkey, pork, shrimp, chicken, and beef just keep coming. Lo mein noodles, rice, and dumplings are among the accompaniments, and the fresh pineapple dipped in caramel sauce is a fine dessert (or try the passion fruit crème brûlée from the à la carte menu). To make the most of 'Ohana's romantic setting, which features exotic wood carvings under a vast thatched roof, request a table that's right up against the windows overlooking Seven Seas Lagoon. This puts you a comfortable distance from the sweltering grill and the route where the exuberant children's coconut-rolling contest is held, but still in prime position to be serenaded by traditional Polynesian songs. Breakfast is a character affair. Priority seating suggested. Expensive. B, D.

PALIO (Swan; 407-934-1609): A spirited Italian trattoria that's a trusty source for imaginatively prepared homemade pasta, tasty pizza baked in wood-fired ovens, and traditional veal and seafood dishes. Beers and Italian wines are also served. Reservations suggested. Expensive. D.

WHISPERING CANYON CAFE (Wilderness Lodge): For savory eating that does not stop until you say "when," consider this family-style restaurant a good (if rowdy) candidate. At dinner, apple-rosemary rotisserie chicken, barbecued pork spareribs, and smoked barbecued beef brisket are sure to satisfy. Homemade desserts come with an extra charge. The waitstaff is as engaging as the menu. (Breakfast, lunch, and dinner selections are also available à la carte.) Priority seating suggested. Expensive. B, L, D.

Other World Options

Standouts

FULTON'S CRAB HOUSE (between Pleasure Island and Downtown Disney Marketplace; 407-934-2628): Walk the gangplank onto this would-be riverboat (formerly the *Empress Lilly*) and with one glance around you're prepared to book passage. Still, the polished woods, brass detailing, and nautical nostalgia of the restaurant are secondary to the impressively fresh seafood served therein. The extensive dinner menu changes with the day's arrivals. Suffice it to say that it's not unusual for Hawaiian albacore tuna (accompanied by, say, crab bordelaise and corn-whipped potatoes) to be spotted next to Great Lakes walleye pike (with garlic chips and herb rice). Standbys include Dungeness crab cakes; cioppino, a San Francisco-style stew with seafood galore in a tomato broth; garlic chicken; crab and lobster platters; and filet mignon. For a quicker fix, the ravishing raw bar at the adjoining Stone Crab lounge suits; for a reasonably priced lunch, it's lounge or bust. Operated by Levy Restaurants of Chicago. Priority seating suggested for dinner. Very expensive. B, L, D, S.

HOUSE OF BLUES (Downtown Disney West Side; 407-934-2583): An eclectic menu with New Orleans taste buds (think étouffée, jambalaya, barbecue, and crispy catfish nuggets) distinguishes this folk art-studded restaurant, attached at the hip, to the club also part-owned by Dan Aykroyd. It's a great spot for a late-night bite (try the Mississippi Cat Bites with Cajun tartar sauce or the surprisingly tasty brick-oven pizzas). Air-conditioning phobes will enjoy the Voodoo Garden. The lively Sunday gospel brunch is a winner. First-come seating. Moderate. L,D, S.

PLANET HOLLYWOOD (Downtown Disney West Side): Ensconced inside a 120-foot-diameter sphere, this restaurant gave the World's dining lineup its first celestial jolt. The hordes who assemble to gain entry to this restaurant are rewarded with a mind-boggling three-dimensional collage of movie memorabilia that couldn't possibly be digested in one meal. But there's more to

---

Dinner in Bed

Sometimes it doesn't matter how great a restaurant's ambience is. You want the next knock on the door to be a person with a platter. Room service at Disney's deluxe hotels is as grand as you want to make it; ask nicely and your appetite for most anything on a house restaurant menu can be sated. With the exception of Wilderness Lodge and the Polynesian (last knock: midnight), the deluxe hotels will rustle something up for you around the clock. Even at the moderate and value hotels, room service isn't just about breakfast; from 6 P.M. to 11 P.M. you may order sandwiches, pizza, salads, and the like. Note that deliveries generally come within an hour.

Dining Rooms with Knockout Views

Boma—Flavors of Africa (Animal Kingdom Lodge)

California Grill (Contemporary)

Cantina de San Angel (Mexico, Epcot's World Showcase)

Cap'n Jack's Restaurant (Downtown Disney Marketplace)

Cinderella's Royal Table (Magic Kingdom)

Coral Reef (The Living Seas, Epcot's Future World)

Fulton's Crab House (between Pleasure Island and Downtown Disney Marketplace)

Garden Grill (The Land, Epcot's Future World)

Jiko—The Cooking Place (Animal Kingdom Lodge)

Narcoossee's (Grand Floridian)

'Ohana (Polynesian)

Planet Hollywood (Downtown Disney West Side)—No windows needed here!

Rose & Crown Dining Room (United Kingdom, Epcot's World Showcase)

this fun-filled planet than meets the eye: The menu has creative flair and depth (consider blackened shrimp and Shanghai chicken salad). Desserts are outstanding. No reservations or priority seating, alas, just extremely long lines (try between 1 P.M. and 5 P.M.). Moderate to expensive. L, D, S.

PORTOBELLO YACHT CLUB (between Pleasure Island and Downtown Disney Marketplace; 407-934-8888): This polished yet casual piece of nautica is simply one of our favorite places in Downtown Disney to visit on an empty stomach. Menu standouts include a variety of thin-crust pizzas baked in a wood-burning oven, *farfalle primavera*, and *spaghettini alla Portobello*, a seafood medley served over pasta in a light tomato and wine sauce. Portobello also offers a sampling of tasty desserts, some tempting specialty coffees, and an impressive wine list. It's open until 1:30 A.M. Owned and operated by Levy Restaurants of Chicago. Smoking permitted. Priority seating suggested. Expensive. L, D, S.

WOLFGANG PUCK CAFE (Downtown Disney West Side; 407-938-9653): This casual yet groundbreaking restaurant marks the famed L.A. chef's Florida debut and brings trendy California cuisine to the fore. Incidentally, his wife, noted interior designer Barbara Lazaroff, fashioned the geometric patterns, the ceramic mosaics, and the glass expanses that make up the convivial interior. There are actually three dining arenas in this two-story restaurant—an express counter, a cafe, and a more formal dining room on the second floor—plus an attractive sushi bar. All feature the celebrated chef's signature gourmet pizzas, rotisserie chicken, and other specialties prepared in the display kitchen. The **Wolfgang Puck Express** counter here (there's also one at the Marketplace) offers wood-fired pizzas, Chinois Chicken Salad, and focaccia sandwiches that defy most definitions of fast food. First-come seating. Inexpensive. L, D, S. At **Wolfgang Puck Cafe**, the menu extends to sushi, Thai chicken satay, and penne with wild shiitake and oyster mushrooms. First-come seating. Moderate to expensive. L, D, S. **Wolfgang Puck Cafe—The Dining Room** puts hunger pangs happily to rest with such dishes as baby vegetable risotto and roast Cantonese duck with plum sauce, plus a wine list well suited to the cuisine. Priority seating suggested. Expensive. D.

Good Bets

BONGOS CUBAN CAFE (Downtown Disney West Side; 407-850-6999): The tastes and sounds of Cuba and Latin America dovetail at this tropical-themed hot spot, created by singer Gloria Estefan and her husband, Emilio. Specialties include black bean soup, Cuban marinated steak with plantains, and flan beneath the gorgeous mosaic mural or out on the balcony, which wraps around a Deco-inspired, three-story pineapple. A takeout window provides snacks on the go. First-come seating. Moderate to expensive. L, D, S.

CAP'N JACK'S RESTAURANT (Downtown Disney Marketplace; 407-828-3971): This attractive pier house perched over Lake Buena Vista is the place to socialize over mason-jar drafts and fresh seafood. The strawberry margarita's a keeper, as are the peel-and-eat shrimp, clam chowder, and oyster starters. Or try the mahi mahi and crab cake entrées. Besides offering some of the most reasonably priced meals around, the restaurant also fetches some fine sunsets. First-come seating. Moderate. L, D, S.

GOURMET PANTRY (Downtown Disney Marketplace): Okay, so it's not a restaurant. But this shop is bursting with inspiration for casual meals, picnics, and even self-catered boating excursions on Lake Buena Vista. When we mention the terrific heros sold by the inch, specialty salads, Godiva chocolates, cookies, wine, and spirits, we're merely hinting at the soup-to-nuts inventory. Inexpensive. B, L, D, S.

OUTBACK (Wyndham Palace, Hotel Plaza Boulevard; 407-827-3430): Despite its similar meat-and-potatoes inclinations, this place has no relation to the chain of the same name. While gator chowder and kangaroo-shaped butter are certainly among the restaurant's more unforgettable traits, we like it for the baby-back ribs, shrimp, and steak. Smoking permitted. Reservations suggested. Moderate. D.

WILDHORSE SALOON (Pleasure Island; 407-827-4947): Good country cookin' is the draw here. There's chicken fried steak, fried catfish, barbecued ribs, smoked pulled-pork sandwiches, and, of course, grits—the perfect side dish to the live country bands and line-dance lessons. There may be an entertainment charge if you dine here in the evening. First-come seating. Moderate to expensive. L, D, S.

For the Love of Chocolate

When only a chocolate fix will do, the Ghirardelli Soda Fountain and Chocolate Shop makes a sweet retreat—the perfect place to pause between shops at the Marketplace for a root beer float, a malt, or a peek at the chocolate-making equipment.

On the West Side, try the southern-style confections at the Candy Cauldron, or smoothies and desserts at Forty Thirst Street. On Pleasure Island, D-Zertz is the sweetest solution.

Instant Film Festival

The exceptional AMC Theatres cinema at Downtown Disney West Side offers more than a little incentive to give aching feet a rest. First-run motion pictures are shown in a whopping 24 plush theaters, all of them equipped with an advanced sound system called THX that was developed by George Lucas. Call 407-298-4488 for showtimes.

NIGHTLIFE GUIDE

Those who find the energy to hit the town after a hard day's recreation are rewarded with a whole new world of amusements and entertainment. Among the many ways to take advantage of a second wind (and find a third) at Walt Disney World, Pleasure Island is the most obvious. This single-admission complex of clubs and restaurants trumpeted as Disney's playground for adults is just that. It has knockout improvisational comedy, smooth jazz, raging dance clubs, and much more, rolled into one neat package that creates a populace of happy nomads.

And that's just the prix fixe menu; à la carte nightlife options abound. Paramount among them is Downtown Disney West Side, a waterfront entertainment pocket next door to Pleasure Island. Board-Walk, the happening entertainment strip right in Epcot's backyard, has earned its place on our don't-miss list. The theme parks (except the Magic Kingdom) also offer a few notable watering holes for early birds, and the resorts in and around the World rally to the adult cause with a tempting slate of lounges and clubs to suit every taste. Tally it all up and you have sufficient incentive to take even the faintest breeze of a second wind for all it's worth: havens for wine lovers and havens for beer drinkers; gems that enchant and gems that rock; places to shoot the breeze and places to shoot pool; desirable digs for singles and desirable digs for couples. The key is knowing where to find them.

In the pages that follow, we present the best nightlife in the World. First, you'll receive a thorough orientation to Pleasure Island, complete with a walking tour; next, an introduction to Downtown Disney West Side; then an informed briefing on the clubs found along the BoardWalk. The final section of this guide completes the nightlife picture with our report on other recommended clubs and lounges located on WDW property. This is structured as a listing. Under the heading "Standouts," we have singled out those places, both quiet and jumping, that are worth going out of your way for or simply a joy to have nearby. Within the designation "Good Bets," we have corralled the best of the rest—additional clubs and lounges worth checking out, particularly if you're in the area. *Cheers!*

Downtown Disney Pleasure Island

This bustling metropolis—a six-acre island consumed entirely by clubs, stage shows, and live entertainment—can be counted on to fill the entertainment void when Walt Disney World's theme parks and golf courses have closed for the day. We'd liken the atmosphere of this most adult venture to a four-alarm block party. (Guests must be 18 or joined at the hip to a parent to be admitted to clubs, and Mannequins disco and BET SoundStage Club are strictly 21 and up.) Pleasure Island's vigor and longevity are bolstered by its unique interpretation of the calendar—the place celebrates more New Year's Eves in a year than Dick Clark could know in four lifetimes ("Auld Lang Syne" and confetti cannons join special effects-enhanced fireworks as nightly rituals). It tosses a nod to most every nightlife niche. And although it's perhaps more fun once you've cased out your favorite hangouts, it is possible to experience all of Pleasure Island's clubs in one whirlwind night, and this is the course we recommend for first-time visitors.

While the main draw here is certainly the clubs, Pleasure Island's shops are open from 10:30 A.M. to 2 A.M., and some of its restaurants serve lunch as well as dinner. There is no admission fee until 7 P.M., when a single cover charge of $20 (including tax; good for entry to all clubs) applies to all but restaurant-goers. Pleasure Island admission is included in Ultimate Park Hopper Passes and an option for Park Hopper Plus Passes. The drinking age in Florida is 21, and a valid photo ID is required at the gate and at most club entrances. While the clubs don't close down until 2 A.M., note that last call is sounded at about 1:30 A.M.

Before we take you on a club-hopping tour of Pleasure Island, a few words about practicalities are warranted. For starters, the restaurants on and around Pleasure Island are among WDW's best, and Portobello Yacht Club and Fulton's Crab House don't shut down their galleys until after midnight. For reviews of the key dining spots here and throughout Downtown Disney, consult this chapter's "Restaurant Guide" (the immediately relevant section begins on page 205). For snacking, carts stand by with such things as crêpes. Of the several clubs that serve food, the Pleasure Island Jazz Company and Wildhorse Saloon venture the furthest beyond pub grub. The Missing Link Sausage Co. sates with hot dogs and sausages, and D-Zertz serves the sweet tooth. For details about transportation to and from Pleasure Island, consult the "Transportation" section of the *Planning Ahead* chapter.

To give you a sense of location, clubs are described here in the order they are encountered after you pass through the turnstiles closest to the Marketplace. But Pleasure Island is an open invitation to serendipity—truly a club-hopper's

A Sense of Place

Pleasure Island's clubs are described here in the order they are encountered after you pass through the turnstiles closest to the Marketplace.

Pleasure Island Tips

■ Adventurers Club, Wildhorse Saloon, BET SoundStage Club, Comedy Warehouse, and Rock N Roll Beach Club are up and running by 7 P.M. The rest kick into gear at 8 P.M. Times are subject to change.

■ It's fun to club-hop, but you can't do it with a glass in your hand. Plan ahead, and ask that your last drink be served in plastic. Most places keep a stack of cups near the door.

■ Caught with your pockets empty? Rendezvous with the ATM located out front at the Rock N Roll Beach Club.

■ The Adventurers Club and the Comedy Warehouse are the island's only non-smoking venues.

•CONTINUED ON NEXT PAGE

paradise—and its varied venues are ideally explored according to mood and energy level. Generally, you'll find that Mannequins, right inside the gate, is not one best encountered cold. Better warm-ups are the Comedy Warehouse, the Rock N Roll Beach Club, 8TRAX, Wildhorse Saloon, and BET SoundStage Club. For a relaxing interlude, we suggest the Pleasure Island Jazz Company and the Adventurers Club.

A Walking Tour

As you bear down on Pleasure Island, note that the parking lot here is a highly trafficked place requiring pedestrian vigilance. Either take advantage of valet parking ($6) or resist the urge to look up at the cluster of neon lights and skyward lasers until you've crossed over to the sidewalk where the ticket booth sits.

After presenting your ticket at the main entrance, in exchange for a lovely paper bracelet, you pass (limbo if you like) under a neon archway and into the pleasuredom itself. The first building on the left houses **Mannequins**, a pulsating den of incredible special effects and current techno-pop tracks that puts a unique spin on the standard club scene with a huge, rotating dance floor. It takes its name from the many mannequins, all related to the dance world, found throughout. Reserved strictly for patrons 21 and older, Mannequins is a club in the urban mold, and it attracts a dressed-to-impress crowd. The music here is cranked so loud that a jet could pass through virtually unnoticed, yet somehow the place is packed all night long with revelers who actually employ verbal communication in their flirtations. If you can stand the volume, you may take pleasure in the fact that the circulating dance floor gives a little boost to your dance skills and allows for exceptionally easy scoping, whether you're dancing or on the sidelines.

Explosive modern dance shows are staged here nightly, and on Thursday night the music is retro-progressive. The club is entered (via an elevator) on the third floor, a level that offers little beyond a bit of privacy and a perch from which to view the action below. Ditto the second floor. As for drinks, Mannequins offers a full bar but emphasizes the bubbly, serving champagne by the glass or the bottle, from Piper Sonoma to Dom Perignon. This club is popular with locals and visitors, so be prepared to encounter a line at the door, especially on weekends.

Directly across from Mannequins you'll see a warehouse-like structure. This is the site of the **Pleasure Island Jazz Company**, the island's most sophisticated entity. Cool, uninhibited jazz and blues are the order at this live-music venue, which runs the gamut from 1930s to contemporary tunes, and features local and national talent. Good for a relaxing interlude, the place is dimly lit and dotted with small cocktail tables that encourage intimate conversation. If you're up for some quality entertainment in a romantic atmosphere; if you're too pooped for anything beyond snapping your fingers; if you're hankering for a jazzy libation, a nice bottle of wine, or a bite on the other side of the fast-food tracks, the Jazz Company will take care of you. The menu here covers all bases. For under $10 you'll find blackened bacon-wrapped shrimp, spinach and artichoke dip, salmon cakes, honey-bourbon barbecue wings, tomato bruschetta, and portobello mushroom with crabmeat stuffing. Desserts include cheesecake (different flavors featured nightly) and chocolate-banana bread. For a specialty drink, try The Nuclear Fallout or The Eye of the Storm. To snag a good table, aim to arrive about 20 minutes before showtime.

Onward. Make a right turn out of the Jazz Company, and when you hit Pleasure Island's main strip, another right. The galloping horses ahead signal that you've reached **Wildhorse Saloon**, a combo club and restaurant. The folks dressed in cowboy boots and Stetsons who have (clearly) come to Pleasure Island with one thing in mind have a new space for two-stepping, with live performances by rising country artists (call 407-827-4947 for schedules), daily line-dance lessons, and a full menu of home-style barbecue all day long. At midnight, the saloon takes a breather from its country music format to celebrate Wildtime, two hours of songs from *all* walks of music. Note that an additional cover is charged for some concerts; a separate Wildhorse Saloon pass may also be purchased.

When you leave Wildhorse Saloon, you're on due course for the **Rock N Roll Beach Club**. At the top of the surfboard stairway, you enter a rollicking dance spot that is substantially more laid-back than Mannequins (perhaps due to its surfer sensibility and excellent live bands). Between sets, some of the wackiest deejays you'll ever see keep the classic rock and current pop coming even as they're bouncing like oversize Super Balls off the walls of the prominent audio booth. While dancing is definitely a big deal here—the dance floor is generally packed with twentysomethings—there's more to do than twist and shout the night away. Many guests enjoy the three-story club's great music and casual atmosphere without so much as stepping onto the lowest level. They shoot pool, play air hockey and pinball, and hang out at tables overlooking the dance floor

---

•*CONTINUED FROM PREVIOUS PAGE*

■ A deejay mixes popular tunes for dancing along the waterfront behind 8TRAX during select summer weekends and special events.

■ To snag a good table at Pleasure Island Jazz Company, arrive about 20 minutes before showtime (listed on the entertainment schedule).

■ At the Comedy Warehouse, aim to see an earlier show for the shortest queue or a later show for the most adult humor.

After-Dark Dazzle

■ The Magic Kingdom's extended curfew during busy seasons (generally summers and holiday periods) means the relaxed atmosphere and romance of the park in the early-evening hours are more accessible. It also means nightly fireworks and performances of the nighttime parade.

The Fantasy in the Sky fireworks display is six minutes of pyrotechnics worthy of a Fourth of July finale. And the evening parade is not to be missed; if there are two performances, aim for the later one, when the prime viewing spots (anywhere along Main Street) arc easier to snare, thanks to little ones' needing to go beddie-bye.

•CONTINUED ON NEXT PAGE

to people-watch and sip a beer. Roving souls should note that the specialty drinks here (try the Great White) are available in 16-ounce squeeze bottles.

From the Rock N Roll Beach Club it's a right turn, then a short walk to our next gig on your left. **8TRAX** is a place so thoroughly seventies that "YMCA" is a scheduled event (12:30 A.M.). In this rather rocking joint, you'll see a lot of people with goofy (lowercase, that is) grins on their faces and hear a continual stream of "Omigod, this is the song . . . We have to dance to this one . . . No way . . . I completely forgot about this song." Suffice it to say that the *Saturday Night Fever*-style dance floor is not only an extraordinarily popular destination but an infinitely fascinating eyeful. Decor tends toward the psychedelic. Specialty drinks include Brady Bunch Punch and Pez (a green sweet-and-sour concoction). And some off-the-beaten-vinyl-sofa nooks are given over to Rubik's Cube tables and a built-in game of Twister. On Thursdays, the club rocks to the beat of a different decade: the eighties. **Note:** The small courtyard out back is a good place to sneak a kiss or have a quiet conversation.

Moving along, the next club on the horizon (veer left out of 8TRAX and cross the street) is Pleasure Island's biggest enigma—the **Adventurers Club**. This elegant and eccentric parlor takes after the salons of 19th-century explorers' clubs, and is decked out with photos, trinkets, and furnishings that document the awfully far-reaching (and farfetched) travels of its card-carrying members. On the surface, it's a quiet place, filled with comfortable chairs; the official club drink, the Kungaloosh, is a tasty frozen number with strawberry and orange juice, blackberry brandy, and rum. But penetrate the recesses of the Adventurers Club and you'll notice some pretty odd characters milling about, stumble upon some rather curious corners and goings-on, and, ultimately, be invited into a hideaway library (where those odd characters put on a rather curious show, complete with haunted organ). A few hints to making the most of this intriguing parlor: Grab a stool at the main bar downstairs, and ask the bartender for a raise; read the captions for the displayed photos; and don't miss the mask room. Finally, note that this is a nonsmoking venue.

Right next door to the Adventurers Club is the **BET SoundStage Club**. This urban den for rhythm and blues and hip-hop has the too-cool aura of an unstoppable after-hours party. Reserved strictly for patrons 21 and older, it's the kind of place you'd like to think Aretha Franklin might frequent, with all due respect (pun intended). A mix of music videos keeps the energy level high and the crowd pumped to dance all night. The club's snack menu favors Caribbean-style munchables sure to cure even the worst case of the blues.

Our next order of business is not a club but a forum known as the **West End Stage**, which provides much of the juice for Pleasure Island's street party. Live bands perform here nightly (there are a few big-name acts a month). While you won't find any seating to speak of in the plaza that fronts this stage, you may very well sight full-blown adults dancing under the stars. Unless you are allergic to confetti, this is the place to be when the nightly New Year's Eve countdown reaches its pyrotechnic climax (showtime is 11:45 P.M.). Sure, the premise is a bit contrived, but you'd be surprised how many couples leap at the chance for an extra New Year's Eve smooch before joining the rest of the crowd in singing "Auld Lang Syne."

In any case, the most strategic spot to take it all in (since you'll be standing, anyway) is the queue for the **Comedy Warehouse**, located right across the plaza from the BET SoundStage Club. Get there no later than 11:30 P.M. (the next show is at 12:20 A.M.) to get a jump on any New Year's revelers who might have the same idea. The Comedy Warehouse, a perennial favorite, is the sort of club in which you prop yourself on a stool in a tiered studio and hope you don't fall off laughing. The rule here: Drink in sips, because the troupe of five lightning-quick improvisational comedians does absolutely hilarious things with assorted suggestions from the audience, and the zingers usually come without warning.

•*CONTINUED FROM PREVIOUS PAGE*

■ Epcot's World Showcase, which stays open until at least 9 P.M. year-round, assumes a sparkling beauty at night. For this reason, Disney presents a special show, IllumiNations: Reflections of Earth. This simulation of our planet's evolution features a three-story globe, intense fireworks, and emotionally charged music. The 13-minute show, typically ignited at closing time, is visible from any point along the promenade.

■ Sure to top the after-dark A-list is Fantasmic!, served up in an amphitheater behind The Twilight Zone Tower of Terror at the Disney-MGM Studios. The 26-minute show takes you inside Mickey's dreams as he conducts dancing fountains, swirling stars, and a delightful musical score. Animation projected onto water screens on the lake helps tell the story, which climaxes with a visit from Disney villains. A battle powered by flaming special effects leads to a character-filled finale.

■ The Electrical Water Pageant, a 1,000-foot-long string of illuminated floating creatures, makes its way around Bay Lake each night. You can usually view the pageant at 9 P.M. from the Polynesian, 9:15 P.M. from the Grand Floridian, 9:35 P.M. from Wilderness Lodge, 9:45 P.M. from Fort Wilderness, and 10:05 P.M. from the Contemporary.

More Reasons to Go West

Downtown Disney West Side has more than just restaurants, nightclubs, and movie theaters. It's also home to some interesting shops (open until 11 P.M.; see the margin on page 166 for details) and DisneyQuest (described on the opposite page).
But most notably, it has a permanent tent for a Cirque du Soleil show called La Nouba. Wipe out all thoughts of Bozo-style antics; this circus ensemble is not your typical big-top production. Cirque features a cast of 60 performing a mix of acrobatics and modern dance. Wild costumes and dramatic original music add to the fun. Cirque fans consider it The Greatest Show in Downtown Disney. Call 407-939-7600 for tickets (up to six months in advance).

Every performance is different, but you can expect the audience to provide some pretty challenging raw material ("Okay, we need an occupation" nets the likes of "rutabaga farmer"), and count on the troupe to rise to the occasion with spontaneously composed songs and skits. Suffice it to say that when these comics go head-to-head in do-it-or-die improv competitions (and they do), they do not go down quickly.

Beer, wine, and mixed drinks are served; popcorn is the preferred snack. While the performances here are worth waiting for, hard-core humorists will often begin lining up a good hour before curtain time for the later shows, making it a tough seat to get. A queue attendant keeps count, so you won't wait for nothing. Some additional tips: Know that it's possible but not likely to get in on the fly, so aim for the earlier shows. However, note that later shows might venture into decidedly more "adult" humor. Also be aware that this is a nonsmoking venue.

Downtown Disney West Side

The newest kid on the entertainment block, the West Side forges with the Marketplace and Pleasure Island to make a triple-header of the alluring distraction zone known as Downtown Disney. Like Pleasure Island, its neighbor to the east, Downtown Disney West Side is a colorful lakeside strip of clubs, restaurants, shops, and energy. Unlike Pleasure Island, this be-there-or-be-square area is ungated, even after dark.

Here, guests pay as they play, springing for cover charges only at establishments they decide to patronize. Puffer's alert: Smoking is permitted in designated sections of House of Blues, Bongos Cuban Cafe, and Planet Hollywood. Night owl's alert: Whereas Planet Hollywood takes orders right up to 1 A.M., Bongos and House of Blues serve until 2 A.M. For more details about the restaurants here, see our "Restaurant Guide."

The easternmost spot at Downtown Disney West Side is the **AMC Theatres** complex, a colossal celebration of the silver screen (make that *screens*—there are 24 of them). The marquee is au courant, the seats are roomy and plush (there's stadium seating in most theaters), and the sound system, developed by George Lucas, is first-rate. Call 407-298-4488 for showtimes, the earliest of which start about 1 P.M. (There's also a Guest Services desk here.)

If you prefer a diversion with an added dimension, start a conga line and head for the three-story pineapple directly across the promenade. **Bongos Cuban Cafe**, created by singer Gloria Estefan and her husband, Emilio, is a bright, boisterous restaurant that parades the flavors and rhythms of Cuba and other Latin American countries. It's a place in which mere foot-tapping is uncommon (sit still and your friends are apt to begin shaking you). So count on swaying in your seat to the sizzling sounds of live salsa and, should the mood strike you, pushing back the tables to dance beside the big pineapple.

When you've had your fill of the fruit-fly fandango, plot a moonlight stroll along the shore of Lake Buena Vista. Melt away the Miami mentality with a dose of cool: **House of Blues**. The massive music hall here is like a songbird that's constantly changing its tune—only much funkier. It has capacity for 2,000 soul men and women. Inspired by one of America's proudest musical traditions, the club also serves up country, with an occasional R & B, gospel, or rock medley tossed into the mix. You may buy tickets in advance through TicketMaster (407-839-3900; *www.ticketmaster.com*) or at the box office up until showtime; cost is $5 to $30, depending on the act. Can't live without a House of Blues cap or T-shirt? Take It Easy Baby—that's the name of the shop stocking all things blues-related. Incidentally, the powers behind House of Blues include actor, Blues Brother, and world-renowned Conehead Dan Aykroyd.

BoardWalk

While merely strolling the boards of this nostalgic entertainment district a short walk from Epcot provides a delightful escape to simpler times, the temptations en route are tough to resist. Cotton candy vendors, savory dining, and surrey bike rides aside, BoardWalk gives the World things it has long needed—a sports bar, a brewpub, a sing-along piano bar, and more. In addition to being an appealing resort (see *Checking In* for a complete description), Board-Walk is a great adult hangout. Although there's no general admission fee, Jelly-rolls charges a cover (usually about $3 to $5), as does Atlantic Dance (about $5),

DisneyQuest: A Virtual Toy Box

Call it a virtual reality check. An ode to flippers and joysticks. A bumper-car blast from your arcade past. DisneyQuest at Downtown Disney West Side is five stories of rampant interactivity that could test the supple wrists of The Who's Pinball Wizard. A sampling: You paddle a buoyant raft around rugged rocks, not to mention dinosaurs, on the Virtual Jungle Cruise. After rediscovering Centipede, you ride a simulated self-made roller coaster—a hair-raising excuse for a Virtual Makeover at Magic Mirror. DisneyQuest is open from 10:30 A.M. to midnight. One-day admission is about $29, including tax (prices may change).

Virgin Daiquiri, Anyone?

Soft drinks, fruit juices, and tasty specialty drinks sans alcohol are available at all Walt Disney World clubs. Just ask the bartender.

and you must be 21 or older to enter Jellyrolls. Valet parking is available free for WDW resort guests, $6 for others. All of the bars and clubs, described below, stay open until 2 A.M. Smoking is permitted in many spots.

High on the hit list is **ESPN Club**, a sports bar so over-the-top it practically has referees. Between the live sports commentators, the ballpark fare, and the more than 80 televisions (some in the restrooms) broadcasting any number of games, no unnecessary time-outs are taken. Check an entertainment schedule for news on any major-league special events that might be happening. And try those hot wings.

Several first downs away, the **Big River Grille & Brewing Works** invites you to bend the ol' elbow right under the brewmaster's nose. Five first-rate specialty ales, including two that change with the seasons, are crafted on the premises. It's a tough job, but someone's got to polish off the beer bread and raise a glass to the hardworking brew maestro. After trying the beer sampler (tastes of all five ales for $4.75), we heartily waved on the Tilt Pale Ale house brew. Hot beer pretzels and other appetizers from the restaurant menu are available at the bar until the kitchen closes around 11 P.M., providing fitting accompaniments to tastings. (Stick around and you'll see that the sleek metal stools are surprisingly comfortable.)

Walk a few short strides into the dueling-pianist realm of **Jellyrolls** and you're soon crooning and swaying along with the rest of the congregation to songs from the 1970s to the present. As an example of the musicians' versatility, consider this sampling of one set: "The Devil Went Down to Georgia," "Joy to the World," and a Kermit the Frog rendition of "Rainbow Connection." The music comes uninterrupted (except by the wisecracking pianists themselves). Soon you're wondering how you got so hoarse.

So you head next door to **Atlantic Dance**, a club out to prove that it don't mean a thing if you ain't got that swing. One look at the elbow room quotient and you'll be itching to jump and jive. The deejay supplies a sound track of old favorites, with a swing band filling in on auspicious nights. You're free to dance, order hors d'oeuvres or desserts, and, if you like, enjoy one of 25 specialty drinks on a balcony overlooking the water. From this perspective,

the game highlights on ESPN Club's monitors seem miles away. But they're not, and so, when your mood shifts, you venture back to settle the score. Such is an evening at BoardWalk.

Other World Options

Standouts

CALIFORNIA GRILL LOUNGE (Contemporary): The companion lounge to the exceptional California Grill restaurant offers what amounts to box seats for the Magic Kingdom fireworks in a casual setting that does California wine country proud. What more could you want? Every wine is available by the glass, and you can often order from the California Grill menu. Doors close: 1 A.M.

CREW'S CUP (Yacht Club): When it comes to beer, the Crew's Cup runneth over with 35 international brews. Consider the warm copper-accented decor, the scintillating aromas wafting in from the neighboring Yachtsman Steakhouse, and the potential for four-cheese garlic bread and New England clam chowder, and you have an even better idea of why we are putty in this lounge's hands. Doors close: midnight.

THE LAUGHING KOOKABURRA GOOD TIME BAR (Wyndham Palace, Buena Vista Drive): At "The Kook," a live band plays Top 40 music Wednesday through Saturday for a crowd hovering in the 25-to-40 age range. If you'd rather listen than dance, snag a spot in one of four seating areas, including a small bar with a skylight on the upper level. Some 80 beers are on hand. Daily happy hour. Doors close: 2 A.M.

MARTHA'S VINEYARD (Beach Club): Although appetizers and desserts are served, the main reason you're here is the wine. Selections from a real Martha's Vineyard winery, as well as selections from California, Long Island, and European vineyards make for tough decisions, but it helps to know that wine can be ordered in sample sizes, as well as full glasses. Doors close: 11 P.M.

MATSU NO MA (Japan, Epcot's World Showcase): A serene setting where—in addition to sake, beer, cocktails, and green tea—you can imbibe a stunning vista of Epcot. Sushi and sashimi are also served. Doors close at park closing.

Whatever Ales You . . .

In addition to BoardWalk's brewpub, the Big River Grille & Brewing Works, visiting beer lovers should remember these names: Crew's Cup (at the Yacht Club, with three beers on tap and 35 worldly brews) and The Laughing Kookaburra Good Time Bar (at the Wyndham Palace, with 80 labels). For a roundup of WDW microbrews, see page 203.

WDW Dinner Shows

When it comes to dinner shows, the Catskills have nothing on Disney. The elaborately themed nightly productions offer set menus with generous portions, accompanied by unlimited alcoholic and nonalcoholic beverages, and they welcome guests in casual attire.

Reservations are required and may be booked up to two years in advance by calling 407-WDW-DINE (939-3463). Special dietary requests are honored at all shows, with advance notice. Prices are subject to change.

The best of the lot (and toughest reservation) is the **Hoop-Dee-Doo Musical Revue**, held in Pioneer Hall at Fort Wilderness.

•CONTINUED ON NEXT PAGE

ONLY'S BAR & JAIL (Dolphin): While certainly a restaurant bar, this atmospheric slammer is a good place to do time, especially if you're a margarita lover. The different kinds are based on tequila gradations rather than fruity flavors; steer toward the Tijuana Cadillac. Sangria by the pitcher and hot tortilla chips with salsa complete the picture. Doors close: 11:30 P.M.

ROSE & CROWN PUB (United Kingdom, Epcot's World Showcase): We've always loved this cheeky classic—for its pretty polished-wood and brass decor; its rich Irish, Scottish, and British drafts; and its neighborly feel. So we weren't too surprised during one of many visits to overhear a gentleman asking a fellow behind the bar to please let Jerry (a bartender not present) know that he was sorry he'd missed him. "Next time," he said hopefully. You needn't be a fan of shandies or black and tans to appreciate that. There's even a pub singer. Doors close at park closing.

STONE CRAB (Fulton's Crab House, between Pleasure Island and Downtown Disney Marketplace): Like the local heartthrob who happens to be loaded, this gorgeous riverboat-bound bar stacks the odds even more in its favor with an excellent raw bar, prime water views, and a honey-wheat house brew. It doesn't just make Bloody Marys from scratch (as in hand-squeezed tomatoes and fresh-grated horseradish), it garnishes them with shrimp. No wonder it attracts so many sophisticated stowaways. Doors close: 2 A.M.

TERRITORY (Wilderness Lodge): This scenic spot of wilderness is marked by wood-carved grizzlies and a muraled map of the western frontier that "unfolds" over the ceiling. While this lounge can be swamped with diners-in-waiting during prime mealtimes, it more often inspires lingering. Hearty appetizers and sandwiches add to the appeal. But the true toast of the Territory lounge is Lodge House Brew, a microbrewed light beer with a hint of honey that's a Wilderness Lodge exclusive. Doors close: midnight.

TUNE-IN LOUNGE (Disney-MGM Studios): This Formica-laden spot, the family den to 50's Prime Time Cafe, serves Dad's Super Snacks and spirits from Dad's Liquor Cabinet, while vintage TV sets show clips from the decade's most popular sitcoms. A baby-boomer's paradise. Doors close: park closing.

TOP OF THE PALACE (Wyndham Palace, Buena Vista Drive): Show up to toast the setting sun and you're provided with a complimentary glass of champagne, not to mention fine wines by the glass and delectable desserts courtesy of the adjacent Arthur's 27 restaurant. Miss the sunset and you've still got reason to propose a toast: live entertainment (Wednesday through Saturday) and an enviable view of Epcot's fireworks. Doors close: 1 A.M.

Good Bets

CAP'N JACK'S RESTAURANT (Downtown Disney Marketplace): This pier house jutting out over Lake Buena Vista scores with a convivial atmosphere, a mean strawberry margarita, and a bar conducive to people-watching. It also offers reasonably priced sunsets and beautiful seafood (or is it the reverse?). Note that if you want to sit at the bar, any line out the door doesn't apply. Doors close: 10:30 P.M.

COTTON CO-OP (Dixie Landings): This one's nothing fancy. Just your unassuming nook that happens to have a fireplace, ready access to chicken wings and spicy Cajun onion straws, and a sing-along-inspiring entertainer with a steady gig Tuesday through Saturday. Anyway, we've cottoned to the place in general and to the Mississippi Mud Slide (a frozen Chambord-Bailey's blend in a chocolate-swirled glass) in particular. Drinks and music stop at midnight, but the doors never close.

•CONTINUED FROM PREVIOUS PAGE

The show incorporates whoopin', singin', dancin', and audience participation in a frontier hoedown. Country vittles include ribs, fried chicken, salad, corn, and strawberry shortcake. There are three seatings, at 5 P.M., 7:15 P.M., and 9:30 P.M.; adults pay $46.33, including tax and tip.

At the Polynesian resort, hula skirts, ukuleles, and fire dances add to the fun at the lakeside **Polynesian Luau**, which takes guests on a whirlwind journey from New Zealand to Samoa. The meal, served family-style, features tropical bread, roasted chicken, spareribs, rice, and a tropical fruit dessert. The outdoor show—presented rain or shine, and canceled only when temperatures drop below 50 degrees—is performed Tuesday through Saturday at 5:15 P.M. and 8 P.M.; adults pay $46.33, including tax and tip.

While not a full dinner show, the nightly **Oktoberfest** celebration at the Biergarten restaurant in the Germany pavilion at Epcot's World Showcase features performers in lederhosen or dirndls yodeling and playing everything from accordions to cowbells. Seating here is family-style (eight to a table), and guests have full run of a buffet that includes bratwurst, rotisserie chicken, homemade spaetzle, red cabbage, and German potato salad. Adults pay $18.95, plus tax and tip; desserts cost extra. A musical trio entertains during the lunch buffet ($12.95 for adults).

Scenic Cocktail Spots

Atlantic Dance
(BoardWalk)

California Grill Lounge
(Contemporary)

Cap'n Jack's Restaurant (Downtown Disney Marketplace)

Matsu No Ma
(Japan, Epcot's World Showcase)

Narcoossee's
(Grand Floridian)

Outer Rim
(Contemporary)

Stone Crab
(Fulton's Crab House between Pleasure Island and the Marketplace)

Top of the Palace
(Wyndham Palace)

GURGLING SUITCASE (Old Key West): This travel-size bar is too small to warrant a special trip, but it has such a great name, we'll take any excuse to mention it. For drinks, we like the one with amaretto, crème de banana, pineapple and orange juices, and a dash of cherry brandy. Tell the bartender you're looking for a Sultry Seahorse. Doors close: midnight.

MIZNER'S (Grand Floridian): If you look past the house orchestra that sets up shop nightly outside this second-floor alcove, you'll find a mahogany bar with fine ports, brandies, and appetizers. Doors close: 1 A.M.

NARCOOSSEE'S (Grand Floridian): You've got to love a lounge that's thoroughly steeped in Victoriana on the inside, and framed by a lake that lies like a picnic blanket beneath the Magic Kingdom fireworks on the outside veranda. Worldly wines by the glass. Doors close: 10 P.M.

RAINFOREST CAFE (Two locations: Downtown Disney Marketplace and Animal Kingdom): When the restaurant is mobbed, we like to take in the thunderstorms and waterfalls from the central mushroom-capped bar. We simply saddle an unwitting zebra or giraffe (the animal bar stools are strictly hooves-to-hips) and chase our tails. Try a Raspberry Rainfall or fresh-squeezed juice. Doors close: 11 P.M., weekdays; midnight, weekends.

SHULA'S (Dolphin): Enjoy a beer at the adjoining bar of this restaurant that proclaims itself to be "one of the Top 10 steakhouses in America." Former Miami Dolphins Coach Don Shula scores big with bar appetizers ranging from barbecued shrimp to steak soup. Doors close: 11 P.M.

Two-Step to the Table

At Mickey's Backyard Barbecue, your favorite Fourth of July grub is forti-fied by live entertainment. As an instructor gives line-dance lessons, a country band whoops it up Nashville-style. Disney characters kick up their heels on the dance floor. As for the chow, it's a a picnic spread of chicken and ribs, corn-on-the-cob, baked beans, corn bread, and other savory reminders of summer, plus as many cold drafts as you need to wash it all down. This seasonal show, presented near River Country, costs $37 for adults (including tax and tip). For reservations, call 407-WDW-DINE (939-3463) up to a year in advance.

Index